John Tinker

ESSAYS ON LANGUAGE AND USAGE

ESSAYS ON LANGUAGE AND USAGE

EDITED BY

LEONARD F. DEAN
University of Connecticut

AND

KENNETH G. WILSON
University of Connecticut

New York / OXFORD UNIVERSITY PRESS / 1959

Printed in the United States of America

Preface

From the early grades through the first year of college, the text-books and lessons in grammar and usage scarcely change. The repetition is well meant and apparently necessary: if they won't learn what's good for them, make them do it again. Certainly habits are formed and re-formed by repetitive drill, but it is clear from the record that repetition is not enough.

This book is based on the conviction that knowledge must be added to drill so that repetition may open into growth. Everyone aims at this, at confidence and pleasure in the use of language rather than at anxiety about being correct; the problem has been to get the liberating knowledge, which is scattered through books and journals, into the hands of the students. We have tried to solve that problem by bringing together here a generous number of readable, authoritative essays on language and usage. These essays put the usual handbooks in perspective, and they provide a proper linguistic foundation for the study of rhetoric and composition. They have been arranged in an order which we hope will be useful for the teacher of composition and his students.

We are indebted to colleagues, students, and former teachers; to critics, known and anonymous; and to the authors and publishers of the essays reprinted here.

LEONARD F. DEAN
KENNETH G. WILSON

Storrs, Connecticut
February 1959

ESSAYS ON LANGUAGE AND USAGE

I.

DICTIONARIES, WORDS, AND MEANINGS

A knowledge of the history of dictionaries is part of a liberal education: it liberates us from the false notion of *the* dictionary. Harold Whitehall, author of the first essay in this section and professor of English linguistics at Indiana University, reminds us that there have been different kinds of dictionaries to serve different users and needs, that dictionaries vary in quality, and that dictionaries must change as the language grows and changes.

The notion that any dictionary of a living language can be a permanent and final authority has been promoted in modern times by exploiting through advertising our latent fears of being "incorrect" in writing and speaking. Samuel Johnson's *Dictionary of the English Language* (1755) carries only the old-fashioned definition of *advertise:* to inform. In the Preface to that *Dictionary,* the second essay in this Section, he informs us with refreshing candor that he had dreamed of permanently purifying and regulating the language but that he finally found it impossible to embalm something which was living and changing. Words are the daughters of earth, as he puts it, and even with the most modern methods they cannot be completely brought to book.

But despite their necessary limitations, dictionaries do contain much more accurate and useful information than many of us may realize. Mitford Mathews, editor of a *Dictionary of Americanisms* (1951) and author of the third essay in this section, proves this by leading us into the fine print in four kinds of modern dictionaries: abridged, unabridged, encyclopedic, and historical. The fascinating information in an historical dictionary, one which traces the changing meanings of words, is the subject of the fourth essay by Stuart Robertson and Frederic Cassidy, professor of English at the University of Wisconsin. They show through examples how meanings shift over the years between special and general, respectable and disreputable. In the fifth essay the late H. L. Mencken describes in humorous detail how the names of things change because of our genteel use of euphemisms, words chosen or invented to prettify and ennoble the appearance of life.

Dr. Johnson remarks sharply in his Preface that some words have vague meanings through no fault of dictionary makers but because most men think indistinctly and therefore cannot speak or write with exactness. An up-to-date illustration of that fact is provided in the sixth selection by the American humorist, Frank Sullivan, posing as Mr. Arbuthnot, the cliché expert. A cliché is a stereotype which is literally a printing plate; hence when we think and speak in clichés, we reduce ourselves to machines. One way to come alive again in thought and language is to learn more about the lost or faded meanings of words, a kind of rejuvenation described in the last essay of this section by Margaret Schlauch, formerly professor of English at New York University, and now at the University of Warsaw.

HAROLD WHITEHALL

The Development of the English Dictionary

The evolution of the English dictionary is rooted in the general evolution of the English language. In this development the chief pressures were exerted by the steady increase in the word stock of English from the 50,000–60,000 words of Anglo-Saxon through the 100,000–125,000 words of the Middle-English vocabulary to the huge total of some 650,000 words which could theoretically be recorded in an exhaustive dictionary of contemporary English. Such an overall increase as this made the dictionary *necessary*. The pressure of vocabulary, however, has always been influenced and reinforced by the intellectual climate of each successive period of the language. A dictionary is not exactly a work of art, yet it bears as strongly as an artistic production the impress of the age that bore it. For that reason, the history of the dictionary is a fascinating chapter in the history of ideas.

The beginnings of dictionary history are neither national nor concerned with any of the national languages. They are concerned with the international language of medieval European civilization: Latin. Our first word books are lists of relatively difficult Latin terms, usually those of a Scriptural nature, accompanied by glosses in easier or more familiar Latin. Very early in the Anglo-Saxon period, however, we find glosses containing native English (i.e., Anglo-Saxon) equivalents for the hard Latin terms, and it may be that two of these—the *Leiden* and *Erfurt Glosses*—repre-
. . . .

From the Introduction to *Webster's New World Dictionary of the American Language*. College Edition, © 1958 by The World Publishing Company. Reprinted by permission of the publishers.

sent the earliest written English we possess. Such glosses, whether Latin-Latin or Latin-English, continued to be compiled during the entire Anglo-Saxon and most of the Middle-English period.

The next stage of development, attained in England around 1400, was the collection of the isolated glosses into what is called a *glossarium*, a kind of very early Latin-English dictionary. As it chances, our first example of the glossarium, the so-called *Medulla Grammatica* written in East Anglia around 1400, has never been printed; but two later redactions were among our earliest printed books, and one of these, the *Promptorium Parvulorum sive Clericorum*, issued by Wynkyn de Worde in 1499, was the first work of a dictionary nature ever to be printed on English soil. Significantly enough, this version of the *Medulla* places the English term first and its Latin equivalent second.

The first onset of the Renaissance worked against rather than in favor of the native English dictionary. The breakdown of Latin as an international language and the rapid development of international trade led to an immediate demand for foreign-language dictionaries. The first of such works, Palsgrave's *Lesclaircissement de la Langue Francoyse* (1523), was rapidly followed by Salesbury's Welsh-English dictionary (1547), Percival's English-Spanish dictionary (1591), and finally, by the best known of all such works, Florio's Italian-English dictionary (1599). Meanwhile, the first great classical dictionary, Cooper's *Thesaurus* (1565), had already appeared. The history of dictionaries is larded with strange occurrences: we are not surprised, therefore, that the publication of Cooper's work was delayed five years because his wife, fearing that too much lexicography would kill her husband, burned the first manuscript of his magnum opus. It should be noted, in passing, that none of these various word books of the 16th century actually used the title *dictionary* or *dictionarium*. They were called by various kinds of fanciful or half-fanciful names, of which *hortus* "garden," and *thesaurus* "hoard" were particularly popular.

During the late 16th century, the full tide of the Renaissance had been sweeping a curious flotsam and jetsam into English literary harbors. Constant reading of Greek and Latin bred a race of Holofernes pedants who preferred the Latin or Greek term to the English term. Their principle in writing was to use Latino-Greek polysyllabics in a Latino-English syntax. Their strange vocabulary—studded with what some critics call "inkhorn" terms—eventually affected English so powerfully that no non-Latinate Englishman could ever hope to read many works in his own language unless he was provided with explanations of elements unfamiliar to him. The "Dictionary of Hard Words," the real predecessor of the modern dictionary, was developed to provide precisely such explanations. It is significant that the first English word book to use the name *dictionary*, Cokeram's *The English Dictionary* (1623), is subtitled "An Interpreter of Hard Words." Among those explained on its first few pages are *Abequitate*, *Bulbulcitate*, and *Sullevation*. In point of time, the first "dictionary of hard words" was Robert Cawdrey's *Table Alphabeticall of Hard Words* (1604). Of the various works of the same class appearing after this date may be mentioned John Bullokar's *English Expositor* (1616) and Edward Phillip's *New World of Words* (1658), both of which reveal a strong interest in the reform of spelling, Blount's *Glossographia* (1656) containing the first etymologies ever to appear in a printed English dictionary, and Thomas Kersey's *Dictionarium Anglo-Brittanicum* (1708), which also includes legal terms, provincialisms, and archaisms. If the 16th was the century of the foreign-language dictionary, the 17th was the century of the dictionary of hard words.

Between 1708 and 1721, hard-word dictionaries began to be replaced by word books giving ever-increasing attention to literary usage. The Latino-Greek borrowings of the earlier century had been either absorbed into the language or sloughed away. The French influence, from 1660 onwards, had replaced Renaissance stylistic ideas with notions of a simple elegance in syntax and a quiet effectiveness in vocabularly. These stylistic virtues were actually achieved in the works of Swift, Addison, Steele, and lesser writers. The literary mind of the early 18th century, therefore, was convinced that English had finally attained a standard of purity such as it had never previously known; it was also convinced that the brash outgrowth of mercantile expansionism, later to be reinforced by the infant Industrial Revolution, might very well destroy this hard-won standard of literary refinement. What more natural than that the standard should be enshrined in a dictionary for the admiration and guidance of posterity?

The first word book to embody the ideals of the age was Nathaniel Bailey's *Universal Etymological Dictionary of the English Language,* originally published in 1721, and then, in a beautiful folio volume with illustrations by Flaxman, in 1731. This, one of the most revolutionary dictionaries ever to appear, was the first to pay proper attention to current usage, the first to feature etymology, the first to give aid in syllabification, the first to give illustrative quotations (chiefly from proverbs), the first to include illustrations, and the first to indicate pronunciation. An interleaved copy of the 1731 folio edition was the basis of Samuel Johnson's *Dictionary* of 1755; through Johnson, it influenced all subsequent lexicographical practice. The position of dictionary pioneer, commonly granted to Johnson or to Noah Webster, belongs in reality to one of the few geniuses lexicography ever produced: Nathaniel Bailey.

Johnson's *Dictionary* (1755) enormously extends the techniques developed by Bailey. Johnson was able to revise Bailey's crude etymologies on the basis of Francis Junius' *Etymologicon Anglicanum* (first published in 1743), to make a systematic use of illustrative quotations, to fix the spelling of many disputed words, to develop a really discriminating system of definition, and to exhibit the vocabulary of English much more fully than had ever been attempted before. In his two-volume work, the age and following ages found their ideal word book. Indeed, a good deal of the importance of the book lies in its later influence. It dominated English letters for a full century after its appearance and, after various revisions, continued in common use until 1900. As late as the '90's, most Englishmen used the word *dictionary* as a mere synonym for Johnson's *Dictionary;* in 1880 a Bill was actually thrown out of Parliament because a word in it was not in "the Dictionary."

One of the tasks taken upon himself by Johnson was to remove "improprieties and absurdities" from the language. In short, he became a linguistic legislator attempting to perform for English those offices performed for French by the French Academy. From this facet of his activities we get the notion, still held by many dictionary users, and fostered by many dictionary publishers, that the dictionary is a "supreme authority" by which to arbitrate questions of "correctness" and "incorrectness." The dictionaries of the second half of the 18th century extended this notion particularly to the field of pronunciation. By 1750, the increasing wealth of the middle classes was making itself felt in the social and political worlds. Those who possessed it, speakers, for the most part, of a middle-class dialect, earnestly desired a key to the pronunciations accepted in polite society. To provide for their needs, various pronunciation experts—usually of Scottish or Irish extraction—edited a series of pronunciation dictionaries. Of these, the most important are James Buchanan's *New English Dictionary* (1769), William Kenrick's *New Dictionary of the English Language* (1773), Thomas Sheridan's *General Dictionary of the English Language* (1780), and, above all, John Walker's *Critical Pronouncing Dictionary and Expositor of the English Language* (1791). In such works, pronunciation was indicated by small superscript numbers referring to the "powers" of the various vowel sounds. Despite the legislative function exercised by the authors of almost all of these works, we must admit that they did indicate contemporary pronunciation with great accuracy, and when Walker's pronunciations were combined with Johnson's definitions the result was a dictionary which dominated the wordbook field, both in England and the United States, until well after 1850.

If the chief contributions of the 18th century to dictionary making were (1) authoritative recording of literary vocabulary and (2) accurate recording of pronunciation, those of the 19th were unmistakably (1) the recording of word history through dated quotations and (2) the development of encyclopedic word books. Already in 1755, Samuel Johnson had hinted in his preface that the sense of a word "may easily be collected entire from the examples." During the first twenty-five years of the century, the researches of R. K. Rask, J. L. C. Grimm, and F. Bopp clearly defined the historical principle in linguistic. It was only a question of time, therefore, before someone combined Johnson's perception with the findings of the new science of historical linguistics. That person was Charles Richardson, who, in his *New Dictionary of the English Language* (1836), produced a dictionary completely lacking definitions but one in which both the senses and the historical evolution of the senses were accurately indicated by dated defining quotations. Richardson's work leads directly to the great *New English Dictionary on Historical Principles*, first organized in 1858, begun under Sir James Murray in 1888, and completed under Sir William Craigie in 1928. With its supplement (1933), the *New English Dictionary* or *Oxford English Dictionary* (N.E.D. or O.E.D.) covers the vocabulary of English with a completeness of historical evidence and a discrimination of senses unparalleled in linguistic history. No other language has ever been recorded on anything approaching this scale, and no dictionary of English since the *New English Dictionary* was completed has failed to reveal a profound debt to this monumental work. As compared with the effort represented by the N.E.D., the attempt to record the technological vocabularies of the language as first seen in John W. Ogilvie's *Universal Dictionary of the English Language* (1850) seems to be of minor importance, although it has had great practical effect on subsequent American dictionaries.

Since the publication of the O.E.D., the only important British dictionary has been Henry Cecil Wyld's *Universal Dictionary of the English Language* (1932), a work of somewhat restricted vocabulary coverage but one which may well point the way to the dictionary of the future. Wyld has discarded the older logical definitions for definitions of a more functional nature; his examples delve deeply into idiom; his etymologies are of a completeness and modernity unparalleled until this present dictionary in any medium-sized word book. The failure of Wyld's book to achieve much popularity on this side of the Atlantic underlines the fact that the typical American dictionary of the English language is a work *differing in kind* from any of those so far mentioned. It differs because the conditions of American life and culture differ from those of English life and culture.

The modern American dictionary is typically a single compact volume published at a relatively modest price containing: (1) definitive American spellings, (2) pronunciations indicated by diacritical markings, (3) strictly limited etymologies, (4) numbered senses, (5) some illustrations, (6) selective treatment of synonyms and antonyms, (7) encyclopedic inclusion of scientific, technological, geographical, and biographical items. It owes its development, within the general framework of the evolution sketched above, to the presence of a large immigrant population in this country, to the elaborate American system of popular education, and to the vast commercial opportunities implicit in both of these.

The first American dictionaries were unpretentious little schoolbooks based chiefly on Johnson's *Dictionary* of 1755 by way of various English abridgments of that work. The earliest of these were Samuel Johnson Junior's *School Dictionary* (1798), Johnson and Elliott's *Selected Pronouncing and Accented Dictionary* (1800), and Caleb Alexander's *Columbian Dictionary* (1800). The most famous work of this class, Noah Webster's *Compendious Dictionary of the English Language* (1806) was an enlargement of Entick's *Spelling Dictionary* (London, 1764), distinguished from its predecessors chiefly by a few encyclopedic supplements and emphasis upon its (supposed) Americanism. The book was never popular and contributed little either to Webster's own reputation or to the development of the American dictionary in general.

The first important date in American lexicography is 1828. The work that makes it important is Noah Webster's *An American Dictionary of the English Language* in two volumes. Webster's book has many deficiencies—etymologies quite untouched by the linguistic science of the time, a rudimentary pronunciation system actually inferior to that used by Walker in 1791, etc.—but in its insistence upon American spellings, in definitions keyed to the American scene, and in its illustrative quotations from the Founding Fathers of the Republic, it provided the country with the first *native* dictionary comparable in scope with that of Dr. Johnson. It was not, as is often claimed, the real parent of the modern American dictionary; it was merely the foster-parent. Because of its two-volume format and its relatively high price it never achieved any great degree of popular acceptance in Webster's own lifetime. Probably its greatest contribution to succeeding American dictionaries was the style of definition writing—writing of a clarity and pithiness never approached before its day.

The first American lexicographer to hit upon the particular pattern that distinguishes the American dictionary was Webster's lifelong rival, Joseph E. Worcester. His *Comprehensive Pronouncing, and Explanatory Dictionary of the English Language* (1830), actually a thoroughly revised abridgment of Webster's two-volume work of 1828, was characterized by the addition of new words, a more conservative spelling, brief, well-phrased definitions, full indication of pronunciation by means of diacritics, use of stress marks to divide syllables, and lists of synonyms. Because it was compact and low priced, it immediately became popular—far more popular, in fact, than any of Webster's own dictionaries in his own lifetime. As George P. Krapp, in his *The English Language in America,* says: "If one balances the faults of the Webster of 1828 against the faults of the Worcester of 1830, the totals are greatly in the favor of Worcester." One might feel the same about its merits as compared with those of Webster's own revision of his *American Dictionary* (1841), which featured the inclusion of scientific terms compiled by Professor W. Tully. The first Webster dictionary to embody the typical American dictionary pattern was that of 1847, edited by Noah Webster's son-in-law, Chauncey A. Goodrich, and published by the Merriams.

Temperamentally the flamboyant Noah Webster and the cautious Joseph Worcester were natural rivals. Their rivalry, however, was as nothing compared with that which developed between the rival publishers of the Webster and Worcester dictionaries. By 1845, the great flood of immigration and the vast extension of the school system had suddenly lifted dictionary making into the realm of big business. In a "war of the dictionaries" that reflects the rudimentary business ethics of the period, the rival publishers used every device of advertisement and every stratagem of high-powered salesmanship to drive each other off the market. Unsavory as this war appears in retrospect, it certainly helped to force rapid improvement of the dictionaries that these publishers controlled. Worcester's initial advantages were surpassed in the Merriam-Webster of 1847; the innovations in Worcester's edition of 1860 were more than paralleled in the Merriam-Webster of 1864, one of the best dictionaries ever to appear, but one from which almost everything really characteristic of Noah Webster himself was deleted. The battle was finally decided in favor of the Webster dictionaries, chiefly because the popularity of Webster's "Little Blue Back Speller" had put their name in every household, partly because of the death of Joseph Worcester, and partly because of the merit of the Merriam product from 1864 onwards.

Since about 1870, the climate of American dictionary making has been much more peaceful. In the field of unabridged dictionaries, the most important accretion is the *Century Dictionary* (1889), edited by the great American linguist, William Dwight Whitney, and issued in six volumes. Unfortunately, this magnificent work, considered by many authorities to be basically the finest ever issued by a commercial publisher, has lost much of its popularity because of inadequate subsequent revision. The fact that it was not in a one-volume format undoubtedly also worked against its popular success. The only other new unabridged dictionaries that have appeared in the period are Webster's *Imperial Dictionary of the English Language* (1904), and Funk and Wagnalls *New Standard Dictionary* (1893). The first of these, the only unabridged dictionary ever published west of the Appalachians, was issued in Chicago by George W. Ogilvie, a publisher who carried on his own private guerrilla "war of the dictionaries" against the Merriam Company between 1904 and circa 1917. At the moment, the most important advances in lexicography are taking place in the field of the abridged collegiate-type dictionaries.

Meanwhile the scholarly dictionary has not been neglected. Once the *New English Dictionary* was published, scholarly opinion realized the need to supplement it in the various periods of English and particularly in American English. The first of the proposed supplements, edited by Sir William Craigie and Professor J. R. Hulbert, is the *Dictionary of American English on Historical Principles*, completed in 1944. This was followed by a *Dictionary of Americanisms*, edited by Mitford M. Mathews and published in 1951. A *Middle English Dictionary*, a *Dictionary of the Older Scottish Tongue*, and a *Dictionary of Later Scottish* are in preparation, and work on the *American Dialect Dictionary* of the American Dialect Society is now finally under way.

SAMUEL JOHNSON

Preface to the Dictionary (1755)

It is the fate of those who toil at the lower employments of life,
to be rather driven by the fear of evil, than attracted by the
prospect of good; to be exposed to censure, without hope of
praise; to be disgraced by miscarriage, or punished for neglect,
where success would have been without applause, and diligence
without reward.

Among these unhappy mortals is the writer of dictionaries;
whom mankind have considered, not as the pupil, but the slave
of science, the pioneer of literature, doomed only to remove
rubbish and clear obstructions from the paths through which
Learning and Genius press forward to conquest and glory, without bestowing a smile on the humble drudge that facilitates their
progress. Every other author may aspire to praise; the lexicographer can only hope to escape reproach, and even this negative
recompense has been yet granted to very few.

I have, notwithstanding this discouragement, attempted a Dictionary of the *English* language, which, while it was employed
in the cultivation of every species of literature, has itself been
hitherto neglected; suffered to spread, under the direction of
chance, into wild exuberance; resigned to the tyranny of time
and fashion; and exposed to the corruptions of ignorance, and
caprices of innovation.

When I took the first survey of my undertaking, I found our
speech copious without order, and energetick without rules:
wherever I turned my view, there was perplexity to be disen-
tangled, and confusion to be regulated; choice was to be made
out of boundless variety, without any established principle of

selection; adulterations were to be detected, without a settled test of purity; and modes of expression to be rejected or received, without the suffrages of any writers of classical reputation or acknowledged authority.

Having therefore no assistance but from general grammar, I applied myself to the perusal of our writers; and noting whatever might be of use to ascertain or illustrate any word or phrase, accumulated in time the materials of a dictionary, which, by degrees, I reduced to method, establishing to myself, in the progress of the work, such rules as experience and analogy suggested to me; experience, which practice and observation were continually increasing; and analogy, which, though in some words obscure, was evident in others.

In adjusting the ORTHOGRAPHY, which has been to this time unsettled and fortuitous, I found it necessary to distinguish those irregularities that are inherent in our tongue, and perhaps coeval with it, from others which the ignorance or negligence of later writers has produced. Every language has its anomalies, which, though inconvenient, and in themselves once unnecessary, must be tolerated among the imperfections of human things, and which require only to be registered, that they may not be increased, and ascertained, that they may not be confounded: but every language has likewise its improprieties and absurdities, which it is the duty of the lexicographer to correct or proscribe.

As language was at its beginning merely oral, all words of necessary or common use were spoken before they were written; and while they were unfixed by any visible signs, must have been spoken with great diversity, as we now observe those who cannot read to catch sounds imperfectly, and utter them negligently. When this wild and barbarous jargon was first reduced to an alphabet, every penman endeavoured to express, as he could, the sounds which he was accustomed to pronounce or to receive, and vitiated in writing such words as were already vitiated in speech. The powers of the letters, when they were applied to a new language, must have been vague and unsettled, and therefore different hands would exhibit the same sound by different combinations.

From this uncertain pronunciation arise in a great part the various dialects of the same country, which will always be observed to grow fewer, and less different, as books are multiplied; and from this arbitrary representation of sounds by letters, proceeds that diversity of spelling observable in the *Saxon* remains, and I suppose in the first books of every nation, which perplexes or destroys analogy, and produces anomalous formations, that, being once incorporated, can never be afterwards dismissed or reformed.

Of this kind are the derivatives *length* from *long*, *strength* from *strong*, *darling* from *dear*, *breadth* from *broad*, from *dry*, *drought*, and from *high*, *height*, which *Milton*, in zeal for analogy, writes *highth; Quid te exempta juvat spinis de pluribus una?* to change all would be too much, and to change one is nothing.

This uncertainty is most frequent in the vowels, which are so capriciously pronounced, and so differently modified, by accident or affectation, not only in every province, but in every mouth, that to them, as is well known to etymologists, little regard is to be shown in the deduction of one language from another.

Such defects are not errours in orthography, but spots of barbarity impressed so deep in the *English* language, that criticism can never wash them away: these, therefore, must be permitted to remain untouched; but many words have likewise been altered by accident, or depraved by ignorance, as the pronunciation of the vulgar has been weakly followed; and some still continue to be variously written, as authors differ in their care or skill: of these it was proper to inquire the true orthography, which I have always considered as depending on their derivation, and have therefore referred them to their original languages: thus I write *enchant, enchantment, enchanter*, after the *French*, and *incantation* after the *Latin;* thus *entire* is chosen rather than *intire*, because it passed to us not from the *Latin integer*, but from the *French entier*.

Of many words it is difficult to say whether they were immediately received from the *Latin* or the *French*, since at the time when we had dominions in *France*, we had *Latin* service in our churches. It is, however, my opinion, that the *French* generally supplied us; for we have few *Latin* words, among the terms of domestick use, which are not *French;* but many *French*, which are very remote from *Latin*.

Even in words of which the derivation is apparent, I have been often obliged to sacrifice uniformity to custom; thus I write, in compliance with a numberless majority, *convey* and *inveigh*, *deceit* and *receipt*, *fancy* and *phantom;* sometimes the derivative varies from the primitive, as *explain* and *explanation*, *repeat* and *repetition.*

Some combinations of letters having the same power, are used indifferently without any discoverable reason of choice, as in *choak, choke; soap, sope; fewel, fuel*, and many others; which I have sometimes inserted twice, that those who search for them under either form, may not search in vain.

In examining the orthography of any doubtful word, the mode of spelling by which it is inserted in the series of the dictionary, is to be considered as that to which I give, perhaps not often rashly, the preference. I have left, in the examples, to every author his own practice unmolested, that the reader may balance suffrages, and judge between us: but this question is not always to be determined by reputed or by real learning; some men, intent upon greater things, have thought little on sounds and derivations; some, knowing in the ancient tongues, have neglected those in which our words are commonly to be sought. Thus *Hammond* writes *fecibleness* for *feasibleness*, because I suppose he imagined it derived immediately from the *Latin;* and some words, such as *dependant, dependent; dependance, dependence*, vary their final syllable, as one or another language is present to the writer.

In this part of the work, where caprice has long wantoned without control, and vanity sought praise by petty reformation, I have endeavoured to proceed with a scholar's reverence for antiquity, and a grammarian's regard to the genius of our tongue. I have attempted few alterations, and among those few, perhaps the greater part is from the modern to the ancient practice; and I hope I may be allowed to recommend to those, whose thoughts have been perhaps employed too anxiously on verbal singularities, not to disturb, upon narrow views, or for minute propriety, the orthography of their fathers. It has been asserted, that for the law to be *known*, is of more importance than to be *right*. Change, says *Hooker*, is not made without inconvenience, even from worse to better. There is in constancy and stability a general and lasting advantage, which will always overbalance the slow improvements of gradual correction. Much less ought our written language to comply with the corruptions of oral utterance, or copy that which every variation of time or place makes different from itself, and imitate those changes, which will again be changed, while imitation is employed in observing them.

This recommendation of steadiness and uniformity does not proceed from an opinion, that particular combinations of letters have much influence on human happiness; or that truth may not be successfully taught by modes of spelling fanciful and errone-ous: I am not yet so lost in lexicography, as to forget that *words are the daughters of earth, and that things are the sons of heaven.* Language is only the instrument of science, and words are but the signs of ideas: I wish, however, that the instrument might be less apt to decay, and that signs might be permanent, like the things which they denote.

In settling the orthography, I have not wholly neglected the pronunciation, which I have directed, by printing an accent upon the acute or elevated syllable. It will sometimes be found, that the accent is placed by the author quoted, on a different syllable from that marked in the alphabetical series; it is then to be under-stood, that custom has varied, or that the author has, in my opinion, pronounced wrong. Short directions are sometimes given where the sound of letters is irregular; and if they are sometimes omitted, defect in such minute observations will be more easily excused, than superfluity.

In the investigation both of the orthography and signification of words, their ETYMOLOGY was necessarily to be considered, and they were therefore to be divided into primitives and deriva-tives. A primitive word, is that which can be traced no further to any *English* root; thus *circumspect, circumvent, circumstance, delude, concave,* and *complicate*, though compounds in the Latin, are to us primitives. Derivatives, are all those that can be referred to any word in *English* of greater simplicity.

The derivatives I have referred to their primitives, with an accuracy sometimes needless; for who does not see that *remoteness* comes from *remote, lovely* from *love, concavity* from *concave,* and *demonstrative* from *demonstrate?* but this grammatical exuberance the scheme of my work did not allow me to repress. It is of great importance, in examining the general fabric of a language, to trace one word from another, by noting the usual modes of derivation and inflection; and uniformity must be preserved in systematical works, though sometimes at the expense of particular propriety.

Among other derivatives I have been careful to insert and elucidate the anomalous plurals of nouns and preterites of verbs, which in the *Teutonick* dialects are very frequent, and, though familiar to those who have always used them, interrupt and embarrass the learners of our language.

The two languages from which our primitives have been derived are the *Roman* and *Teutonick:* under the *Roman* I comprehend the *French* and provincial tongues; and under the *Teutonick* range the *Saxon, German,* and all their kindred dialects. Most of our polysyllables are *Roman,* and our words of one syllable are very often *Teutonick.*

In assigning the *Roman* original, it has perhaps sometimes happened that I have mentioned only the *Latin,* when the word was borrowed from the *French;* and considering myself as employed only in the illustration of my own language, I have not been very careful to observe whether the *Latin* word be pure or barbarous, or the *French* elegant or obsolete. . . .

Our knowledge of the northern literature is so scanty, that of words undoubtedly *Teutonick,* the original is not always to be found in any ancient language; and I have therefore inserted *Dutch* or *German* substitutes, which I consider not as radical, but parallel, not as the parents, but sisters of the *English.*

The words which are represented as thus related by descent or cognation, do not always agree in sense; for it is incident to words, as to their authors, to degenerate from their ancestors, and to

change their manners when they change their country. It is sufficient, in etymological inquiries, if the senses of kindred words
be found such as may easily pass into each other, or such as may
both be referred to one general idea.

The etymology, so far as it is yet known, was easily found in
the volumes where it is particularly and professedly delivered;
and, by proper attention to the rules of derivation, the orthography was soon adjusted. But to COLLECT the WORDS of our
language was a task of greater difficulty: the deficiency of dictionaries was immediately apparent; and when they were ex-
hausted, what was yet wanting, must be sought by fortuitous and
unguided excursions into books, and gleaned as industry should
find, or chance should offer it, in the boundless chaos of a living
speech. My search, however, has been either skilful or lucky;
for I have much augmented the vocabulary. . . .

The words, thus selected and disposed, are grammatically considered; they are referred to the different parts of speech; traced,
when they are irregularly inflected, through their various termina-
tions; and illustrated by observations, not indeed of great or
striking importance, separately considered, but necessary to the
elucidation of our language, and hitherto neglected or forgotten
by *English* grammarians.

That part of my work on which I expect malignity most frequently to fasten, is the *Explanation;* in which I cannot hope to
satisfy those, who are perhaps not inclined to be pleased, since
I have not always been able to satisfy myself. To interpret
a language by itself is very difficult; many words cannot be
explained by synomimes, because the idea signified by them has
not more than one appellation; nor by paraphrase, because simple
ideas cannot be described. When the nature of things is unknown, or the notion unsettled and indefinite, and various in
various minds, the words by which such notions are conveyed, or
such things denoted, will be ambiguous and perplexed. And
such is the fate of hapless lexicography, that not only darkness,
but light, impedes and distresses it; things may be not only
too little, but too much known, to be happily illustrated. To
explain, requires the use of terms less abstruse than that which

is to be explained, and such terms cannot always be found; for as nothing can be proved but by supposing something intuitively known, and evident without proof, so nothing can be defined but by the use of words too plain to admit a definition. . . .

All the interpretations of words are not written with the same skill, or the same happiness: things equally easy in themselves, are not all equally easy to any single mind. Every writer of a long work commits errours, where there appears neither ambiguity to mislead, nor obscurity to confound him; and in a search like this, many felicities of expression will be casually overlooked, many convenient parallels will be forgotten, and many particulars will admit improvement from a mind utterly unequal to the whole performance.

But many seeming faults are to be imputed rather to the nature of the undertaking, than the negligence of the performer. Thus some explanations are unavoidably reciprocal or circular, as *hind, the female of the stag; stag, the male of the hind:* sometimes easier words are changed into harder, as *burial* into *sepulture* or *interment, drier* into *desiccative, dryness* into *siccity* or *aridity, fit* into *paroxysm;* for the easiest word, whatever it be, can never be translated into one more easy. But easiness and difficulty are merely relative, and if the present prevalence of our language should invite foreigners to this dictionary, many will be assisted by those words which now seem only to increase or produce obscurity. For this reason I have endeavoured frequently to join a *Teutonick* and *Roman* interpretation, as to CHEER, to *gladden,* or *exhilarate,* that every learner of *English* may be assisted by his own tongue.

The solution of all difficulties, and the supply of all defects, must be sought in the examples, subjoined to the various senses of each word, and ranged according to the time of their authors.

When I first collected these authorities, I was desirous that every quotation should be useful to some other end than the illustration of a word; I therefore extracted from philosophers principles of science; from historians remarkable facts; from chymists complete processes; from divines striking exhortations; and from poets beautiful descriptions. Such is design, while it is yet at a distance from execution. When the time called upon me to range this accumulation of elegance and wisdom into an alphabetical series, I soon discovered that the bulk of my volumes would fright away the student, and was forced to depart from my scheme of including all that was pleasing or useful in *English* literature, and reduce my transcripts very often to clusters of words, in which scarcely any meaning is retained; thus to the weariness of copying, I was condemned to add the vexation of expunging. Some passages I have yet spared, which may relieve the labour of verbal searches, and intersperse with verdure and flowers the dusty deserts of barren philology.

The examples, thus mutilated, are no longer to be considered as conveying the sentiments or doctrine of their authors; the word for the sake of which they are inserted, with all its appendant clauses, has been carefully preserved; but it may sometimes happen, by hasty detruncation, that the general tendency of the sentence may be changed: the divine may desert his tenets, or the philosopher his system.

Some of the examples have been taken from writers who were never mentioned as masters of elegance or models of style; but words must be sought where they are used; and in what pages, eminent for purity, can terms of manufacture or agriculture be found? Many quotations serve no other purpose, than that of proving the bare existence of words, and are therefore selected with less scrupulousness than those which are to teach their structures and relations.

My purpose was to admit no testimony of living authors, that I might not be misled by partiality, and that none of my cotemporaries might have reason to complain; nor have I departed from this resolution, but when some performance of uncommon excellence excited my veneration, when my memory supplied me, from late books, with an example that was wanting, or when my heart, in the tenderness of friendship, solicited admission for a favourite name.

So far have I been from any care to grace my pages with modern decorations, that I have studiously endeavoured to collect examples and authorities from the writers before the restoration, whose works I regard as *the wells of English undefiled,* as the pure sources of genuine diction. Our language, for almost a century, has, by the concurrence of many causes, been gradually departing from its original *Teutonick* character, and deviating towards a *Gallick* structure and phraseology, from which it ought to be our endeavour to recal it, by making our ancient volumes the ground-work of style, admitting among the additions of later times, only such as may supply real deficiencies, such as are readily adopted by the genius of our tongue, and incorporate easily with our native idioms.

But as every language has a time of rudeness antecedent to perfection, as well as of false refinement and declension, I have been cautious lest my zeal for antiquity might drive me into times too remote, and crowd my book with words now no longer understood. I have fixed *Sidney's* work for the boundary, beyond which I make few excursions. From the authors which rose in the time of *Elizabeth,* a speech might be formed adequate to all the purposes of use and elegance. If the language of theology were extracted from *Hooker* and the translation of the Bible; the terms of natural knowledge from *Bacon;* the phrases of policy, war, and navigation from *Raleigh;* the dialect of poetry and fiction from *Spenser* and *Sidney;* and the diction of common life from *Shakespeare,* few ideas would be lost to mankind, for want of *English* words, in which they might be expressed.

It is not sufficient that a word is found, unless it be so combined as that its meaning is apparently determined by the tract and tenour of the sentence; such passages I have therefore chosen, and when it happened that any author gave a definition of a term, or such an explanation as is equivalent to a definition, I have placed his authority as a supplement to my own, without regard to the chronological order, that is otherwise observed.

Some words, indeed, stand unsupported by any authority, but they are commonly derivative nouns, or adverbs, formed from their primitives by regular and constant analogy, or names of things seldom occurring in books, or words of which I have reason to doubt the existence.

There is more danger of censure from the multiplicity than

paucity of examples; authorities will sometimes seem to have been accumulated without necessity or use, and perhaps some will be found, which might, without loss, have been omitted. But a work of this kind is not hastily to be charged with superfluities: those quotations, which to careless or unskilful perusers appear only to repeat the same sense, will often exhibit, to a more accurate examiner, diversities of signification, or, at least, afford different shades of the same meaning: one will show the word applied to persons, another to things; one will express an ill, another a good, and a third a neutral sense; one will prove the expression genuine from an ancient author; another will show it elegant from a modern: a doubtful authority is corroborated by another of more credit; an ambiguous sentence is ascertained by a passage clear and determinate; the word, how often soever repeated, appears with new associates and in different combinations, and every quotation contributes something to the stability or enlargement of the language.

When words are used equivocally, I receive them in either sense; when they are metaphorical, I adopt them in their primitive acceptation.

I have sometimes, though rarely, yielded to the temptation of exhibiting a genealogy of sentiments, by showing how one author copied the thoughts and diction of another: such quotations are indeed little more than repetitions, which might justly be censured, did they not gratify the mind, by affording a kind of intellectual history.

The various syntactical structures occurring in the examples have been carefully noted; the license or negligence with which many words have been hitherto used, has made our style capricious and indeterminate; when the different combinations of the same word are exhibited together, the preference is readily given to propriety, and I have often endeavoured to direct the choice.

Thus have I laboured by settling the orthography, displaying the analogy, regulating the structures, and ascertaining the signification of *English* words, to perform all the parts of a faithful lexicographer: but I have not always executed my own scheme, or satisfied my own expectations. The work, whatever proofs of diligence and attention it may exhibit, is yet capable of many improvements: the orthography which I recommend is still controvertible, the etymology which I adopt is uncertain, and perhaps frequently erroneous; the explanations are sometimes too much contracted, and sometimes too much diffused, the significations are distinguished rather with subtilty than skill, and the attention is harassed with unnecessary minuteness.

The examples are too often injudiciously truncated, and perhaps sometimes, I hope very rarely, alleged in a mistaken sense; for in making this collection I trusted more to memory, than, in a state of disquiet and embarrassment, memory can contain, and purposed to supply at the review what was left incomplete in the first transcription.

Many terms appropriated to particular occupations, though necessary and significant, are undoubtedly omitted; and of the words most studiously considered and exemplified, many senses have escaped observation.

Yet these failures, however frequent, may admit extenuation and apology. To have attempted much is always laudable, even when the enterprise is above the strength that undertakes it: To rest below his own aim is incident to every one whose fancy is active, and whose views are comprehensive; nor is any man satisfied with himself because he has done much, but because he can conceive little. When first I engaged in this work, I resolved to leave neither words nor things unexamined, and pleased myself with the prospect of the hours which I should revel away in feasts of literature, with the obscure recesses of northern learning which I should enter and ransack; the treasures with which I expected every search into those neglected mines to reward my labour, and the triumph with which I should display my acquisitions to mankind. When I had thus inquired into the original of words, I resolved to show likewise my attention to things; to pierce deep into every science, to inquire the nature of every substance of which I inserted the name, to limit every idea by a definition strictly logical, and exhibit every production of art or nature in an accurate description, that my book might be in place of all other dictionaries whether appellative or technical. But these were the dreams of a poet doomed at last to wake a lexicographer. I soon found that it is too late to look for instruments, when the work calls for execution, and that whatever abilities I had brought to my task, with those I must finally perform it. To deliberate whenever I doubted, to inquire whenever I was ignorant, would have protracted the undertaking without end, and, perhaps, without much improvement; for I did not find by my first experiments, that what I had not of my own was easily to be obtained: I saw that one inquiry only gave occasion to another, that book referred to book, that to search was not always to find, and to find was not always to be informed; and that thus to pursue perfection, was, like the first inhabitants of Arcadia, to chase the sun, which, when they had reached the hill where he seemed to rest, was still beheld at the same distance from them.

I then contracted my design, determining to confide in myself, and no longer to solicit auxiliaries, which produced more incumbrance than assistance: by this I obtained at least one advantage, that I set limits to my work, which would in time be ended, though not completed.

Despondency has never so far prevailed as to depress me to negligence; some faults will at last appear to be the effects of anxious diligence and persevering activity. The nice and subtle ramifications of meaning were not easily avoided by a mind intent upon accuracy, and convinced of the necessity of disentangling combinations, and separating similitudes. Many of the distinctions, which to common readers appear useless and idle, will be found real and important by men versed in the school philosophy, without which no dictionary can ever be accurately compiled, or skilfully examined.

Some senses however there are, which, though not the same, are yet so nearly allied, that they are often confounded. Most men think indistinctly, and therefore cannot speak with exactness; and consequently some examples might be indifferently put to either signification: this uncertainty is not to be imputed to me, who do not form, but register the language; who do not teach men how they should think, but relate how they have hitherto expressed their thoughts.

The imperfect sense of some examples I lamented, but could not remedy, and hope they will be compensated by innumerable passages selected with propriety, and preserved with exactness; some shining with sparks of imagination, and some replete with treasures of wisdom.

The orthography and etymology, though imperfect, are not imperfect for want of care, but because care will not always be successful, and recollection or information come too late for use.

That many terms of art and manufacture are omitted, must be frankly acknowledged; but for this defect I may boldly allege that it was unavoidable: I could not visit caverns to learn the miner's language, nor take a voyage to perfect my skill in the dialect of navigation, nor visit the warehouses of merchants, and shops of artificers, to gain the names of wares, tools and operations, of which no mention is found in books; what favourable accident, or easy inquiry brought within my reach, has not been neglected; but it had been a hopeless labour to glean up words, by courting living information, and contesting with the sullenness of one, and the roughness of another. . . .

Nor are all words which are not found in the vocabulary to be lamented as omissions. Of the laborious and mercantile part of the people, the diction is in a great measure casual and mutable; many of their terms are formed for some temporary or local convenience, and though current at certain times and places, are in others utterly unknown. This fugitive cant, which is always in a state of increase or decay, cannot be regarded as any part of the durable materials of a language, and therefore must be suffered to perish with other things unworthy of preservation.

Care will sometimes betray to the appearance of negligence. He that is catching opportunities which seldom occur, will suffer those to pass by unregarded, which he expects hourly to return; he that is searching for rare and remote things, will neglect those that are obvious and familiar: thus many of the most common and cursory words have been inserted with little illustration, because in gathering authorities, I forbore to copy those which

I thought likely to occur whenever they were wanted. It is remarkable that, in reviewing my collection, I found the word SEA
unexemplified.

Thus it happens, that in things difficult there is danger from
ignorance, and in things easy from confidence; the mind, afraid
of greatness, and disdainful of littleness, hastily withdraws herself
from painful searches, and passes with scornful rapidity over
tasks not adequate to her powers, sometimes too secure for caution, and again too anxious for vigorous effort; sometimes idle
in a plain path, and sometimes distracted in labyrinths, and dis-
sipated by different intentions.

A large work is difficult because it is large, even though all its
parts might singly be performed with facility; where there are
many things to be done, each must be allowed its share of time
and labour, in the proportion only which it bears to the whole;
nor can it be expected, that the stones which form the dome of
a temple, should be squared and polished like the diamond of a
ring.

Of the event of this work, for which, having laboured it with
so much application, I cannot but have some degree of parental
fondness, it is natural to form conjectures. Those who have been
persuaded to think well of my design, will require that it should
fix our language, and put a stop to those alterations which time
and chance have hitherto been suffered to make in it without
opposition. With this consequence I will confess that I flattered
myself for a while; but now begin to fear that I have indulged
expectation which neither reason nor experience can justify.
When we see men grow old and die at a certain time one after
another, from century to century, we laugh at the elixir that
promises to prolong life to a thousand years; and with equal
justice may the lexicographer be derided, who being able to
produce no example of a nation that has preserved their words
and phrases from mutability, shall imagine that his dictionary can
embalm his language, and secure it from corruption and decay,
that it is in his power to change sublunary nature, and clear
the world at once from folly, vanity and affectation.

With this hope, however, academies have been instituted, to

guard the avenues of their languages, to retain fugitives, and repulse intruders; but their vigilance and activity have hitherto been vain; sounds are too volatile and subtle for legal restraints; to enchain syllables, and to lash the wind, are equally the undertakings of pride, unwilling to measure its desires by its strength. The *French* language has visibly changed under the inspection of the academy; the style of *Amelot's* translation of father *Paul* is observed by *Le Courayer* to be *un peu passé;* and no *Italian* will maintain, that the diction of any modern writer is not perceptibly different from that of *Boccace, Machiavel,* or *Caro.*

Total and sudden transformation of a language seldom happen; conquests and migrations are now very rare: but there are other causes of change, which, though slow in their operation, and invisible in their progress, are perhaps as much superiour to human resistance, as the revolutions of the sky, or intumescence of the tide. Commerce, however necessary, however lucrative, as it depraves the manners, corrupts the language; they that have frequent intercourse with strangers, to whom they endeavour to accommodate themselves, must in time learn a mingled dialect, like the jargon which serves the traffickers on the *Mediterranean* and *Indian* coasts. This will not always be confined to the exchange, the warehouse, or the port, but will be communicated by degrees to other ranks of the people, and be at last incorporated with the current speech.

There are likewise internal causes equally forcible. The language most likely to continue long without alteration, would be that of a nation raised a little, and but a little, above barbarity, secluded from strangers, and totally employed in procuring the conveniencies of life; either without books, or, like some of the *Mahometan* countries, with very few: men thus busied and unlearned, having only such words as common use requires, would perhaps long continue to express the same notions by the same signs. But no such constancy can be expected in a people polished by arts, and classed by subordination, where one part of the community is sustained and accommodated by the labour of the other. Those who have much leisure to think, will always be enlarging the stock of ideas; and every increase of knowledge, whether real or fancied, will produce new words, or combinations of words. When the mind is unchained from necessity, it will range after convenience; when it is left at large in the fields of speculation, it will shift opinions; as any custom is disused, the words that expressed it must perish with it; as any opinion grows popular, it will innovate speech in the same proportion as it alters practice.

As by the cultivation of various sciences a language is amplified, it will be more furnished with words deflected from their original sense; the geometrician will talk of a courtier's zenith, or the eccentrick virtue of a wild hero, and the physician of sanguine expectations and phlegmatick delays. Copiousness of speech will give opportunities to capricious choice, by which some words will be preferred, and others degraded; vicissitudes of fashion will enforce the use of new, or extend the signification of known terms. The tropes of poetry will make hourly encroachments, and the metaphorical will become the current sense: pronunciation will be varied by levity or ignorance, and the pen must at length comply with the tongue; illiterate writers will, at one time or other, by public infatuation, rise into renown, who, not knowing the original import of words, will use them with colloquial licentiousness, confound distinction, and forget propriety. As politeness increases, some expressions will be considered as too gross and vulgar for the delicate, others as too formal and ceremonious for the gay and airy; new phrases are therefore adopted, which must, for the same reasons, be in time dismissed. *Swift*, in his petty treatise on the *English* language, allows that new words must sometimes be introduced, but proposes that none should be suffered to become obsolete. But what makes a word obsolete, more than general agreement to forbear it? and how shall it be continued, when it conveys an offensive idea, or recalled again into the mouths of mankind, when it has once become unfamiliar by disuse, and unpleasing by unfamiliarity?

There is another cause of alteration more prevalent than any other, which yet in the present state of the world cannot be obviated. A mixture of two languages will produce a third distinct from both, and they will always be mixed, where the chief part of education, and the most conspicuous accomplishment, is skill in ancient or in foreign tongues. He that has long cultivated another language, will find its words and combinations crowd upon his memory; and haste and negligence, refinement and affectation, will obtrude borrowed terms and exotick expressions.

The great pest of speech is frequency of translation. No book was ever turned from one language into another, without imparting something of its native idiom; this is the most mischievous and comprehensive innovation; single words may enter by thousands, and the fabrick of the tongue continue the same; but new phraseology changes much at once; it alters not the single stones of the building, but the order of the columns. If an academy should be established for the cultivation of our style, which I, who can never wish to see dependance multiplied, hope the spirit of *English* liberty will hinder or destroy, let them, instead of compiling grammars and dictionaries, endeavour, with all their influence, to stop the license of translators, whose idleness and ignorance, if it be suffered to proceed, will reduce us to babble a dialect of *France*.

If the changes that we fear be thus irresistible, what remains but to acquiesce with silence, as in the other insurmountable distresses of humanity? It remains that we retard what we cannot repel, that we palliate what we cannot cure. Life may be lengthened by care, though death cannot be ultimately defeated: tongues, like governments, have a natural tendency to degeneration; we have long preserved our constitution, let us make some struggles for our language.

In hope of giving longevity to that which its own nature forbids to be immortal, I have devoted this book, the labour of years, to the honour of my country, that we may no longer yield the palm of philology, without a contest, to the nations of the continent. The chief glory of every people arises from its authors: whether I shall add any thing by my own writings to the reputation of *English* literature, must be left to time: much of my life has been lost under the pressures of disease; much has been trifled away; and much has always been spent in provision for the day that was passing over me; but I shall not think my employment useless or ignoble, if by my assistance foreign nations, and distant ages, gain access to the propagators of knowledge, and understand the teachers of truth; if my labours afford light to the repositories of science, and add celebrity to *Bacon*, to *Hooker*, to *Milton*, and to *Boyle*.

When I am animated by this wish, I look with pleasure on my book, however defective, and deliver it to the world with the spirit of a man that has endeavoured well. That it will immediately become popular I have not promised to myself: a few wild blunders, and risible absurdities, from which no work of such multiplicity was ever free, may for a time furnish folly with laughter, and harden ignorance in contempt; but useful diligence will at last prevail, and there never can be wanting some who distinguish desert; who will consider that no dictionary of a living tongue ever can be perfect, since while it is hastening to publication, some words are budding, and some falling away; that a whole life cannot be spent upon syntax and etymology, and that even a whole life would not be sufficient; that he, whose design includes whatever language can express, must often speak of what he does not understand; that a writer will sometimes be hurried by eagerness to the end, and sometimes faint with weariness, under a task, which *Scaliger* compares to the labours of the anvil and the mine; that what is obvious is not always known, and what is known is not always present; that sudden fits of inadvertency will surprise vigilance, slight avocations will seduce attention, and casual eclipses of the mind will darken learning; and that the writer shall often in vain trace his memory at the moment of need, for that which yesterday he knew with intuitive readiness, and which will come uncalled into his thoughts tomorrow.

In this work, when it shall be found that much is omitted, let it not be forgotten that much likewise is performed; and though no book was ever spared out of tenderness to the author, and the world is little solicitous to know whence proceeded the faults of that which it condemns; yet it may gratify curiosity to inform it, that the *English Dictionary* was written with little assistance of the learned, and without any patronage of the great; not in the soft obscurities of retirement, or under the shelter of academick bowers, but amidst inconvenience and distraction, in sickness and in sorrow. It may repress the triumph of malignant criticism to observe, that if our language is not here fully displayed, I have only failed in an attempt which no human powers have hitherto completed. If the lexicons of ancient tongues, now immutably fixed, and comprised in a few volumes, be yet, after the toil of successive ages, inadequate and delusive; if the aggregated knowledge, and co-operating diligence of the *Italian* academicians, did not secure them from the censure of *Beni;* if the embodied criticks of *France*, when fifty years had been spent upon their work, were obliged to change its economy, and give their second edition another form, I may surely be contented without the praise of perfection, which, if I could obtain, in this gloom of solitude, what would it avail me? I have protracted my work till most of those whom I wished to please have sunk into the grave, and success and miscarriage are empty sounds. I therefore dismiss it with frigid tranquility having little to fear or hope from censure or from praise.

MITFORD M. MATHEWS

Meanings and Etymologies

> In a single written sentence, a hundred elusive meanings obscurely palpitate.
>
> —GILES LYTTON STRACHEY

There is an old saying that the same man never crossed the same river twice. The man is bound to be a little different on his second crossing. He is at least a little older and more experienced. For one thing, he knows more about crossing rivers. Also, the river is not quite the same. It may be much higher, or lower, than it was when the man crossed it before. It would be impossible for the man to find and pass through or over just the same water he crossed earlier.

This old saying occurs to one who contemplates the manifold meanings words have. No word is ever used twice in just the same sense. The matter is perplexing in the extreme, and we need not go into it here, but it is a well-known fact that many words, especially those that are old in the language, have more than one clearly recognizable meaning.

One of the most important things a lexicographer has to do is to record the meanings of words. He has the task of arranging these meanings in the order he thinks will be of most help to those who use his work.

Different editors solve this problem of arrangement in different ways. In the prefatory part of your dictionary you will find some

. . . .

indication of the plan that has been followed in arranging the meanings. In the Merriam-Webster dictionaries, the meanings are arranged, as far as possible, in the order in which they arose. In those dictionaries, the first meanings given are the earliest a word is known to have had, and the more modern meanings come later.

The arrangement of meanings is difficult, no matter what plan is used. Students not instructed about this aspect of dictionaries sometimes suppose that the first meaning given for a word is the most common one, but that is not always the case. The only safe course is to examine the forematter of your dictionary to see what plan has been followed.

Many of those who consult a dictionary search through the meanings, often in haste, hoping to find the one in which they are interested or one that will satisfy their immediate need. Such a method is not to be recommended. Such flutterings about leave only a meager residue of information and interest in the mind of the searcher. The most fruitful way to approach the meanings is by way of etymologies. Many times the etymology will illuminate not only a particular meaning but all the meanings a word has, and will show the way to related words and their meanings.

For example, *nausea* is a classical Greek word in English dress. It is based upon another Greek word meaning a ship. The Greeks were acquainted with the miseries of sea-sickness, which their word *nausia* meant, but in thinking of this distress they focused attention on a ship rather than on the sea. Dictionaries in their etymologies point out that *nausea* is closely related to *nave* (of a church or cathedral), *nautical, naval,* each of them having this basic idea of a ship.

Clinic is from a Greek word meaning a bed, and the meanings of the word and those of its derivatives and combinations stem from this significance. *Longitude* is based upon a Latin word for *long,* and this sense colors all its meanings. The same is true of *latitude,* from a Latin word for *broad,* and, indeed, of an avalanche of others.

Sometimes the original meaning of a word is markedly different from some of its later ones. *Scene* started out in classical Greek meaning a tent and later a booth before which actors played and into which they retired to change their costumes. As the art of acting became more elaborate, the scene of a Greek theater became the permanent structure forming the background of the stage (cf. our expression "to look behind the scene"). The extension of the meaning of the word has continued until it now means anything that lies open to view. The idea of a tent is not felt at all.

One who does not pay attention to etymologies misses surprising and fascinating information about word relationships. For example, *hyena* is a Greek word in modern English form. It was the name the Greeks applied to the animal still so called. Dictionaries dismantle this Greek name for the hyena and show that it was the feminine form of the Greek word for hog and consequently meant sow. When the Greeks called a hyena a sow, they no doubt did so in allusion to its pronounced mane, suggesting the bristling arched mane of a wild sow.

The Greek word *hys*, without any feminine suffix, meant hog or swine. Latin had the same word with the same meaning but spelled it *sus*. The Greek word, with its feminine suffix, appears now in English as *hyena*, and the Latin *sus* accounts for our *sow*. *Hyena* and *sow* certainly do not at first glance appear to be cognates, but they are. Similarly *six* and the first part of *hexagon* are cognates, *six* being from the Germanic *sex*, and *hex-* coming from Greek *hex* meaning six.

Let us now look carefully at some dictionary entries in an effort to secure from them all the information they contain. We shall begin by looking closely at the entry *anecdote* in the College Edition of *Webster's New World Dictionary*.[1]

> **an·ec·dote** (an′ik-dōt′), *n.* [Fr.; ML. *anecdota;* Gr. *anekdota*, neut. pl. of *anekdotos*, unpublished; *an-*, not + *ekdotos* < *ekdidonai; ek-*, out + *didonai*, to give], **1.** *pl.* originally, little-known, entertaining facts of history or biography; hence, **2.** a short, entertaining account of some happening, usually personal or biographical.—*SYN.* see **story.**

This dictionary makes etymology one of its strong features and so serves exceptionally well for our purpose.

The following things about this entry are of interest.

1. The entry word, printed in boldface to give it more prominence, is divided by periods into its three syllables. This form of division not only helps out with the pronunciation of a word, but it also gives assistance to one who has to divide a word at the end of a line of writing or printing. In such cases, words should be divided with respect to their syllables.

2. Then, within curves, the word is rewritten, this time in symbols that show pronunciation. A heavy accent mark, ' immediately follows the syllable which receives most stress, and a lighter mark indicates the syllable getting minor stress. A syllable, here *ik*, which gets no stress is followed by a hyphen.

Following the indication of pronunciation comes the abbreviation of the part of speech to which the word belongs. It is the conventional practice to give these abbreviations in italics.

3. It is well-accepted dictionary procedure to place etymologies in square brackets just after the indictation of the part of speech of the word involved. The etymologies are perhaps the parts of dictionaries least often looked at, especially by younger students who are in such a hurry to get an education that they often miss fine opportunities to learn something. How much is missed by those who fail to give attention to etymologies may be seen by examining somewhat closely the one given here.

To show in a simpler way what it means, let us write the etymology in a much more expanded form, making no use of the abbreviations with which it is generously provided and with which we have become familiar on previous pages, and retaining the transliterated forms of the Greek words that occur. It may make this expanded version of the etymology easier to follow if we begin at the very end of it and proceed back to its beginning, just as it is sometimes easier to follow a stream from its source to its mouth than it is to explore it beginning at the mouth.

> In Greek there was a verb, *didonai*, meaning to give. A common prefix, *ek-*, was often used before this verb and it then became *ekdidonai* to give out. From this expanded form of the verb, Greek formed an adjective, *ekdotos*, given out. In

Greek it was customary to prefix *an-* to adjectives beginning with a vowel and thus reverse or negate their meanings. So the Greeks formed *anekdotos,* not given out.

Greek adjectives had masculine, feminine, and neuter forms. The neuter plural of *anekdotos* was *anekdota,* unpublished things, that is, things not given out. Latin, during the medieval period, borrowed *anekdota* in the form *anecdota.* This Latin term passed into French, where it was spelled *anecdote.* From French the word, unchanged in form, passed into English.

The etymology we began with has about twenty words in it; the expanded form above has many times as many. It is easy, however, for anyone who looks at the etymology in the dictionary to see that *anecdote* comes from French, which derived it from Latin, which obtained it from Greek, and that the basic meaning of it is things not published or given out. Anyone who considers this etymology thoughtfully may well be puzzled over the fact that *anecdote* began its career with such an odd meaning. A fuller account of the word is needed before this puzzle can be cleared up.

4. The definitions are numbered and begin with small letters. The numbering is of course a great convenience. The use of small letters at the beginnings of the definitions is a mere stylistic device, those charged with producing this dictionary feeling that the looks of the page justified the use of the small letters rather than capitals in such cases. The meanings are given in the order of their ages, the oldest meaning being given first. Observe how the original meaning led on to sense 2, the one which nowadays the word usually has.

5. At the very end of the entry there is a reference to *story* for a presentation of the synonyms of *anecdote.* English abounds in words that mean about the same thing. Dictionaries perform a useful service by giving such groups of words and distinguishing between such terms as *anecdote, narrative, tale, story.*

Of course, the larger a dictionary is, the more information one can obtain from it. Here is the entry *anecdote* as it appears in the current large unabridged *Webster's New International Dictionary, Second Edition.*[2]

an'ec·dote (ăn'ĕk·dōt; ăn'ĭk-), *n.* [F., fr. Gr. *anekdotos*
not published, fr. *an-* not + *ekdotos* given out, fr.
ekdidonai to give out, to publish, fr. *ek* out + *didonai*
to give. See DATE point of time.] **1.** *pl.* Literally, unpublished items; narratives of secret or private details
of history;—often in book titles. *Now Rare.*
2. A narrative, usually brief, of a separable incident or
event of curious interest, told without malice and usually with intent to amuse or please, often biographical
and characteristic of some notable person, esp. of his
likable foibles.
   Some modern *anecdotes* aver, He nodded in his elbow chair.
Prior.
Syn.—See STORY.

The attention already given to *anecdote* as it appears in a
smaller dictionary makes it unnecessary to do more here than to
point out some features of the present entry not taken account
of in the one previously examined.

Notice that the etymology here ends with a reference to the
entry DATE, meaning a point of time. An inspection of the etymology given of that entry reveals that *anecdote* belongs to a
group of words that are related because they all trace their
ancestry, in whole or in part, back to the same IE root that is
seen in the Greek verb *didonai*, meaning to give. Here is the list
of words Webster cites as being related in the manner indicated:
*anecdote, condone, dado, damn, dative, datum, die, n., donate,
dose, dower, edit, pardon, render, sacerdotal.*

All these words have in them the basic idea of giving. In some
of them this primary notion is quite obvious, as it clearly is in
donate and *dose.* In some of the words, other ideas are involved
along with that of giving, and it is interesting to work these out
by looking at a good dictionary. For example, the first syllable
of *condone* adds the idea of "altogether" to that of giving and
suggests giving entirely. The first syllable in *pardon* has nearly
the same significance, and the word suggests giving thoroughly or
completely. The case is different with *render.* Here the *re-* suggests "back" or "again." To *render* something is to give it back.
The *e-* in *edit* imparts the idea of "out" to that of *give.* To *edit*
a thing is to give it out.

It should not be supposed that these are all the English words that are related because they all have in them this idea of giving. Even in a large dictionary, space is limited. Words suggested by those in the list are left out. For example, *antidote* is omitted. The first element, *anti-*, is easily recognized as having in it the idea of "against." An *antidote* is something given against something, usually a poison.

One of the unique and highly valuable features of the unabridged Merriam-Webster is that it often groups words basically related because they, or parts of them, go back to a common ancestor word. No other English dictionary gives so much of this kind of information. Some of the commonest words in the language have a surprisingly large number of relatives. Here is a list of a few words related to *stand, v.*:

> assist, circumstance, consist, constant, contrast, cost, desist, destine, distant, exist, extant, instant, obstacle, obstinate, persist, stage, stalwart, stamen, standard, state, station, statue, steed, stool, subsist, substance, superstition, system, vassal

The entry *stand, v.* in *Webster's New International Dictionary, Second Edition,* should be seen for the full list.

Those interested in becoming acquainted with a large number of words should cultivate the habit of considering them as related to other words. Making the acquaintance of words by mastering them in isolation is slow and laborious, to be done only when absolutely necessary.

The next dictionary in which we shall examine the word *anecdote* is the *Century* [3] in which the entry is as follows:

> **anecdote** (an′ek-dōt), *n.* [< F. *anecdote,* first in pl. *anecdotes,* M.L. *anecdota,* < Gr. ἀνέκδοτα, pl., things unpublished, applied by Procopius to his memoirs of Justinian, which consisted chiefly of gossip about the private life of the court; prop. neut. pl. of ἀνέκδοτος, unpublished, not given out, < Gr. ἀν- priv. + ἔκδοτος, given out, verbal adj. of ἐκδιδόναι, give out, publish, < ἐκ, out (= L. *ex:* see ex-), + διδόναι, give, = L. *dare,* give: see *dose* and *date.*] **1.** *pl.* Secret history; facts relating to secret or private affairs, as of governments or of individuals: often used (commonly in the form *anecdota*) as the title of works treating of such mat-

ters.—2. A short narrative of a particular or detached
incident or occurrence of an interesting nature; a
biographical incident; a single passage of private life.
=Syn. *Anecdote, Story.* An *anecdote* is the relation of an
interesting or amusing incident, generally of a private nature,
and is always reported as true. A *story* may be true or fictitious,
and generally has reference to a series of incidents so arranged and related as to be entertaining.

In this treatment of the word there are some things not observed
before.

1. As is often done in dictionaries, the sign < is used freely in
the sense of "from." One instance of its use is seen in the etymology on page 41.

2. According to the etymology given here, the form which
anecdote had in French was the plural, a form to be expected
from the word's being derived from a plural in Latin and in
Greek. With this information, it is easier to understand why it
was in its plural form that the word made its first appearance in
English.

3. The fuller meaning of the source word, *anecdota,* is here
made clear—"applied by Procopius to his memoirs of Justinian,
which consisted chiefly of gossip about the private life of the
court." What is needed now is some information about Procopius
and Justinian. In 1894 the *Century* was completed by a *Cyclopedia of Names.* By referring to this volume we find that Procopius (?490–565 A.D.) was a historian in the old city of By-
zantium, now Istanbul, during the time (527–565 A.D.) Justinian
was emperor there.

Without letting the ruler find out about it, Procopius wrote the
gossip about the goings-on at the court. The historian did not
like Justinian, and he knew his head would roll if his manuscript
came to the attention of the emperor. He selected a title for his
collection of choice scandal that would indicate that the work
was not designed for giving out or publishing.

4. The remainder of the *Century* entry is easily understood with
the possible exception of the abbreviation "priv." for *privative,*
a word used in grammar in connection with those prefixes which
change the sense of a word from a positive to a negative one, as
do *un-, il-, in-, ir-,* in English. Compare such words as *lawful,*

unlawful; legal, illegal; tolerant, intolerant; regular, irregular.
On page 39 we mentioned that Greek made use of a prefix of this
kind, *a-*, which might also appear as *an-*. In Greek grammars this
prefix is referred to as "alpha privative."

It may appear to the beginner that by this time we have certainly found out all there is to know about *anecdote*, but we have
not. Here is how the entry looks in the *Oxford English Dictionary*.[4]

Anecdote (æ·nèkdoᵘt). [a. Fr. *anecdote*, or ad. its
source, med. L. *anecdota* (see sense I), a. Gr. ἀνέκδοτα
things unpublished, f. ἀν priv. + ἔκδοτ-ος published, f.
ἐκδιδόναι to give out, publish: applied by Procopius to
his 'Unpublished Memoirs' of the Emperor Justinian,
which consisted chiefly of tales of the private life of the
court; whence the application of the name to short stories
or particulars.]

1. *pl.* Secret, private, or hitherto unpublished narratives
or details of history. (At first, and now again occas.
used in L. form *anecdota* (ăne·kdotă.)
1676 MARVEL *Mr. Smirke* Wks. 1875 IV. 71 A man . . might
make a pleasant story of the *anecdota* of that meeting. **1686** F.
SPENCE (*title*) Anecdotes of Florence, or the secret History of the
House of Medicis [a translation of Varillas' *Anecdotes de Florence*].
1727 SWIFT *Gulliver* III. viii. 230 Those who pretend to write
anecdotes, or secret history. **1727-51** CHAMBERS *Cycl.*, *Anecdotes*,
Anecdota, a term used by some authors, for the titles of Secret
Histories; that is, of such as relate the secret affairs and transactions
of princes; speaking with too much freedom, or too much sincerity,
of the manner and conduct of persons in authority, to allow
of their being made public. **1769** BURKE *State Nat.* Wks. II. 157
Professing even industriously, in this publick matter, to avoid
anecdotes, I say nothing of those famous reconciliations and
quarrels which weakened the body. **1882** *Pall Mall G.* 23 Oct. 5
To dispel by means of 'anecdota' the common impression that
Mdme. de Staël and her mother did not get on very well together.

2. The narrative of a detached incident, or of a single
event, told as being in itself interesting or striking. (*At
first,* An item of gossip.)
1761 YORKE in Ellis *Orig Lett.* II. 483 IV. 429 Monsieur Coccei
will tell you all the anecdotes of London better than I can. **1769**
Junius Lett. xxix. 133 The anecdote was referred to, merely to
show how ready a man, etc. **1789** BOSWELL *Lett.* (1857) 311 It
[life of Johnson] will certainly be . . full of literary and charac-
teristical anecdotes (which word, by the way, Johnson always condemned, as used in the sense that the French, and we from them,
use it, as signifying particulars). **1806** MAR. EDGEWORTH *Forester*
(1832) 160 Telling little anecdotes to his disadvantage. **1832** HT.
MARTINEAU *Demerara* i. 12 He told some anecdotes of Alfred's
childhood. **Mod.** An after-dinner anecdote.

b. *collect.*
1826 DISRAELI *Viv. Grey* III. ii. 95 A companion who knew
everything, everyone, full of wit and anecdote.

3. *Comb.*, as *anecdote-book, -loving;* **anecdote-monger**
a retailer of anecdotes.

1862 BURTON *Bk.-hunter* II. 125 Irish bulls . . manufactured
for the . . anecdote-books betray their artificial origin. **1836** *Edin.
Rev.* LXIII. 364 By no means so explanatory as his anecdote-loving
master could desire. **1807** *Ibid.* X. 43 The large tribe of anecdote-
mongers. **1850** MAURICE *Mor. Philos.* 164 The gossiping anecdote-
mongers of later Greece.

1. With the information already given, it is easy to understand
the etymology of this entry. It should be observed that according
to it, *anecdote* may not have come into English from French, but
directly from medieval Latin. That this source is likely is suggested by the spelling the word has in the earliest example found
of its use in English. Had it come from the French *anecdotes*, it is
not easy to see why Marvell in 1676 spelled it *anecdota*. Of
course, it may have come into English both from French and from
Latin.

2. The most noteworthy feature of this entry, and of the dictionary from which it comes, is that the definitions are followed
by examples of the use of the word in the senses given. These
examples all follow the same pattern. First comes the date, then
the author's name in small capitals, then the title of the work
cited, usually abbreviated, followed by the number of the page.
Some sources are cited in a manner slightly different from this,
as is seen in the last quotation given under 1. The use of illustrative quotations is a marked feature of historical dictionaries. They
are given generously in the *OED*, there being about 1,827,306 of
them in that great work.

It would be a mistake, however, to conclude that the earliest
example given in the *OED* for a word in a particular sense is
really the first time the word occurs in print. The *OED* is a
remarkable dictionary, but it would be much more so if those
who collected material for it had been able to find the very first
printed uses of all the words with which the dictionary deals.
It is extremely useful to have such dates as are given, but they
should not be misinterpreted.

3. Under 3 in the above entry there are given combinations
into which *anecdote* has entered. The first two of these, *anecdote-
book*, and *anecdote-loving*, are illustrated by only one example

each. Neither of the expressions appears to have been much used. The same may be said of *anecdote-monger*, which is treated slightly differently because two examples of its use were available.

NOTES

1. This entry is reproduced here by permission of The World Publishing Co.

2. By permission. From *Webster's New International Dictionary, Second Edition*, copyright, 1934, 1939, 1945, 1950, 1953, 1954, by G. & C. Merriam Co.

3. This entry is reproduced here with the permission of Appleton-Century-Crofts Inc., successors to The Century Co., publishers of *The Century Dictionary and Cyclopedia*.

4. This entry is reproduced here with the permission of The Clarendon Press, Oxford, England, publishers of the *Oxford English Dictionary*.

MITFORD M. MATHEWS

Dictionaries Contain Surprises

> Neither is a dictionary a bad book to read. There is no cant in it, no excess of explanation, and it is full of suggestion,—the raw material of possible poems and histories.
>
> —RALPH WALDO EMERSON

Our explanation of *anecdote* as it appears in a good desk-size dictionary, a good unabridged one, in the encyclopedic *Century Dictionary*, and in the historical *Oxford English Dictionary* has afforded a glimpse of four distinct types of general dictionaries. Very little, of course, can be found out about a dictionary from looking up one word in it. Unabridged dictionaries contain about a half-million entries, so it is difficult in a brief space to give a good characterization of their chief features.

It is remarkable how much information about words is packed into such a dictionary as the current *Webster's New International, Second Edition.* Any entry in it is likely to be a revelation. Those who never examine words in dictionaries until they are confronted with some kind of problem about them, never know what they are missing in the way of intriguing information about words they have known all their lives. For example, here is merely the etymological treatment which the *New International* gives for the very common verb *sit:* [1]

ME. *sitten,* fr. AS. *sittan;* akin to OS. *sittian,* OFris. *sitta,* D. *zitten,* G. *sitzen,* OHG. *sizzan,* ON. *sitja,* Sw. *sitta,* Dan. *sidde,* Goth. *sitan,* Lith. *sėdėti,* L. *sedēre* to sit, *sedes* seat, Gr. *hezesthai* to sit, *hedra* seat, Skr. *sadas* a seat, *sīdati* he sits. Cf. ASSIDUOUS, ASSIZE, CEDE, CHAIR, DISSIDENT, INSIDIOUS, NEST, OBSESS, POLYHEDRON, POSSESS, PRESIDENT, RESIDENCE, SADDLE, SANHEDRIN, SÉANCE, SEAT, SEDATE, SEDENTARY, SEDIMENT, SEE, *n.*, SESSION, SET, SEWER, SERVANT, SIEGE, SIZAR, SOOT, SUBSIDY, SUPERSEDE.

Following this etymology and enumeration of terms related to *sit* comes a long list of meanings of the word and explanations of its use in more than a dozen phrases.

But the *New International* with its more than 3,000 pages cannot give as full treatment to terms as that given by the *Oxford English Dictionary* with its more than 15,000 pages. One of the outstanding characteristics of this dictionary is that it gives information about how words have been spelled throughout their history. Under the entry *thief* that word is shown to have had a perfect welter of spellings, a few of them being *thef, thif, theyf, thefe, theef, thife, theyff, theaf, theiff.*

Often interesting things have happened to the spellings of words. For example, *abominable* came into English from Old French which had taken it from Latin *abominabilis.* It was not immediately apparent that *abominable* is based ultimately on the two Latin terms, *ab* off, away and *omen* sign, token. The erroneous impression became widespread that the word was from the Latin *ab homine,* signifying away from man, inhuman, beastly. Therefore a new spelling, *abhominable* became current. The word occurs in this spelling 18 times in the first folio of Shakespeare. In *Love's Labour's Lost* Holophernes speaks contemptuously of the "rackers of ortagriphie" who were beginning to write *abominable* for the time-honored *abhominable.*

From this it is seen that the present spelling of this word is recent and came in over the sarcastic protest of Shakespeare and no doubt others. Inquisitiveness about words is amply rewarded by the *OED.* Here is the story of *cobalt.*[2]

    a. Ger. *kobalt,* formerly also *kobald,* -*olt,* -*old,* -*elt,* -*el,* app. the same word as *kobold,* etc., goblin or demon of the mines; the ore of cobalt having been so called by the miners on account of the trouble which it gave them, not only from its worthlessness (as then supposed), but from its mischievous effects upon their own health and upon silver ores in which it occurred, effects due mainly to the arsenic and sulphur with which it was combined. From the miners of the Harz or Erzgebirge the name became common German, and thence passed into all the European langs., F. *cobalt,* It., Sp., Pg. *cobalto,* Du., Da., Russ., Pol., Boh., etc., *kobalt,* Sw. *kobolt.*

In order to demonstrate more fully some of the characteristic features of this dictionary, we reproduce with the publisher's permission a somewhat longer entry from it.

In examining the *Deer* entry, notice that immediately after the listing of the word comes the respelling for pronunciation in a system not used in American dictionaries. Next there is a full display of the spellings *deer* has had throughout its history. In this presentation, numbers are used to denote centuries, 1 standing for "before the year 1100 A.D.," 2 for the twelfth century (*i.e.* 1100 to 1200), 3 for the thirteenth century, etc. Notice that in the fourteenth century the modern spelling became dominant though after that time such spellings as *dere, dur, deere* and others are found. From the beginning, the plural form has been the same as the singular, though sporadic plurals such as *deore, deoran, deers*, have been used.

Next, within square brackets the etymology is given, in which abundant use is made of abbreviations. It is instructive to look at this etymology closely. It begins by pointing out that *deer* is common to the Teutonic, *i.e.* Germanic languages. The etymological treatment then enumerates the forms or spellings *deer* had in some of these Germanic languages, not omitting to give the word as it now exists in Dutch, German, Icelandic, Swedish, and Danish. It is difficult to see how more information could have been given in such a small space.

> **Deer** (dīᵊɹ). Forms: 1 díor, déor, 2–3 deor, (2 dær), 2–4 der, (2–3 dor, 3 dier, 3–4 duer, 4 dur, 5 dure, deure), 4–6 dere, (4–7 deere, 5, 7 diere, 5– (*Sc.*) deir, 6–7 deare), 4– deer, (5 theer). *Pl.* 1–9 normally same as sing.; also 2 deore, deoran, 2–3 -en; 3–4 deores, dueres, 7–9 *occas.* deers. [A Comm. Teut. sb.: OE., *díor, déor* = OS. *dier,* OFris. *diar, dier* (MDu. and Du. and LG. *dier*), OHG. *tior* (MHG. *tier,* Ger. *tier, thier*):—WG. *dior,* ON. °*djúr* (Icel. *dýr,* Sw. *djur,* Da. *dyr*); Goth. *dius, diuz*- :—OTeut. *deuzoᵐ*:—pre-Teut. *dheusoᵐ.*
> Generally referred to a root *dhus* to breathe (cf. *animal* from *anima*), and thought by some etymologists to be the neuter of an adj. used subst. Cf. DEAR *a.*² (Not connected with Gr. θηρ wild beast.)]
> †1. A beast: usually a quadruped, as distinguished from birds and fishes; but sometimes, like *beast,* applied to animals of lower orders. *Obs.*
> c 950 *Lindisf. Gosp.* Luke xviii. 25 Se camal þæt micla dear.

a **1000** *Boeth. Metr.* xxvii. 24 Swa swa fuðl oððe dior. *c* **1000** ÆLFRIC *Voc.* in Wr.-Wülcker 118/31 *Fera,* wild deor. *Bellua,* reðe deor . . *Unicornis,* anhyrne deor. **1154** *O. E. Chron.* (Laud MS.) an. 1135 Pais he makede men & dær. *c* **1200** ORMIN 1176 Shep iss..stille der. *Ibid.* 1312 Lamb iss soffte & stille deor. *a* **1250** *Owl & Night.* 1321 Al swo deth mani dor and man. *c* **1250** *Gen. & Ex.* 4025 Also leun is miðful der. **1482** CAXTON *Reynard* (Arb.) 18 The rybaud and the felle diere here I se hym comen.

B. *plural.*

c **1000** ÆLFRIC *Gen.* i. 25 And he sið ofer þa deor. *c* **1175** *Lamb. Hom.* 43 Innan þan ilke sea weren un-aneomned deor, summe feðerfotetd, summe al bute fet. *Ibid.* 115 þene bið his erd ihened..on wilde deoran. *c* **1200** *Trin. Coll. Hom.* 177 Oref, and deor, and fishshes, and fugeles. *Ibid.* 209 Hie habbeð geres after wilde deore. *Ibid.* 224 Of wilde diere. *c* **1350** *Gen. & Ex.* 4020 On ilc brend eft twin der. *Ibid.* 4032 Efte he sacrede deres mor. *a* **1310** in Wright *Lyric P.* xiii. 44 Deores with huere derne rounes. *Ibid.* xiv 45 In dounes with this dueres plawes. *c* **1340** *Gaw. & Gr. Kt.* 1151 Der drof in þe dale . . bot heterly þay were Restayed with þe stablye.

2. The general name of a family (*Cervidæ*) of ruminant quadrupeds, distinguished by the possession of deciduous branching horns or antlers, and by the presence of spots on the young: the various genera and species being distinguished as *rein-deer, moose-deer, red deer, fallow deer;* the MUSK DEER belong to a different family, *Moschidæ.*

A specific application of the word, which occurs in OE. only contextually, but became distinct in the ME. period, and by its close remained as the usual sense.

[*c* 893 K. ÆLFRED Oros. I. i. (Sw.) 18 He [Ohthere] hæfde þa ðyt ða he þone cyningc sohte, tamra deora unbebohtra syx hund. þa deor hi hatað hranas.] *a* **1131** [see *der fald* in 4]. *c* **1205** LAY. 2586 To huntien after deoren [*c* 1275 after deores]. **1297** R. GLOUC. (Rolls) 9047 He let [make] þe parc of Wodestoke, & der þer inne do. *c* **1325** *Song on Passion* 59 (*O. E. Misc.*) He was todrawe so dur islawe in chace. **1375** BARBOUR *Bruce* VII. 497 [He] went..to purchase venysoun, For than the deir war in sesoun. *c* **1420** *Anturs of Arth.* (Camden) iv, Thay felle to the female dure, feyful thyk fold. **1464** *Mann. & Househ. Exp.* 195 A payr breganderys cueryd wyth whyte deris leder. **1470–85** MALORY *Arthur* x. lxi, He chaced at the reed dere. **1538** STARKEY *England* I. iii. 98 A dere louyth a lene barren..ground. **1601** SHAKS. *Jul. C.* III. i. 209 Like a Deere, strocken by many Princes. **1611** CORYAT *Crudities* 10 A goodly Parke..wherein there is Deere. **1774** GOLDSM. *Nat. Hist.* (1776) III. 80 An hog, an ox, a goat, or a deer. **1855** LONGF. *Hiaw.* III. 169 Where the red deer herd together.

b. occasional plural *deers.*

c **1275** [see **1205** in prec.] **1674** N. Cox *Gentl. Recreat.* II. (1677) 58 The reasons why Harts and Deers do lose their Horns yearly. **1769** HOME *Fatal Discov.* III, Stretch'd on the skins of deers. *c* **1817** HOGG *Tales & Sk.* II. 89 The place of rendezvous, to which the deers weer to be driven.

† **c.** *Deer of ten:* a stag of ten, i. e. one having ten points or tines on his horns; an adult stag of five years at least, and therefore 'warrantable' or fit to be hunted. *Obs.*

1631 MASSINGER *Emp. of East* IV. ii, He will make you royal sport, He is a deer Of ten, at the least.

3. *Small deer:* a phrase originally, and perhaps still by Shakspere, used in sense 1; but now humorously associated with sense **2.**

14. .*Sir Beues* (1885) p. 74/2 (MS.C.) Ratons & myse and soche smale dere, That was hys mete that vii yere. **1605** SHAKS. *Lear* III. iv. 144 But Mice, Rates, and such small Deare, Haue bin Toms food, for seuen long yeare. **1883** G. ALLEN in *Colin Clout's Calender* 14 Live mainly upon worms, slugs, and other hardy small deer.

transf. **1857** H. REED *Lect. Eng. Poets* x. II. 17 The small deer that were herded together by Johnson as the most eminent of English poets.

4. *attrib.* and *Comb.*, as *deer bed, herd, -hide, -keeper, kind, life, -sinew, -snaring,* etc.; *deer-like, deer-loved* adjs. [Several already in OE., as *déor-fald* an enclosure or cage for wild beasts in the amphitheatre, or for beasts of the chase, a deer-park, *déor-edisc* deer-park, *déor-net* net for wild animals, etc.]

1835 W. IRVING *Tous Prairies* xi, The tall grass was pressed down into numerous ° 'deer beds', where those animals had couched. *a* **1000** *Ags. Gloss.* in Wr.-Wülcker 201 *Causea, domus in theatro,* °deorfald. *a* **1131** *O. E. Chron.* an. 1123 Se king rad in his der fald [æt Wudestoke]. **1860** G. H. K. *Vac. Tour.* 123 Peaks..where the scattered remnants of the great °deer herds can repose in security. **1814** SCOTT *Ld. of Isles* III. xix, Goat-skins or °deer-hides o'er them cast. **1849** JAMES *Woodman* vii, I have got my °deer-keepers watching. **1875** LYELL *Princ. Geol.* II. III. xxxix. 359 Animals of the °deer kind. **1860** G. H. K. *Vac. Tour.* **122** The shepherds..see a good deal of °deer life. **1840** MRS. NORTON *Dream* 127 The dark, °deer-like eyes. **1876** GEO. ELIOT *Dan. Der.* IV. liv. 114 Deer-like shyness. **1831** LYTTON *Godolph.* 23 The °deer-loved fern. *c* **1000** ÆLFRIC *Voc.* in Wr.-Wülcker 167 *Cassis,* °deornet. **1856** KANE *Arct. Expl.* II. vii. 79 To walk up Mary River Ravine until we reach the °deer-plains. **1866** KINGSLEY *Herew.* I. vi. 178 Sea-bows of horn and °deer-sinew. **1862** S. ST. JOHN *Forests Far East* II. 34, I have been out °deer-snaring in this neighbourhood.

b. Special comb.: **deer-brush,** an American shrub in Arizona; **deer-cart,** the covered cart in which a tame stag to be hunted is carried to the meet; **deer-dog** = DEER-HOUND; **deer-drive,** a shooting expedition in which the deer are driven past the sportsman; so *deer-driving;* **deer-eyed** *a.*, having eyes like deer, having soft or languid eyes; **deer-fence,** a high railing such as deer cannot leap over; **deer-flesh,** venison; **deer-forest,** a 'forest' or extensive track of unenclosed wild land reserved for deer; † **deer-goat,** an old name for the capriform or caprine antelopes; **deer-grass,** species of Rhexia (N.O. *Melastomaceæ*); **deer-leap,** a lower place in a hedge or fence where deer may leap; **deer-meat** = *deer-flesh;* **deer-neck,** a thin neck (of a horse) resembling a deer's; **deer-park,** a park in which deer are kept; † **deer-reeve,** a township officer in New England in the colonial days, whose duty it was to execute the laws as to deer; **deer-plain,** a plain inhabited by deer; **deer-saddle,** a saddle on which a slain deer is carried away; **deer's-eye** = BUCK-EYE (the tree); **deer's foot** (*grass*), the fine grass *Agrostis setacea;* **deer's hair** = DEER-HAIR; **deer's milk**, a local name of the wood spurge, *Euphorbia amygdaloides;* **deer's tongue**, deer-tongue, a N. American Cichoraceous plant, *Liatris odoratissima;* **deer-tiger**, the puma or cougar; **deer-yard**, an open spot where deer herd, and where the ground is trodden by them.

1883 W. H. BISHOP in *Harper's Mag.* Mar. 502/2 The °'deer brush' resembles horns. **1840** HOOD *Up the Rhine* 186 The hearse, very like a °deer-cart. **1814** SCOTT *Ld. of Isles* v. xxiii, Many a °deer-dog howl'd around. **1882** *Society* 21 Oct. 19/1 Setting out for a °deer-drive. **1860** G. H. K. *Vac. Tour.* 143 Mr. Scrope..was a great hand at °deer-driving. **1884** Q. VICTORIA *More Leaves* 14 The gate of the °deer-fence. *a* **1300** *Cursor M.* 3603 (Cott.) If þou me °dere flesse [*v. r. venisun*] ani gete. **1854** *Act* 17–8 *Vict.* c. 91 § 42 Where such shootings or °deer forests are actually let. **1892** E. WESTON BELL *Scot. Deerhound* 80 Probably not more than twenty deer forests, recognized as such, were in existence prior to the beginning of the present century. **1607** TOPSELL *Four-f. Beasts* (1658) 93 Of the first kinde Tragelaphvs which may be called a °Deer-goat. **1693** SIR T. P. BLOUNT *Nat. Hist.* 30 The Deer-Goat..being partly like a deer partly like a Goat. **1866** *Treas. Bot.* 972/2 Low perennial often bristly herbs, commonly called °Deer-grass, or Meadow-beauty, [with] large showy cymose flowers. **1540–2** *Act* 31 *Hen. VIII*, c. 5 To make °dere leapes and breakes in the sayde hedges and fences. **1838** JAMES *Robber* i, In front appeared a °deer-park. **1860** G. H. K. *Vac. Tour.* 172 It is no light business to get our big stag..on the °deer saddle. **1762** J. CLAYTON *Flora Virginica* 57 *Æsculus floribus octandris* Linn . . . °Dear's Eye, and Bucks Eyes. **1883** *Century Mag.* XXVI. 383 Among the lily-pads, °deer-tongue, and other aquatic plants. **1880** *7th Rep. Surv. Adirondack Reg. N. Y.* 159 We reached an open forest plateau on the mountain, where we were surprised to find a °'deer-yard.' Here the deep snow was tramped down by deer into a broad central level area.

Then, still within the brackets, there comes a note in smaller type, from which we learn that *deer* is believed to go back to a root, *i.e.* the earliest ideal form that can be inferred from existing words, and that this root had in it the sense "to breathe." A reference is then made to *animal* as being related to *anima*, the Latin word for air, breath, life. The basic meaning of *animal* therefore is something living. Similarly, as some scholars think, *deer* may have in it the idea of breathing, and mean, basically, anything that lives or breathes.

The etymology, in conclusion, warns us not to think that the Greek word meaning a wild beast is the source of *deer*.

Only advanced students are likely ever to need such detailed information about the early forms and etymological history and connections of words shown in this treatment of *deer*. But it is well for anyone to know that such information is available and where it may be found. Look at the etymology of *deer* in your desk dictionary and see how brief it necessarily is.

The enumeration of senses follows. Sense 1 is preceded by a dagger, (†), to indicate that it is now obsolete. We no longer use *deer* in the general sense of a beast, especially a quadruped as distinguished from birds and fishes. Note however that this sense has remained in the German *Tier* to this day. It may well be, however, that *deer* in the early sense of an animal is preserved in our word *wilderness*. See what your dictionary says about the make-up of this word.

To illustrate this first sense, a quotation of about the year 950 is given from the *Lindisfarne Gospels*, the book of Luke in the New Testament being cited, Chapter 18, Verse 25, "The camel that large animal." The passage is the familiar one about the camel's going through the eye of a needle, but only so much of it is quoted as shows that a camel was, in Old English, called a deer.

The latest example of this original sense is from a work by Caxton, famous for the role he played in English printing. Then come nearly a dozen passages written from about 1000 A.D. to about 1340 A.D., showing early plural forms of the word.

Sense 2 shows the narrowing down of the meaning of *deer* to an animal of a particular family of "ruminant quadrupeds." Among the quotations given to illustrate this sense of the word, notice that the last one, of 1855, is from a well-known American work, Longfellow's *Hiawatha*. Under Sense 2 there are subdivisions marked b. and c. which are self-explanatory.

Attributive and combinative uses are given under 4. Among the authors drawn upon in this section there are two Americans, Irving and Kane. A little further, under 4. b., special combinations are given and defined. These differ from the ones under 4 in being better established as fixed expressions. The first of them is *deer-brush*, pointed out as an American name for a shrub found in Arizona. Notice that further down in this list *deer-reeve* occurs as an obsolete term once used in New England for "a township officer . . . whose duty it was to execute the laws as to deer."

Deer's tongue, deer tongue is listed as a North American plant and the supporting evidence is from American sources. The last combination, *deeryard*, is also an American term and is illustrated by American evidence.

A close examination of such an entry as this—and it is among the simpler ones in the *OED*—is likely to surprise one not accustomed to such fullness of treatment of terms. Students often go through college, and even much beyond, without ever becoming aware of the richness of treatment of words in this dictionary.

NOTES

1. By permission. From *Webster's New International Dictionary, Second Edition*, copyright, 1934, 1939, 1945, 1950, 1953, 1954, by G. & C. Merriam Co.

2. This part of the entry *Cobalt* and the following entry *Deer* are reproduced by permission of The Clarendon Press, Oxford, England, publishers of the *Oxford English Dictionary*.

STUART ROBERTSON AND FREDERIC G. CASSIDY

Changing Meanings and Values of Words

Even though it is generally recognized that meanings change, many people still cling, curiously enough, to the quite contradictory notion that words all have "true" meanings, that changes somehow take us away from the "true" meaning, and that the way to find out what a word "really means" is to find out what it once meant. This is particularly true in respect to borrowed words in English, the belief evidently being that the meaning of the word in contemporary English and the meaning of the Latin or Greek word from which the English word is derived must be one and the same. A little reflection should show that an appeal to etymology in order to establish the present meaning of the word is as untrustworthy as an appeal to spelling in order to establish its present pronunciation. And for a reason that is almost exactly parallel: change of *meaning* is likely to have altered the etymological sense, which is thereby rendered archaic or obsolete, just as change of *sound* is likely to be unrecorded in the "antiquarian" spelling that so frequently characterizes Modern English. The study of etymology has great value and interest—a point to which we shall later return—but its usefulness in settling the question of what a word means is subject to considerable qualification.

Let us see what results when one ignores the idea that a word may change its meaning, and appeals to its etymology in order to determine its present meaning. A handbook of only twenty-odd

. . . .

years ago on "correct English" [1] sets forth the following dictum: "*Dilapidated* . . . Said of a building or other structure. But the word is from the Latin *lapis*, a stone, and cannot properly be used of any but a stone structure." One might just as reasonably argue that because *candidate* is related to the Latin *candidus* (white), it cannot properly be used of an aspirant for political office unless he is clothed in a suit of white material. More clearly even, one might protest that *holiday* properly describes Christmas or Easter, but should never be used of Independence Day or Labor Day; or that *bonfire* should not be applied except where the combustible material is bone. These arguments are not much more grotesque than some that have been seriously maintained in defense of an etymological crotchet, while ignoring the fact of change of meaning. Indeed, one who argues on this basis is a victim of the "etymological fallacy."

The fact is that what a word once meant is not necessarily what it now means; the etymological meaning has often died out, and a quite new development is the living descendant. This is particularly true of words in common or popular use. Words, after all, are for the most part purely conventional symbols. They mean only what those who are using them agree to make them mean. Exactly the same principles apply to "learned" words, but because their traditional users have generally known the language from which they were borrowed, or of whose elements they were composed, they have tended to preserve the etymological meaning—indeed, it is conventional to use such words with an eye to their source; thus they are less prone to alterations of meaning than are popular words. It is in this way, incidentally, that a cultural tradition holds in check, to some extent, the constant tendency of language to change.[2]

Change of meaning, however, though usually unpredictable, is not utterly arbitrary; as we shall see in a moment, it often proceeds along familiar paths. Furthermore, though it takes place in all languages, it does not proceed at the same rate even in related ones. If we look at cognate words in English and German, for example, which might have been expected to have the same meaning, we often find them widely different, and the difference is most commonly the result of some radical change of sense in the English word. Opposite instances can be found, admittedly, in which the English word has stood still and the German one changed; yet it is usually the latter which is conservative. Examples of this characteristic English shift in meaning are the following: *Schlagen* and *slay* are originally the same word, but the German word retains the general meaning of "smite" or "strike" while the English word has become narrowed to mean "strike with fatal consequences" or "kill." [3] *Knabe* is the cognate in German of Old English *cnapa* or *cnafa*, and has the same meaning, "boy"; but Modern English *knave* has a radically different one; the German *Tier* means any kind of animal, as did the cognate Old English *deor*, but in Modern English *deer* means one particular kind of animal.

Generalization and Specialization. One very common type of change is that in which the "area" of the meaning is changed. When a word that has referred broadly or inclusively begins instead to refer narrowly or exclusively, this is an example of "specialization" of meaning; the contrary is called "generalization." Interestingly enough, the same word may undergo both processes at different stages of the development of its meaning. *Go*, for example, is a verb of motion that seems as general as possible in meaning, and presumably this is also the basic meaning; early in its history in English, however, it must have specialized, for Old English *gān* sometimes means "walk," and in Middle English *ryde or gon* (ride or walk) is a familiar formula. Although the present meaning is the generalized one, the specialization "walk" was still possible in the late seventeenth century, as we see in these phrases from Bunyan: "I am resolved to run when I can, to go when I cannot run, and to creep when I cannot go." [4]

Borrowed words are quite as likely as native ones to undergo such transformations in meaning. *Virtue* [5] is connected with Latin *vir* (man). Thus, *virtue* first meant "manliness" in general; but its meaning later specialized to stand for the manly quality most in demand in the military state, namely "fortitude" or "warlike prowess"—the meaning familiar in Caesar's *Commentaries*. But a still later Latin meaning is more comprehensive, and it was this very general meaning that was attached to *virtue* when it was borrowed in English through French. One possible specialization was "power," as in "Virtue had gone out of him," or even "magical power," as in "the virtue of the spell" or Milton's "virtuous ring and glass." More commonly, however, the word in English retained a general sense of "noble quality"—though more and more with reference to moral rather than to mental or physical characteristics. But another specialization limits its application to women; for example, "All the sons were brave, and all the daughters virtuous," where *virtuous* is equivalent to "chaste." "A woman's virtue" will today be interpreted in only the last sense. A curious evolution, indeed, when one recalls that the etymological meaning is "manliness."

The foregoing are particularly striking examples, but hundreds of others could be cited. We find generalization in such everyday words as *picture*, once restricted, as the etymology would suggest (compare: the *Picts*, "painted ones"), to a *painted* representation of something seen, but now applicable to photograph, crayon drawing, and so forth; *butcher*, who once slew one animal only, the goat (French *bouc*); the verb *sail*, which has been transferred to *steam* navigation, just as *drive* has been transferred to self-propelled vehicles; *injury*, which once was limited to "injustice"; *zest*, which meant "bit of lemon-peel"; *chest*, which usually meant "coffin"— "He is now deed and nayled in his cheste";[6] *pen*, which meant "feather," but which is now much more likely to mean a writing implement tipped with metal than a quill; *quarantine*, from which the original meaning of a "forty" days' isolation has quite disappeared; and *companion*, which has likewise lost the etymological sense of "one who (shares) bread with" another.

But generalization of meaning does not always stay within bounds; under some conditions the meaning becomes so broad that, in extreme cases, there is hardly any meaning left. We have a whole set of words, used conversationally when we either do not know, or cannot remember, or perhaps will not take the trouble to search for a more precise term: the *what-you-may-call-it* kind of word—*thingumabob, doohickie, jigger*, and so on.[7] Not so long ago *gadget* was imported into the U. S. from England, and has found a very hearty welcome into this company.

Another type, in which generalization goes even farther, has aroused strong opposition from guardians of literary style, who realize that emptiness and "jargon" result from the indiscriminate use of "words that mean little or nothing, but may stand for almost anything": [8] such words are *thing, business, concern, condition, matter, article, circumstance.* As we all recognize at once, these are words that have a fairly exact sense, but which also have acquired the ability to fit into a wide variety of everyday contexts, in which their meaning becomes extremely vague—in fact, almost wholly dependent on the context. The word *deal* is the current American favorite in this group, its gamut of meaning running all the way from perfectly favorable ("Your job sounds like a pretty fine deal") to thoroughly unfavorable ("I won't take part in any of his deals"). This word serves the purpose, and is going through the same general sort of development, that *proposition* did a generation ago.

Even more frequent than generalization, and even more readily illustrated in numberless familiar instances, is the opposite process of specialization. *Steorfan* is an Old English word, cognate with the German *sterben*, which meant "die"; but the standard Modern English meaning ("starve") is a specialized one, namely "die from hunger." Another specialization, "die from cold," is found in certain Modern English dialects: "[he] . . . bid her come . . . sit close by the fire: he was sure she was starved" is from the Yorkshire dialect of *Wuthering Heights* (Chapter XXX). The older meaning of *meat* was "food" in general, as one might suspect from the archaic phrase *meat and drink* and from the compound *sweetmeat.* For the meaning "meat," the older term was *flesh* or *flesh meat.* It is interesting to observe, incidentally, that the German cognate for *flesh, Fleisch,* suggests first of all the specialized sense of "meat"; this is the present meaning, too, of French *viande*, while the English *viands* retains the general sense of "food." *Coast* is a borrowing, through French, from a Latin word for "side" or "rib" (compare Modern English *intercostal*), and once meant "border" or "frontier"—the "coast of

Bohemia" was not always an absurdity. But *coast* in present use not only has the usual specialization "seashore"; as employed in the eastern United States, it means specifically "Pacific coast." *Shore*, on the other hand, means, in parts of the east at any rate, "Atlantic shore." [9] In some of the same localities, however, "eastern shore" means what elsewhere would have to be expanded into "eastern shore of the Chesapeake in Maryland," just as in part of New England "the cape" means definitely "Cape Cod." *Token* formerly had the broad meaning "sign," but was long ago specialized to mean a physical thing that is a sign (of something) —as in *love token*, or the metal tokens used on streetcars or buses.

An *undertaker* once could undertake to do anything; nowadays he only undertakes to manage funerals. So, to people in general, *doctor* stands only for *doctor of medicine*. *Liquor*, which once was synonymous with *liquid*, is now definitely specialized. *Reek*, like the German *rauchen*, once had the broad meaning "smoke," as it still has in the Scotch dialect; but the standard Modern English use limits it quite definitely to unpleasant exhalations. *Disease* meant "discomfort"—"lack of ease" in general. *Girl* meant "young person (of either sex)." The limitation of *corpse* to "*dead* body" made it necessary to re-borrow the word in its Modern French form *corps* for another possible meaning of "body," and to make occasional use of the original Latin, *corpus*, for still another sense, "complete collection of writings." *Corn*, in general American use, will be immediately understood as "Indian corn" or "maize." But the word itself once meant simply "grain," and so, in other parts of the English-speaking world, it is differently specialized [10]—in Scotland, to mean "oats," and in England "wheat." Keats's allusion to "Ruth amid the alien corn" probably calls up, to many American readers, a very different picture from what the poet had in mind.

What are the factors that account for specialization of meaning? One is, of course, that localities and groups of people have their own specialized associations for words that otherwise may convey a broader meaning. It has been well remarked that "every man is his own specializer." [11] *Pipe*, for example, calls up different ideas in the mind of the smoker, the plumber, and the organist.

Ring may be thought of in connection with jewelry, opera, politics, or pugilism—even though, in the last connection, the "squared circle" has long since superseded the original truly circular shape. Quite apart from particular or local specializations, however, there are a great many words whose meaning has become specialized for nearly everybody. A second factor that helps to account for both generalization and specialization is the fading of the etymological significance of the word. Thus, to illustrate the one point, *arrive* [< Lat. *ad* (to) + *ripa* (shore)] originally applied to the end of a voyage only, and was used without the preposition, since this was included in the word. Milton's "ere he arrive the happy isle" illustrates a use that is in strict accord with the etymology of the word. When, however, consciousness of the Latin parts that made up the word was weakened, it was no longer used transitively, but in the phrase "arrive at," and with the more generalized application to the end of any journey.

Yet another factor is the competition among synonymous words. The borrowing of the Latin *animal* and the French *beast* meant that, with the native *deer*, English would have possessed three exactly synonymous terms for one idea; it is obviously in the interests of economy that *deer* should have specialized to mean one particular species of animal rather than "animal" in general, and that *beast* should have acquired connotations that limit its sphere. *Bird* and *fowl*, *dog* and *hound*, *boy* and *knave*, *chair* and *stool* are further instances of words that were once synonyms but that have been differentiated in meaning here by the specialization of the second term of each pair.

A further remark about generalization and specialization is suggested by some of the words just alluded to. The degree of specialization which a language exhibits seems to depend on cultural need. In a culture in which the coconut is essential—as in Polynesia—an extremely complex vocabulary is said to have grown up, with different terms for many stages or ripeness of the fruit. So also, the Eskimos have different terms for falling snow, snow on the ground, snow packed hard like ice, slushy snow, wind-driven flying snow, and other kinds.[12] Many similar examples could be cited, for the languages of peoples of undeveloped culture appear to be particularly rich in specialized terms. At one time in the course of the English language it must have seemed desirable to speakers to make verbal distinctions in connection with groups of animals—mostly those of interest to farmers and hunters. An elaborate set of what are called "company terms" was accordingly developed, some (but by no means all) of which survive today. The better known ones include a *herd* or a *drove* of cattle, but a *flock* of sheep (or birds), a *school* of fish, a *pack* of wolves (or hounds), a *covey* of partridges, and a *swarm* of bees. But there are others far more esoteric,[13] such as *nye* of pheasants, *cete* of badgers, *sord* of mallards, *wisp* of snipe, *doylt* of tame swine, *gaggle* of geese, *harras* of horses, and *kennel* of raches. There is a similar profusion of names for the same animal (*cow, heifer, bull, calf, steer,* and *ox*), the young of various animals (*puppy, kitten, kid, calf, colt, lamb,* and so forth), and the male and female of the same species (*gander* and *goose, drake* and *duck, horse* and *mare, cock* and *hen, dog* and *bitch*.)[14] The need for a generic term is of course particularly felt here, and it is supplied, not quite satisfactorily, by the convention of making either the name of the male (*horse* and *dog*) or of the female (*cow, duck,* and *goose*), or even that of the young of the species (*chicken* and *pig*), perform a larger duty.

Elevation and Degradation. If generalization and specialization may be said to involve a change in the "area" of meaning, elevation and degradation [15] involve the rising or falling of meaning in a scale of values. Thus a word which once denominated something bad (or at least neutral) but comes to refer to something good, has undergone *elevation* of meaning; the reverse of this process, obviously, represents a *degradation* of meaning.

And here a word of warning: we must not confuse the linguistic signal with the thing it stands for, though that error is too often made. It is not the word as such which is bad or good, or which becomes elevated or degraded, but only the meaning which society chooses to put upon it. As we shall see, society often reverses itself in the course of time, and words which were once disapproved may become "respectable," while others that had social favor may lose it. This would not be possible if the value were inherent in the word. With this in mind, then, let us illustrate degradation of meaning.

Many terms that are now descriptive of moral depravity were once quite without this suggestion. *Lust*, for example, meant simply "pleasure," as in German; *wanton* was "untaught"; *lewd* was merely "ignorant," "lerned and lewed" being a phrase commonly standing for "clergy and laity"; *immoral* was "not customary"; *vice*, "flaw"; *hussy*, "housewife"; *wench*, "young girl"; and *harlot*, "fellow" (of either sex). In a similar way, words that impute rascality have often been thoroughly innocent labels: *villain*, for example, was "farm laborer"; *counterfeiter*, "imitator" or "copyist"; *pirate* (at least in its earlier Greek sense), "one who adventures or tries"; *buccaneer*, "one who smokes meat"; *ringleader*, simply "leader" (in a good or a neutral sense); *varlet*, *knave*, and *imp* meant merely "boy"; and *sly*, *crafty*, and *cunning* all implied the compliment "skilful." A perennial form of humor —the city man's ridicule of the countryman—is witnessed in the degradation of such nouns as *peasant*, *boor* (compare German *Bauer* and Dutch *Boer*), and *churl*, and in the frequent implication of such adjectives as *bucolic*, *rural*, *rustic*, and *provincial*.

When a word may be applied in two possible ways, one favorable or complimentary and the other reverse, it is extremely likely that it will specialize in the less desirable sense. Thus, *suggestive* is likely to mean only "evilly suggestive," though it *may* still mean "informative" or "illuminating," and though the noun *suggestion* has escaped any such specialization—just as the verb *to harbor* is limited to unworthy or illegal concealment (as in "harboring a criminal" or "harboring thoughts of revenge"), while the noun *harbor* retains the old broad and literal meaning of "haven." *Asylum*, through association with the idea of "refuge for the insane," has followed a course like that of the verb *harbor*. A *libel*, in Middle English and early Modern English, was simply a "brief bit of writing" (from Lat. *libellum*, little book); now it is definitely limited to something malicious or defamatory. *Doom* once meant "judgment"; now it means only "condemnation." *Reek*, as we have seen, can now stand only for unpleasant distillations; *stink* and *stench* have specialized in the same way from a formerly neutral meaning, and *smell* and even *odor* seem likely to follow their lead. A *smirk* was once merely a smile, without the suggestion of affectation. One could formerly *resent* benefits as well as injuries, and *retaliate* for favors as well as slights; compare with the present meanings of these words the ordinary implications of the phrase "get even with" or "get square with."

On the other hand, instances of words that have traveled an opposite path, from the humble to the exalted, or from the base to the refined, are not far to seek. The institution of chivalry brought about the elevation of *knight* (youth) and *squire* (shield-bearer); and *chivalry* itself was invested by the Romantic Revival with a glamor that the word (as we see from its source, Fr. *cheval*, horse) did not originally possess. "Romantic" ideas in the late eighteenth and early nineteenth centuries were similarly responsible for the gain in dignity of such words as *bard*, once a term of contempt like *vagabond*; *minstrel*, once applicable to juggler and buffoon as well as musician; and *enthusiasm*, in the earlier eighteenth century akin to *fanaticism*. Like *knight*, other terms for rank or position have had the good fortune to take on added prestige when the offices for which they stood changed their character, and when their own etymological meanings were forgotten. Such is the history of *marshal* (originally, "horse-serv-ant"), *chamberlain* (room-attendant), *minister* (servant), *con-stable* (stable-attendant), *governor* (pilot), and *steward* (sty-guardian). It is true that in a number of these words the extent of the elevation fluctuates: *marshal* is a less dignified title when it is applied to the lone policeman of an American village than when it is applied to the highest ranking officers of the English or the French army; there is a similar variation between the American and the British connotations for *constable*, just as *steward* may suggest a club attendant as well as the Lord High Steward of England, or even the royal dynasty of the *Stewarts* (or Stuarts); [16] likewise, *governor* may mean the warden of an English prison or the chief administrative officer of one of our American states. On the whole, however, the fact that any present implica-tion of these words represents a gain in dignity over the etymological one is patent enough. So too it is with a number of political and religious labels: *Tory, Whig, Puritan, Quaker,* and *Methodist* are well-known examples of names that were originally applied in contempt but that have taken on dignified associations (though, to some, *Puritan* and perhaps *Tory* still convey a derisive significance). Archbishop Trench long ago pointed out that the influence of Christianity elevated *angel* from merely "messenger," *martyr* from "witness," and *paradise* from "park," through the Biblical application to the abode of our first parents (as in *Paradise Lost* and "*earthly* paradise") to the "blisful waiting-place of faithful departed spirits." [17] Miscellaneous further illustrations of elevation are *pretty* from an early meaning "sly," through "clever," to something approaching "beautiful"; *nice* from an etymological meaning "ignorant," through its earliest English sense "foolish," and later ones like "particular," to its present broad and vague colloquial meaning of "pleasant" or "acceptable"; and *fond* from "foolish" to "affectionate."

The usual view of degradation and elevation has been that the downward path is far the more common. Despite McKnight's protest to the effect that elevation has been less noticed simply because it is less dramatic,[18] there seems to be every reason to agree with the general verdict. Examples of elevation, after all, are far less easy to find than examples of degradation, which indeed meet us at every turn. Besides, most of the words that have been cited as undergoing elevation fall into a few obvious categories, while the types of degradation are extremely various. The truth of the matter would appear to be that degradation has been more noticed not because it is more spectacular but simply because it is omnipresent, as elevation is not. Why should this be so, and why should the use of words be made difficult by a lurking leer, a hint of unpleasant connotation that makes a word that appears to be absolutely right in denotation impossible for a given occasion? It is hard to escape the conclusion that there is a disagreeable commentary on human nature here. How difficult it is for superlatives to retain their superlative force—because the general tendency is to apply them on light occasion and hence to weaken their meaning! So *fair* comes to mean "passable," and indeed is often equivalent to "not good"; and *quite* has passed, in its usual American application at least, from "entirely" or "completely" to "moderately." The tendency to procrastinate finds illustration in a whole series of words or phrases—*by and by, presently, anon, immediately, directly,* and *soon* itself—that have "slowed up," changing their meaning from "now" or "at once" to "soon" or "after a time." It is scarcely a farfetched interpretation to see in the narrowing of *demure* to apply to *mock* modesty, of *genteel* to *spurious* gentility, of *sophistication* to *worldly* wisdom, of *egregious* to notoriety rather than fame, of *sanctimonious* to *pretended* holiness, and of *grandiose* to *tinsel* (itself an example of degradation) grandeur—to see in all these, and dozens of others that might be mentioned, the workings of human motives like suspicion, contempt, and general pessimism.

NOTES

1. *Write It Right,* by Ambrose Bierce, New York (Neale), 1928. The work is well worth investigating as a striking demonstration of what pedantry, combined with ignorance of linguistic processes, will do for one. To much of it, a witty definition of Bierce's own is curiously applicable: "*positive*—mistaken at the top of one's voice."

2. Some of this holding in check is unconscious, some conscious; we shall have to postpone to a later chapter the question of the values and judgments upon which conscious attempts to control language are based.

3. The Latin word *caedere,* though unrelated to English *slay,* has undergone exactly the same specialization of meaning.

4. Quoted by Bradley, *The Making of English,* p. 182.

5. This history is given in greater detail in Greenough and Kittredge, *Words and Their Ways in English Speech,* pp. 241–242.

6. Chaucer's clerk, speaking of Petrarch (*Clerk's Prologue,* line 30).

7. Louise Pound has collected more than 100 such terms now current in popular speech: "American Indefinite Names," *American Speech,* Vol. VI, No. 4 (April 1931), pp. 257–259.

8. Greenough and Kittredge, *op. cit.,* p. 235.

9. In Philadelphia it is often used in a still more specific sense, "southern New Jersey shore"; it sometimes bears a yet more localized signification: "Atlantic City," which occurs repeatedly in the headlines of Philadelphia newspapers.

10. In other Germanic languages, the cognate word has still different specializations in various places: "barley" in Sweden, "rye" in north Ger-

many, and "spelt" in south Germany. (Jespersen, *Mankind, Nation, and Individual*, p. 212.)

11. Quoted by Greenough and Kittredge, *op. cit.*, p. 251.

12. See B. L. Whorf, "Science and Linguistics," *The Technology Review*, Vol. XLII, No. 6 (April 1940), reprinted in *Four Articles on Metalinguistics*, Washington, D.C. (Foreign Service Institute), 1950, p. 6. For further examples see also Jespersen, *Language*, pp. 429–431.

13. These, and many others, are mentioned in an editorial comment in the *New York Times* for November 20, 1930. All but *doylt* are recorded in the *Oxford Dictionary*.

14. McKnight, *English Words and Their Background*, p. 239, calls attention in greater detail to the lack of generalizing terms in the animal kingdom, and suggests further that the variety of names for sea craft (*sloop, schooner, brig, ship, boat, dinghy, bark,* and so on) is a similar survival of primitive habits of thought.

15. Elevation is also called *aggradation* or *amelioration,* and degradation is also called *degeneration* or *pejoration.*

16. Greenough and Kittredge, *op. cit.*, p. 296.

17. Archbishop Richard Chevenix Trench, *On the Study of Words*, New York (Armstrong), 20th ed. (no date), p. 114.

18. *English Words and Their Background*, p. 292; cf. also Janet Aiken, *English Present and Past*, p. 112, and G. A. Van Dongen, *Amelioratives in English.*

H. L. MENCKEN

Euphemisms

The American, probably more than any other man, is prone to be apologetic about the trade he follows. He seldom believes that it is quite worthy of his virtues and talents; almost always he thinks that he would have adorned something far gaudier. Unfortunately, it is not always possible for him to escape, or even for him to dream plausibly of escaping, so he soothes himself by assuring himself that he belongs to a superior section of his craft, and very often he invents a sonorous name to set himself off from the herd. Here we glimpse the origin of a multitude of characteristic American euphemisms, e.g., *mortician* for *undertaker*, *realtor* for *real-estate agent*, *electragist* for *electrical contractor*, *aisle manager* for *floor-walker*, *beautician* for *hairdresser*, *exterminating engineer* for *rat-catcher*, and so on. *Realtor* was devised by a high-toned real-estate agent of Minneapolis, Charles N. Chadbourn by name. He thus describes its genesis:

> It was in November, 1915, on my way to a meeting of the Minneapolis Real Estate Board, that I was annoyed by the strident peddling of a scandal sheet: "All About the Robbery of a Poor Widow by a Real Estate Man." The "real estate man" thus exposed turned out to be an obscure hombre with desk-room in a back office in a rookery, but the incident set me to thinking. "Every member of our board," I thought, "is besmirched by this scandal article. Anyone, however unworthy or disreputable, may call himself a real estate man. Why do not the members of our board deserve a distinctive

. . . .

title? Each member is vouched for by the board, subscribes to its Code of Ethics, and must behave himself or get out." So the idea incubated for three or four weeks, and was then sprung on the local brethren.[1]

As to the etymology of the term, Mr. Chadbourn says:

> Real estate originally meant a royal grant. It is so connected with land in the public mind that *realtor* is easily understood, even at a first hearing. The suffix *-or* means a doer, one who performs an act, as in *grantor, executor, sponsor, administrator.*

The Minneapolis brethren were so pleased with their new name that Mr. Chadbourn was moved to dedicate it to the whole profession. In March, 1916, he went to the convention of the National Association of Real Estate Boards at New Orleans, and made a formal offer of it. It was accepted gratefully, and is now defined by the association as follows:

> A person engaged in the real estate business who is an active member of a member board of the National Association of Real Estate Boards, and as such, an affiliated member of the National Association, who is subject to its rules and regulations, who observes its standards of conduct, and is entitled to its benefits.[2]

In 1920 the Minneapolis Real Estate Board and the National Association of Real Estate Boards applied to Judge Joseph W. Molyneaux of Minneapolis for an injunction restraining the Northwestern Telephone Exchange Company from using *realtor* to designate some of its hirelings, and on September 10 the learned judged duly granted this relief. Since then the National Association has obtained similar injunctions in Virginia, Utah and other States. Its general counsel is heard from every time *realtor* is taken in vain, and when, in 1922, Sinclair Lewis applied it to George F. Babbitt, there was an uproar. But when Mr. Chadbourn was appealed to he decided that Babbitt was "fairly well described," for he was "a prominent member of the local board and of the State association," and one could scarcely look for anything better in "a book written in the ironic vein of the author of 'Main Street.'" [3] Mr. Chadbourn believes that *realtor* should be capitalized, "like *Methodist* or *American*," [4] but so far it has not been generally done. In June, 1925, at a meeting of the National Association of Real Estate Boards in Detroit, the past presidents of the body presented him with a gold watch as a token of their gratitude for his contribution to the uplift of their profession. On May 30, 1934, the following letter from Nathan William MacChesney, general counsel of the National Association, appeared in the *New Republic:*

> [*Realtor*] is not a word, but a trade right, coined and pro-tected by law by the National Association of Real Estate Boards, and the term is a part of the trade-mark as registered in some forty-four States and Canada. Something over $200,-000 has been spent in its protection by the National Associa-tion of Real Estate Boards in attempting to confine its use to those real estate men who are members of the National Asso-ciation of Real Estate Boards, subject to its code for ethics and to its discipline for violation. It has been a factor in making the standards of the business generally during the past twenty years, and the exclusive right of the National Associa-tion of Real Estate Boards has been sustained in a series of court decisions, a large number of injunctions having been issued, restraining its improper use.

In 1924 the *Realtor's Bulletin* of Baltimore reported that certain enemies of realtric science were trying to show that *realtor* was derived from the English word *real* and the Spanish word *toro*, a bull, and to argue that it thus meant *real bull*. But this obscenity apparently did not go far; probably a hint from the alert general counsel was enough to stop it. During the same year I was informed by Herbert U. Nelson, executive secretary of the Na-tional Association, that "the real-estate men of London, through the Institute of Estate Agents and Auctioneers, after studying our experience in this respect, are planning to coin the word *estator* and to protect it by legal steps." This plan, I believe came to fruition, but *estator* never caught on, and I can't find it in the Supplement to the Oxford Dictionary. *Realtor*, however, is there —and the first illustrative quotation is from "Babbitt"! In March, 1927, J. Foster Hagan, of Ballston, Va., reported to *American*

Speech that he had encountered *realtress* on the window of a real-estate office there, but this charming derivative seems to have died a-bornin'. In 1925 or thereabout certain ambitious insurance solicitors, inflamed by *realtor*, began to call themselves *insurors*, but it, too, failed to make any progress.

Electragist, like *realtor*, seems to be the monoply of the lofty technicians who affect it: "it is copyrighted by the Association of Electragists International, whose members alone may use it." [5] But *mortician* is in the public domain. It was proposed by a writer in the *Embalmers' Monthly* for February, 1895, but the undertakers, who were then *funeral-directors*, did not rise to it until some years later. On September 16, 1916, some of the more eminent of them met at Columbus, O., to form a national association, on the lines of the American College of Surgeons, the American Association of University Professors, and the Society of the Cincinnati, and a year later they decided upon National Selected *Morticians* as its designation.[6] To this day the association remains so exclusive that, of the 24,000 undertakers in the United States, only 200 belong to it. But any one of the remaining 23,800 is free to call himself a *mortician*, and to use all the other lovely words that the advance of human taxidermy has brought in. *Mortician*, of course, was suggested by *physician*, for undertakers naturally admire and like to pal with the resurrection men, and there was a time when some of them called themselves *embalming surgeons*. A *mortician* never handles a *corpse;* he *prepares* a *body* or *patient*. This business is carried on in a *preparation-room* or *operating-room*, and when it is achieved the patient is put into a *casket* [7] and stored in the *reposing-room* or *slumber-room* of a *funeral-home*. On the day of the funeral he is moved to the *chapel* therein for the last exorcism, and then hauled to the cemetery in a *funeral-car* or *casket-coach*.[8] The old-time shroud is now a *négligé* or *slumber-shirt* or *slumber-robe*, the mortician's work-truck is an *ambulance*, and the cemetery is fast becoming a *memorial-park*. In the West cemeteries are being supplanted by public mausoleums, which sometimes go under the names of *cloisters*, *burial-abbeys*, etc.[9] To be laid away in one runs into money. The vehicle that morticians use for their expectant hauling of the ill

is no longer an *ambulance*, but an *invalid-coach*. *Mortician* has
been a favorite butt of the national wits, but they seem to have
made no impression on it. In January, 1932, it was barred from
the columns of the Chicago *Tribune*. "This decree goes forth,"
announced the *Tribune*, "not for lack of sympathy with the
ambition of undertakers to be well regarded, but because of it.
If they haven't the sense to save themselves from their own
lexicographers, we shall not be guilty of abetting them in their
folly." [10] But *mortician* not only continues to flourish; it also begets
progeny, e.g., *beautician*, *cosmetician*, *radiotrician* and *bootician*.[11] The barbers, so far, have not devised a name for themselves in *-ician*, but they may be trusted to do so anon. In my
youth they were *tonsorial artists*, but in recent years some of
them have been calling themselves *chirotonsors*. [12] Practically all
American press-agents are now *public relations counsel, contact-
managers* or *publicists*, all tree-trimmers are *tree-surgeons*, all
milk-wagon and bakery-wagon drivers have become *salesmen*,
nearly all janitors are *superintendents*, many gardeners have become *landscape-architects* (in England even the whales of the
profession are simple *landscape-gardeners*), cobblers are beginning to call themselves *shoe-rebuilders*,[13] and the corn-doctors,
after a generation as *chiropodists*, have burst forth as *podiatrists*.
The American fondness for such sonorous appellations arrested
the interest of W. L. George, the English novelist, when he visited
the United States in 1920. He said:

> Business titles are given in America more readily than in
> England. I know one *president* whose staff consists of two
> typists. Many firms have four *vice-presidents*. In the maga-
> zines you seldom find merely an *editor;* the others need their
> share of honor, so they are *associate* (not *assistant*) *editors*.
> A dentist is called a *doctor*. I wandered into a university,
> knowing nobody, and casually asked for the *dean*. I was
> asked, "Which *dean?*" In that building there were enough
> deans to stock all the English cathedrals. The master of a
> secret society is *royal supreme knight commander*. Perhaps
> I reached the extreme at a theatre in Boston, when I wanted
> something, I forgot what, and was told that I must apply to
> the *chief of the ushers*. He was a mild little man, who had
> something to do with people getting into their seats, rather

a come-down from the pomp and circumstance of his title. Growing interested, I examined my programme, with the following result: It is not a large theatre, but it has a *press-representative*, a *treasurer* (box-office clerk), an *assistant treasurer* (box-office junior clerk), an *advertising-agent*, our old friend the *chief of the ushers*, a *stage-manager*, a *head-electrician*, a *master of properties* (in England called *props*), a *leader of the orchestra* (pity this—why not *president?*), and a *matron* (occupation unknown).[14]

George might have unearthed some even stranger magnificoes in other playhouses. I once knew an ancient bill-sticker, attached to a Baltimore theatre, who boasted the sonorous title of *chief lithographer*. Today, in all probability, he would be called a *lithographic-engineer*. For a number of years the *Engineering News-Record*, the organ of the legitimate engineers, used to devote a column every week to just such uninvited invaders of the craft, and some of the species it unearthed were so fantastic that it was constrained to reproduce their business cards photographically in order to convince its readers that it was not spoofing. One of its favorite exhibits was a bedding manufacturer who first became a *mattress-engineer* and then promoted himself to the lofty dignity of *sleep-engineer*. No doubt he would have called himself a *morphician* if he had thought of it. Another exhilarating specimen was a tractor-driver who advertised for a job as a *caterpillar-engineer*. A third was a beautician who burst out as an *appearance-engineer*. In an Atlanta department-store the *News-Record* found an *engineer of good taste*—a young woman employed to advise newly-married couples patronizing the furniture department, and elsewhere it unearthed *display-engineers* who had been lowly window-dressers until some visionary among them made the great leap, *demolition-engineers* who were once content to be house-wreckers, and *sanitary-engineers* who had an earlier incarnation as garbage-men. The *wedding-engineer* is a technician employed by florists to dress churches for hymeneal orgies. The *commence-ment-e.* arranges college and high-school commencements; he has lists of clergymen who may be trusted to pray briefly, and some sort of fire-alarm connection, I suppose, with the office of Dr. John H. Finley, the champion commencement orator of this or any other age. The *packing-e.* is a scientist who crates clocks, radios and chinaware for shipment. The *correspondence-e.* writes selling-letters guaranteed to pull. The *income-e.* is an insurance solicitor in a new false-face. The *dwelling-e.* replaces lost keys, repairs leaky roofs, and plugs up rat-holes in the cellar. The *vision-e.* supplies spectacles at cut rates. The *dehorning-e.* attends to bulls who grow too frisky. The *Engineering News-Record* also discovered a *printing-e.*, a *furniture-e.*, a *photographic-e.*, a *financial-e.* (a stock-market tipster), a *paint-e.*, a *clothing*-e., a *wrapping-e.* (a dealer in wrapping-paper), a *matrimonial-e.* (a psychoanalyst specializing in advice to the lovelorn), a *box-e.* (the *packing-e.* under another name), an *automotive-painting-e.*, a *blasting-e.*, a *dry-cleaning-e.*, a *container-e.*, a *furnishing-e.*, a *socio-religious-e.* (an uplifter), a *social-e.* (the same), a *feed-plant-e.*, a *milk-e.*, a *surface-protection-e.*, an *analyzation-e.*, a *fiction-e.*, a *psychological-e.* (another kind of psychoanalyst), a *casement-window-e.*, a *shingle-e.*, a *fumigating-e.*, a *laminated-wood-e.*, a *package-e.* (the *packing-e.* again), a *horse-e.*, a *podiatric-e.* (a corn-doctor), an *ice-e.*, a *recreation-e.*, a *tire-e.*, a *paint-maintenance-e.*, a *space-saving-e.*, a *film-e.* (or *filmgineer*), a *criminal-e.* (a criminologist), a *diet-kitchen-e.*, a *patent-e.*, an *equipment-e.*, a *floor-covering-e.*, a *society-e.*, a *window-cleaning-e.*, a *dust-e.*, a *hospitalization-e.*, a *baking-e.*, a *directory-e.*, an *advertising-e.*, a *golf-e.* (a designer of golf-courses), a *human-e* (another variety of psychoanalyst), an *amusement-e.*, an *electric-signe-e.*, a *household-e.*, a *pageant-e.*, an *idea-e.*, a *ballistics-e.*, a *lace-e.* and a *sign-e.*[15] Perhaps the prize should go to the *dansant-e.* (an agent supplying dancers and musicians to nightclubs), or to the *hot-dog-e.*[16] The *exterminating-engineers* have a solemn national association and wear a distinguishing pin; whether or not they have tried to restrain non-member rat-catchers from calling themselves *engineers* I do not know. In 1923 the *Engineering News-Record* printed a final blast against all the pseudo-engineers then extant, and urged its engineer readers to boycott them. But this boycott apparently came to nothing, and soon thereafter it abated its indignation and resorted to laughter.[17] Next to *engineer*, *expert* seems to be the favorite talisman of

Americans eager to augment their estate and dignity in this world. Very often it is hitched to an explanatory prefix, e.g., *housing-, planning-, hog-, erosion-, marketing-, boll-weevil-, or sheep-dip-*, but sometimes the simple adjective *trained-* suffices. When the Brain Trust came into power in Washington, the town began to swarm with such quacks, most of them recent graduates of the far-flung colleges of the land. One day a humorous member of Congress printed an immense list of them in the *Congressional Record*, with their salaries and academic dignities. He found at least one whose expertness was acquired in a seminary for chiropractors. During the John Purroy Mitchel "reform" administration in New York City (1914–18) so many bogus *experts* were put upon the pay-roll that special designations for them ran out, and in prodding through the Mitchel records later on Bird S. Coler discovered that a number had been carried on the books as *general experts*.

Euphemisms for things are almost as common in the United States as euphemisms for avocations. Dozens of forlorn little fresh-water colleges are called *universities*, and almost all *pawnshops* are *loan-offices*. When *movie-cathedral* came in a few scoffers snickered, but by the generality of fans it was received gravely. *City*, in England, used to be confined to the seats of bishops, and even today it is applied only to considerable places, but in the United States it is commonly assumed by any town with paved streets, and in the statistical publications of the Federal government it is applied to all places of 8000 or more population. The American use of *store* for *shop*, like that of *help* for *servant*, is probably the product of an early effort at magnification. Before Prohibition saloons used to be *sample-rooms, buffets, exchanges, cafés* and *restaurants*; now they are *taverns, cocktail-rooms, taprooms, American-bars, stubes* and what not. Not long ago the *Furnished-Room Guide* undertook to substitute *hotelette* for *rooming-house*,[18] and in 1928 President E. L. Robins of the National *Fertilizer* Association proposed that the name of that organization be changed to the National Association of *Plant Food* Manufacturers or the American *Plant Food* Association.[19] In Pasadena the public garbage-wagons bear the legend: *Table-*

Waste Disposal Department. The word *studio* is heavily over-worked; there are *billiard-studios, tonsorial-studios, candy-studios*, and even *shoe-studios*.[20] Nor is this reaching out for sweet and disarming words confined to the lowly. Some time ago, in the *Survey*, the trade journal of the American uplifters, Dr. Thomas Dawes Eliot, associate professor of sociology in Northwestern University, printed a solemn argument in favor of abandoning all such harsh terms as *reformatory, house of refuge, reform school* and *jail*. "Each time a new phrase is developed," he said, "it seems to bring with it, or at least to be accompanied by, some measure of permanent gain, in standards or in viewpoint, even though much of the old may continue to masquerade as the new. The series, *alms, philanthropy, relief, rehabilitation, case work, family welfare*, shows such a progression from cruder to more re-fined levels of charity." Among the substitutions proposed by the learned professor were *habit-disease* for *vice, psycho-neurosis* for *sin, failure to compensate for disease, treatment* for *punishment, dilinquent* for *criminal, unmarried mother* for *illegitimate mother, out of wedlock* for *bastard, behavior problem* for *prostitute, colony* for *penitentiary, school* for *reformatory, psychopathic hospital* for *insane asylum*, and *house of detention* for *jail*.[21] Many of these terms (or others like them) have been actually adopted. Prac-tically all American insane asylums are now simple *hospitals*, many reformatories and houses of correction have been converted into *homes* or *schools*, all *almshouses* are now *infirmaries, county-farms* or *county-homes*, and most of the more advanced American penologists now speak of criminals as *psychopathic personalities*. By a law of New York it is provided that "in any local law, ordi-nance or resolution, or in any public or judicial proceeding, or in any process, notice, order, decree, judgment, record or other public document or paper, the term *bastard* or *illegitimate child* shall not be used, but the term *child born out of wedlock* shall be used in substitution therefor, and with the same force and effect." [22] Mean-while, such harsh terms as *second-hand* and *ready-made* disappear from the American vocabulary. For the former the automobile dealers, who are ardent euphemists, have substituted *recondi-tioned, rebuilt, repossessed* and *used*, and for the latter department stores offer *ready-tailored, ready-to-wear* and *ready-to-put-on*. For *shop-worn* two of the current euphemisms are *store-used* and *slightly-second*.

The English euphemism-of-all-work used to be *lady*. Back in the Seventeenth Century the court-poet Edmund Waller thought it quite proper to speak of actresses, then a novelty on the English stage, as *lady-actors*, and even today the English newspapers frequently refer to *lady-secretaries, lady-doctors, lady-inspectors, lady-golfers* and *lady-champions. Women's wear,* in most English shops, is *ladies' wear.* But this excessive use of lady seems to be going out, and I note *women's singles* and *women's ice hockey* on the sports pages of the *London Daily Telegraph.*[23] The *Times* inclines the same way, but I observe that it still uses *Ladies' International* to designate a golf tournament, *ladies' round* and *ladies' championship* (golf and fencing).[24] In the United States *lady* is definitely out of favor. The *salesladies* of yesteryear are now all *saleswomen* or *salesgirls,* and the female superintendent of a hospital is not the *lady-superintendent,* but simply the *superintendent.* When women were first elected to Congress, the question as to how they should be referred to in debate engaged the leaders of the House of Representatives. For a while the phrase used was "the *lady* from So-and-so," but soon "the *gentlewoman*" was substituted, and this is now employed almost invariably. Its invention is commonly ascribed to the late Nicholas Longworth; if he actually proposed it, it was probably jocosely, for *gentlewoman* is clumsy, and in some cases, as clearly inaccurate as *lady.* The English get round the difficulty by using *the hon. member* in speaking of women M.P.'s, though sometimes the *hon. lady* is used.[25] A member who happens to be a military or naval officer is always, by the way, *the hon. and gallant member,* and a legal officer, say the Attorney-General or Solicitor-General, or a lawyer member in active practice, is *the hon. and learned member.* The English use *gentleman* much more carefully than we do, and much more carefully than they themselves use *lady. Gentleman-author* or *gentleman-clerk* would make them howl, but they commonly employ *gentleman-rider* and *gentleman-player* in place of our *amateur,* though *amateur* seems to be gaining favor. Here the man referred to is always actually a gentleman by their standards.

NOTES

1. Private communication, Sept. 28, 1935.
2. Realtor: Its Meaning and Use; Chicago (National Association of Real Estate Boards), 1925.
3. Letter to W. A. Frisbie, editor of the Minneapolis *Daily News*. This was in 1922. The letter was subscribed "Yours *realtorially*." A copy was sent to Mr. Lewis, who preserves it in his archives.
4. Private communication, Sept. 4, 1935.
5. Eletragist, by Corneil Ridderhof, *American Speech*, Aug., 1927, p. 477. It means, according to Mr. Ridderhof, "a combined electrical dealer and contractor."
6. I am indebted here to Mr. W. M. Krieger, executive secretary of the organization, the headquarters of which are in Chicago.
7. *Casket* seems to have come in during the Civil War Period. In 1863 Nathaniel Hawthorne denounced it in Our Old Home as "a vile modern phrase, which compels a person . . . to shrink . . . from the idea of being buried at all." At the start it had a rival in *case*. The latter was used in the Richmond *Examiner's* report of the funeral of Gen. J. E. B. Stuart, May 13, 1864. But the *Examiner*, in the same report, used *corpse* and *hearse*.
8. Mortuary Nomenclature, *Hygeia*, Nov., 1925, p. 651.
9. The *Mortician*, by Elmer Davis, *American Mercury*, May, 1927.
10. *Editor and Publisher*, Jan. 30, 1932.
11. I proposed the use of bootician to designate a a high-toned big-city bootlegger in the *American Mercury*, April, 1925, p. 450. The term met a crying need, and had considerable success. In March, 1927, the San José *Mercury-Herald* said: "Our bootleggers are now calling themselves *booticians*. It seems that *bootlegger* has some trace of odium about it, while *bootician* has none." (Reprinted in the Baltimore *Evening Sun*, April 4, 1927). On July 23, 1931, according to the Associated Press, a man arrested in Chicago, on being asked his profession, answered proudly that he was a *bootician*.
12. In 1924 representatives of 3000 of them met in Chicago, and voted for *chirotonsor*. See the *Commonweal*, Nov. 26, 1924, p. 58.
13. There is a *Shoe Rebuilders'* Association in Baltimore. See the Baltimore *Evening Sun*, Oct. 17, 1935.
14. Hail, Columbia!; New York, 1921, pp. 92-3.
15. Many other varieties of engineers have been unearthed by other fanciers. On Oct. 19, 1935 the *New Yorker* announced the discovery of a *persuasion-e.*—"a man sent somewhere by his company to try and sell somebody an idea that would be of advantage to the company." A few months before this the *Professional Engineer* found a *pajama-e.* in the *New Yorker's* advertising columns. For this last I am indebted to Mr. M. E. McIver,

secretary of the American Association of Engineers. In *Popular Science,* Aug., 1935 a contributor called himself a *coffee-e.*

16. A curious anticipation of the American misuse of *engineer,* by an Englishman, is to be found in a memorandum submitted to Henry Dundas, first Viscount Melville, by Charles Stuart at the end of 1793. Dundas was Home Secretary from 1791 to 1794, and as such was in charge of the government's relations with the press. "I firmly believe, without any vanity," wrote Stuart, "that I know as much in the engineering of the press as any *press engineer* in Britain." See The History of the *Times;* London, 1925, p. 66. But Stuart's attempt to make the manipulation of the press a branch of engineering was not imitated, and there is no mention of pseudo-engineers in any of the English dictionaries.

17. See the issue for Jan. 15, 1925. Also, Some "Engineers" I Have Known, by a Civil Engineer, *Engineering News-Record,* April 19, 1923, p. 701. The engineers themselves have grossly misused the term designating them. In the Structure of the Engineering Profession, by Theodore J. Hoover, dean of the School of Engineering at Stanford University, *Journal of Engineering Education,* Jan., 1935, appears an exhaustive report upon what the 10,542 listed in "Who's Who in Engineering" call themselves. Mr. Hoover finds 2518 different titles, including such absurdities as *sales-e., sales-promotion-e., promotion-e., application-e., college-e., social-e., technical-publicity-e., bank-management-e.,* and *export-e.* He advocates a complete reform of professional nomenclature, but when I last heard from him he didn't seem to have much hope. On Feb. 21, 1935 the Associated Press reported that the National Society of Professional Engineers was trying to induce the American railroads to call their locomotive-engineers *enginemen.* The New York Central and the Pennsylvania, it was said, were already doing so.

18. See the *New Yorker,* Jan. 9, 1935, p. 74. The *New Yorker* expressed a waggish preference for *furnished-roomateria.*

19. United Press report, Nov. 13, 1928.

20. See *Studio,* by John T. Krumpelmann, *American Speech,* Dec., 1926, p. 158.

21. A Limbo for Cruel Words, *Survey,* June 15, 1922.

22. Laws of 1925, Ch. 515, in force April 9, 1925. I have to thank Mr. Sylvan Baruch of the New York Bar for calling my attention to this statute.

23. March 29, 1935.

24. April 12, 1935, p. 6.

25. I am indebted for the following to Mr. James Bone, London editor of the Manchester *Guardian:* "When a Minister answers a question in the House he says Yes, *sir* or No, *sir,* whether the question is asked by a man or a woman M.P. The reason is that he is supposed to be addressing the Speaker. There was some laughter among young members when a Minister replied Yes, *sir* to a question by Lady Astor, but elderly members wrote to the papers at once, rebuking them and explaining the procedure." Some time ago I heard the trial of a case in one of the London Law Courts, with the Lord Chief Justice of England, Lord Hewart, on the bench. There were two women on the jury, but when they finished their labors he said "Thank you, *gentlemen.*"

FRANK SULLIVAN

The Cliché Expert Testifies on the Atom

Q—Mr. Arbuthnot, you're the very man I want to see. I've been longing to examine you on atomic energy.

A—Well, my boy, you've come to the right party. I believe I can say that I know all the clichés on the subject.

Q—How can you say that?

A—Without fear of successful contradiction.

Q—I'm glad to hear it. I suspected you would be making a study of the atomic cliché.

A—A study! Why I've been doing nothing since V-J Day but listen to the experts explain atomic energy and the bomb on the air, or editorialize about them in the newspapers. Indeed I *am* the cliché expert of the atom. You realize of course what the dropping of that test bomb in the stillness of the New Mexico night did.

Q—What did it do?

A—It ushered in the atomic age, that's what it did. You know what kind of discovery this is?

Q—What kind?

A—A tremendous scientific discovery.

Q—Could the atomic age have arrived by means of any other verb than "usher"?

A—No. "Usher" has the priority.

Q—Mr. Arbuthnot, what will never be the same?

A—The world.

. . . .

Q—Are you pleased?

A—I don't know. The splitting of the atom could prove a boon to mankind. It could pave the way for a bright new world. On the other hand it may spell the doom of civilization as we know it.

Q—You mean that it has—

A—Vast possibilities for good or evil.

Q—At any rate, Mr. Arbuthnot, as long as the bomb had to be discovered, I'm glad we got it first.

A—If you don't mind, I will be the one to recite the clichés here. You asked me to, you know.

Q—I'm sorry.

A—Quite all right. I shudder to think.

Q—What?

A—Of what might have happened if Germany or Japan had got the bomb first.

Q—What kind of race was it between the Allied and German scientists?

A—A close race.

Q—What pressed?

A—Time pressed.

Q—With what kind of energy did the scientists work in their race to get the bomb?

A—Feverish energy. Had the war lasted another six months the Germans might have had the bomb. It boggles.

Q—What boggles?

A—This tremendous scientific discovery boggles the imagination. Also stirs same.

Q—Where do we stand, Mr. Arbuthnot?

A—At the threshold of a new era.

Q—And humanity is where?

A—At the crossroads. Will civilization survive? Harness.

Q—Harness, Mr. Arbuthnot? What about it?

A—Harness and unleash. You had better learn to use those two words, my boy, if you expect to talk about the atom, or write about it, either. They are two words very frequently used. With pea, of course.

Q—Why pea?

A—Oh, everything is in terms of the pea. You know how much U-235 it would take to drive a car to the moon and back?

Q—No, sir. How much?

A—A lump the size of a pea. Know how much U-235 it would take to ring your electric doorbell for twenty million years?

Q—How much, God forbid?

A—A lump the size of a pea. Know how much it would take to lift the Empire State Building twelve miles into the air?

Q—I wish you would let the Empire State Building alone, Mr. Arbuthnot. It is all right where it is.

A—Sorry. It must be lifted twelve miles into the air. Otherwise, do you know who would not be able to understand the practical application, or meaning, of atomic energy?

Q—No. Who?

A—The average layman.

Q—I see. Well, in that case, up she goes. I gather that a lump the size of a pea would do it.

A—Exactly.

Q—You wouldn't settle for a lump the size of a radish, or a bean?

A—Sorry. The pea is the accepted vegetable in these explanations. Do you know what the atomic energy in the lobe of your left ear could do?

Q—What?

A—If harnessed, it could propel a B-29 from Tokyo to San Francisco.

Q—It *could!*

A—Do you know that the energy in every breath you take could send the Twentieth Century Limited from New York to Chicago?

Q—Mercy on us, Mr. Arbuthnot!

A—And the atomic energy in your thumbnail could, if unleashed, destroy a city twice the size of three Seattles. Likewise, the energy in your . . .

Q—For God's sake, stop, Mr. Arbuthnot! You make me feel like a menace to world security in dire need of control by international authority in the interests of world peace. Kindly leave off explaining atomic energy to me in terms so simple a layman can understand. Explain it to me in scientific terms, and the more abstruse the better.

A—Well, listen carefully and I'll give you a highly technical explanation. In the first place the existence of the atom was only suspected. Then Einstein . . . equation . . . nucleus . . . electron . . . bombard . . . proton . . . deuteron . . . radioactive . . . neutron . . . atomic weight . . . beta rays . . . matter . . . split . . . chain reaction . . . gamma rays . . . alpha particles . . . Mme. Curie . . . break down . . . energy . . . end products . . . control . . . impact . . . uranium . . . Dr. Niels Bohr . . . barium . . . orbit . . . Dr. Lise Meitner . . . knowledge pooled . . . Dr. Enrico Fermi . . . military possibilities . . . Dr. Vannevar Bush . . . U-235 . . . isotopes . . . U-238 . . . autocatalytic . . . heavy water . . . New Mexico . . . mushroom-shaped cloud . . . awesome sight . . . fission . . . William L. Laurence . . . and there you had a weapon potentially destructive beyond the wildest nightmares of science. Do I make myself clear?

Q—Perfectly. Now, Mr. Arbuthnot, what is nuclear energy the greatest discovery since?

A—It is the greatest discovery since the discovery of fire. You will find that "Promethean" is the correct adjective to use here.

Q—What does this tremendous scientific discovery do to large armies?

A—It spells the doom of large armies. It also spells the doom of large navies. Likewise, it spells the doom of large air forces. Similarly, as I mentioned earlier, it may spell the doom of civilization. I doubt if so many dooms have been spelled by anything since the phrase was first coined.

Q—When was that, sir?

A—I should imagine at the time gunpowder spelled the doom of the bow and arrow.

Q—What is the atomic bomb a menace to?

A—World order, world peace, and world security.

Q—What must be done to it?

A—It must be controlled by an international authority. The San Francisco Charter must be revised to fit the Atomic Age.

Q—What does the bomb make essential?

A—It makes world unity essential. It makes an international league for peace essential if the world is not to be plunged into a third war which will destroy civilization.

Q—In short, its use must be—

A—Banned.

Q—What kind of plaything is the bomb?

A—A dangerous plaything. A dangerous toy.

Q—What kind of boomerang is it?

A—A potential boomerang.

Q—What else is it?

A—It is the greatest challenge mankind has yet faced. It is also the greatest destructive force in history. It has revolutionary possibilities and enormous significance and its discovery caused international repercussions.

Q—What does the splitting of the atom unleash?

A—The hidden forces of the universe. Vast.

Q—Vast?

A—That's another word you'd better keep at hand if you expect to talk or write about this tremendous scientific discovery. Vast energy, you know. Vast possibilities. Vast implications. Vast prospects; it opens them.

Q—I see. What cannot grasp the full significance of the tremendous scientific discovery?

A—The human mind.

Q—Whose stone is it?

A—The philosopher's stone.

Q—Whose dream?

A—The alchemist's dream

Q—And whose monster?

A—Frankenstein's monster.

Q—What does it transcend?

A—It transcends the wildest imaginings of Jules Verne.

Q—And of who else?

A—H. G. Wells.

Q—The fantastic prophecies of these gentlemen have become what?

A—Stern reality.

Q—What does it make seem tame?

A—The adventures of Superman and Flash Gordon.

Q—Very good, Mr. Arbuthnot. Now, then, in addition to ushering in the Atomic Age, what else does this T.S.D. do?

A—It brightens the prospect for the abolition of war but increases the possibility of another war. It adds to the store of human knowledge. It unlocks the door to the mysteries of the universe. It makes flights into interstellar space a possibility. It endangers our security and makes future aggression a temptation.

Q—What has it done to warfare?

A—It has revolutionized warfare, and outmoded it, and may outlaw it. It has changed all existing concepts of military power. It has made current weapons of war obsolete.

Q—And what may it do to cities?

A—It may drive cities underground.

Q—Mr. Arbuthnot, in the happy event that atomic energy is not used destructively, what kind of role will it play?

A—A peacetime role.

Q—Meaning?

A—Meaning cheap power, cheap fuel. A lump of U-235—

Q—The size of a pea?

A—No, not this time—the size of forty pounds of coal would run the entire nation's heating plants all winter.

Q—What would that result in?

A—Sweeping changes in our daily life and unemployment on a hitherto unheard-of scale.

Q—Bringing about what kind of revolution?

A—An industrial revolution.

Q—Mr. Arbuthnot, should we share the secret with other nations?

A—Yes and no.

Q—If the latter, why?

A—Because we can be trusted with it.

Q—Why can we be trusted with it?

A—Because we would use it only in self-defense and as a last resort.

Q—Who could not be trusted with it?

A—Some future Hitler. Some gangster nation. Some future aggressor.

Q—If we should share it, why that?

A—As a gesture of confidence in other nations.

Q—And anyhow—

A—Anyhow, every nation will possess the secret within five years.

Q—Now, Mr. Arbuthnot, can you tell us what is ironic?

A—It is ironic that several of the major contributions to the bomb were made by scientists whom Hitler and Mussolini had exiled.

Q—In other words, Hitler cooked—

A—His own goose.

Q—What else is ironic?

A—The spending of two billions on the bomb, in contrast to the amounts spent on education, public health, slum clearance, and research on cancer and other diseases.

Q—What kind of commentary is that?

A—A sad commentary on our so-called, or vaunted, civilization.

Q—Mr. Arbuthnot, how ready is man for the Atomic Age?

A—As ready as a child is to handlle dynamite.

Q—What kind of little boys do the atomic scientists remind you of?

A—Of little boys playing with matches.

Q—What is a possibility of the future?

A—Atomic bombs a hundred times more destructive than the one dropped on Nagasaki.

Q—What is such a discovery known as?

A—It is known as man's conquest of natural forces.

Q—What does such a discovery advance?

A—It advances the frontiers of science.

Q—And what does the invention of this key to world suicide constitute?

A—It constitutes scientific progress.

MARGARET SCHLAUCH

Semantic Rejuvenation

Some of the most abstract terms in the language are really faded
metaphors. On examination it turns out that an earlier meaning,
now forgotten, is often lively in the extreme. Hence an obvious
means of invigorating our jejune vocabulary is to fall back on
those lively older meanings. True enough, the average speaker
does not know that they ever existed. He is not *reminded* that
"express" once meant, literally and physically, "to press out." But
he can learn it instantaneously from a context. It may be that only
the archaic literal sense is intended, or it may be that both the
physical and the metaphorical are to be grasped simultaneously.
In any event, the impact of the divergent use on an attentive
reader forces him to a new experience of the word, without sac-
rificing comprehension. An example of the use of "express"
in this revivified fashion will be found in Emily Dickinson:

> Essential oils are wrung;
> The attar from the rose
> Is not expressed by suns alone,
> It is the gift of screws.

In the age of Shakespeare, intensive classical education had
shaped a reading public (among the few, of course) who could
sense the older meaning with less effort than many feel today.
The plays offer repeated vivid uses of etymological rejuvenation
of words. Horatio's "Season thy admiration for a while with an
attent ear" makes use of the Latin sense of *admirari*, "to wonder

. . . .

at" something and of "attent" in the sense of "stretched." "Hast thou no *speculation* in those eyes?" recalls the literal meaning of *speculare*, "to gaze, look upon." "Occulted guilt" means guilt covered over, or hidden. When Troilus says "there's no maculation in thy heart" he reminds us of the concrete meaning of *macula*, namely "spot (of dirt)," and when he refers to his "sequent protestation" it is in the concrete sense of "my calling on witness, which now follows." Hamlet's injunction "Let it be tenable in your silence still" evokes the basic meaning of Latin *tenere*, "to hold"—not merely "to maintain a theoretical position." So when Laertes warns his sister that "nature, crescent, does not grow alone in thews and bulk," the adjective reminds us that *crescrere* meant "to grow," to mature in a physical sense. In *Troilus and Cressida* Ulysses can speak of "deracinating" a political state and thus call upon us to think of *racine*, a root, so that the meaning of "uproot" is conveyed in an unaccustomed startling manner. The usual word having lost emphasis, the learned one infuses new life by causing us to share in the original metaphoric synthesis.

Sophisticated writers still impose the etymological task upon their readers as part of the aesthetic experience. It may be said, in fact, that etymology is one of the devices by which readers are now called upon to share in the creative act. The enormous influence of English metaphysical poets of the seventeenth century on modern writers—notably the influence of Donne—has accentuated this etymological awareness. The reason for a return to metaphysical poets as a source of inspiration is not our subject here. But a consequence of it is certainly a recourse to similar linguistic devices.

James Joyce, for instance, has evinced etymological preoccupations throughout his entire work. When he says that one pugilist's fist is "proposed" under the chin of another, he intends the word as Latin *proponere*, "to place under"; and he is capable of using "supplant" as "to plant under" in describing the Gracehoper (i. e. Grasshopper) of *Finnegans Wake*: "he had a partner pair of findlestilts to *supplant* him." T. S. Eliot expects the same etymological collaboration from his readers in his simile from "The Love Song of J. Alfred Prufrock":

> Streets that follow like a tedious argument
> Of insidious intent
> To lead you to an overwhelming question. . . .

Like Shakespeare, he wishes you to remember that "intent" means a thing that is taut and stretched for action, and that "insidious" (Latin *insidiae*, "sitting or lurking within") means "ambushed" against an enemy. At the same time the literal metaphor of warfare is merged in the image of a verbal argument. In "Preludes" there is another figure of the many he evokes from the streets of a city:

> The conscience of a blackened street
> Impatient to assume the world.

Here it is necessary to remember that "assume" means "to take on" (*ad-sumere*) and hence "to play the part of." In his epithet "maculate giraffe" ("Sweeny among the Nightingales") he is doing exactly as Shakespeare did: reminding us that our faded theological term "immaculate conception" contains a sharp visual image of literal, physical spots.

So C. Day Lewis makes use of both the literal and figurative senses of "derelict mills" in "You that love England." He means lonely and abandoned mills, of course, but also mills that have simply and unmetaphorically been "left behind" (*de-linqui*) by those who formerly worked in them. And W. H. Auden, speaking in "Sir, No Man's Enemy" of "the distortions of ingrown virginity," surely intends us to feel the root meaning of "twist, physical bending from the norm" under the abstract "distortion." When he uses the expression "trains that *fume* in the station" he evokes the literal visual image "to smoke" as well as the later extended meaning "to be impatient."

Hart Crane's strange vigor is in part derived from the reminder of root meanings. Here are a few examples. In a description of an airplane flying over Mount Hatteras, the pilot is thus addressed:

> Remember, Falcon-Ace,
> Thou hast there in thy wrist a Sanskrit charge
> To conjugate infinity's dim marge—
> Anew. . . !

If the general sense is the quasi-magic power of dominating the horizons of infinity, the root meaning of "conjugate" is still felt as "to put a yoke on," rather than "to inflect a verb." In "Garden Abstract" the opening lines are

> The apple on its bough is her desire,—
> Shining suspension, mimic of the sun.

The abstract word "suspension" is to be interpreted as "the thing which is hung." In the haunting phrase "the silken skilled trans-memberment of song" there is an enormous heightening of effect when the trite word "trans-formation" (passing of one form into another) is replaced by "transmemberment" (passing of one member into another). This particular instance shows how readily an acquired skill in etymological rejuvenation will pass into creative independence in handling words.

II.

THE HISTORY OF ENGLISH

Why study the history of our language? Why not ignore the past and simply study today's language, the one we actually use and wish to use more effectively? The essays in this Section say, in effect, that if we know how our language got to be the way it is, we are likely to use it with increased confidence and judgment. Strictly speaking, we are all from the provinces, but we need not be provincial.

In the first essay, Margaret Schlauch takes us across Europe so that we can hear similarities in words and sentences from one country to another which imply descent from a few ancient language families. From one of those families, the Germanic, modern English developed. The stages of that development are outlined by the late E. G. Mathews and J. N. Hook, professor of English at the University of Illinois. A closer view of one stage in both England and the United States is provided in "The Language of the Colonists" by Albert H. Marckwardt, professor of English at the University of Michigan. The eighteenth century with its notions about "correctness" is the point of departure in the fourth essay for a discussion of what attitudes toward the English language should be adopted and what material should be studied. The author, Charles C. Fries, is a distinguished linguist and professor-emeritus from the University of Michigan. In the last essay, Albert H. Marckwardt, looking from the past development of our language toward its future, sees a healthy growth ahead if linguistic anxiety is replaced by knowledge and interest.

MARGARET SCHLAUCH

Family Relationships Among Languages

Families of Languages

In happier times, it was possible to cross the length and breadth
of Europe by train in so few days that the journey could still be
conveniently measured by hours. Paris to Berlin, fifteen hours;
Berlin to Moscow, forty hours; Berlin to Milan, twenty hours. In
certain parts of that complex and explosive continent, it was
necessary to change one's official language three or four times in
the course of a pilgrimage which in the United States would
appear to be, in length, a mere uneventful hop. You could cross
the English Channel and find yourself greeted within a couple
of hours by the slow even courtesy of a Dutch immigration
officer; a few more hours and a Belgian would appear at the
door of your compartment and, in French idiom sounding somehow un-French, make the same routine demands with a courtesy
of a different tang. Then eastwards, you could encounter the
clipped precision of German officialdom, followed by softer ac-
cents emanating from the speakers of a series of Western Slavonic
national languages. And to the south there lay, also easily accessible, the varied music of Mediterranean Romance languages,
maintaining a certain insidious charm even as spoken by the
stampers of passports and openers of trunks. The landscape might
not change perceptibly at the political borders, but there would
be a stir in your compartment, a coming and going of people,
new phrases to be caught on the wing as travelers passed by in
. . . .

the corridor; and as you sat in your corner eagerly experiencing the linguistic kaleidoscope of the continent, you would strain to catch the first sounds of the new idiom as fresh companions settled themselves about you. The Dutch commercial travelers condoling or congratulating with one another in measured tones on the current market would give place to a group of French *permissionaires* exchanging rapid chaff on the exploits of their leave, in an esoteric professional jargon of considerable gayety; their still-warm places might be occupied by a domestic group on the German border, *Vati* and *Mutti* complete with *Bruderlein* and *Schwesterlein* who were sure to be the silent, well-behaved recipients of a series of solicitous imperatives. Cries from the station platforms might echo in your mind in rich polyglot confusion at the end of such a long journey eastwards: *"Cigarren! Cigaretten!"—"Paris-Soir! Figaro!"—"Abfahrt!"—"Het is al tien uur."—"A la aduana . . ." "Agua mineral, chocolade . . ." "Priidjote, pozhaluista!"*

Certainly these differences in tongue would be bewildering in the extreme to any traveler, until instruction and experience could bring order out of the chaos of aural impressions. But an enthusiast who set out to acquire some smattering of the languages in a series of countries to be so traversed would soon begin to observe some curious parallelisms in the words learnt to designate the same object. For two or even more languages he would find repeated similarities, remote but still perceptible, not only in individual words but in the manner in which these words were put together in sentences. Naïve observers explain these similarities by talking of a vague "mixture" or "corruption." When they come across a sentence in Dutch like *"Ik heb het gekoopt voor mijnen zoon"* they are pleased and surprised to observe how much it resembles English "I have bought it for my son" or German *"Ich habe es fur meinen Sohn gekauft."* And so they inform you gleefully, with all the assurance of a non-linguist: "Dutch is a funny language; it's a mixture of English and corrupt German."

A Hollander would of course protest vehemently that Dutch is no more corrupt, funny, or mixed than any other national speech in Europe, and he would be quite right. There is another way of explaining its gratifying resemblance to things we already know.

Let us take a single sentence and follow its land-changes, its mutations, over a fairly wide territory—as territories are reckoned in Europe.

Suppose you begin a trip in Sweden, and you find yourself seated with a mother who is anxiously supervising the box lunch of several small children. She turns solicitously to one of them and says, "Did you get any cookies (or apples, or candies)?" And the child replies: "Yes, Mother, I have three." In Swedish that would be, "*Ja, moder, jag har tre.*" In Norway, to the west, or Denmark, to the south, it would be almost the same: "*Já, mor, jeg ar tre.*"

The slight differences in vowel sound and in sentence melody do not disguise the fact that we are listening to the same words. A moment's reflection will suggest the right explanation. We are not confronted by a borrowing or "mixture" in any case. The three Scandinavian languages mentioned are equally ancient. At one time they were identical, for all practical purposes. A traveler in olden times (let us say the ninth century) could traverse the whole length of Norway or Sweden and pass to the southern extremity of Denmark without any change in his speech. Everywhere he would hear children say: "*Ja, móðir, ek hefi prjá.*" (The last word was pronounced [θrja:].) The changes and differences developed during centuries, rather rapidly in Denmark, more slowly in Sweden. As a result, we now have diversity where once there was unity. Three national languages, equally venerable, have replaced Old Scandinavian. They are extremely close relatives, but none could claim parental precedence over the others. If any branch of Scandinavian could exact respect on the grounds of conservatism (that is, fidelity to the parent, the Old Scandinavian) it would be modern Icelandic, spoken in the distant island which Norwegians settled in the ninth century. Here children still say: "*Já, móðir, ek hefi prjá.*" The values of the vowels have changed slightly; that is all.

When the train crosses from Denmark into Germany, a greater change becomes apparent. Here the maternal inquiry elicits the answer, "*Ja, Mutter, ich habe drei.*" In Holland or the Flemish-speaking parts of Belgium, tow-headed lads murmur, "*Ja, moeder* (or *moer*) *ik heb drie.*" The cleavage is greater, but the separate words still look distinctly familiar. We can even group the versions of our little sentence to show where two or more languages show particular likeness:

ICELANDIC:	*Já, móðir, ek hefi þrjá.*
SWEDISH:	*Ja, moder, jag har tre.*
DANISH:	*Ja, mor, jeg har tre.*
NORWEGIAN:	*Ja, mor, jeg har tre.*
GERMAN:	*Ja, Mutter, ich habe drei.*
DUTCH:	*Ja, Moeder, ik heb drie.*
FLEMISH:	*Ja, Moeder, ik heb drie.*
ENGLISH:	Yes, Mother, I have three.

German stands somewhat apart because its consonants show certain peculiarities: it alone has a [t] between vowels (that is, intervocalic) in the word for mother. Still, it is clear that we are still dealing with variations on the same theme.

Just as the Scandinavian examples revealed close kinship among themselves, so all of those in the extended list show some degree of relationship with one another. Sentences betraying the close linguistic ties within this same group could be multiplied indefinitely. Such being the case, we are justified in speaking of a "family" of languages, borrowing a metaphor from the realm of human relations.

Parent Germanic

Detailed comparisons of this sort indicate that all the members of this Germanic group go back to a single parent language, now lost, spoken as a unity somewhere between the first century B.C. and the first A.D. We call this lost parent language Primitive Germanic. Its modern descendants are grouped into what is known as the Germanic family of European languages. English is one of them. The precise geographical location of Primitive Germanic is not known. We can surmise the nature of its sounds (*phonology*) and inflections (*morphology*) with what is probably fair accuracy, however, because of some early literature and inscriptions dating back to a time when the separate descendants had as yet separated very little from one another. The runic inscription on the Gallebus horn belongs to this early period. It was Old Scandinavian, but it might almost have been composed in an early form of any of the others mentioned.

By comparative study it has been established which sounds in the quoted words are most faithful to the original language. We know that English has preserved the initial consonant of the word "three" [θ] as spoken in Primitive Germanic; but that Icelandic, Flemish, and Dutch have kept the consonant at the end of the first person pronoun singular (*ik*), which has been lost in English and transformed in the others. Back of the multiplicity of extant forms we can feel our way to the existence of the single speech called parent Germanic.

Romance Languages

But now let us continue the journey south. In Belgium our anxious Flemish mother may be replaced by a fellow-country-woman who speaks French. Her child will say something strikingly different from anything heard so far. "*Oui, mère* (or *maman*), *j'en ai trois.*" As the train goes southwards towards that fertile cradle of cultures, the Mediterranean basin, it may be routed towards the Pyrenees, or across the Alps into Italy. If it should cross the Iberian peninsula you would hear in Spain: "*Si madre, (yo) tengo tres;* and in Portugal: "*Sim, mãe, tenho tres.*" But if it should take you across the barrier which Hannibal—even Hannibal—found all but impassable, down the steep slopes to the smiling Lombard plains, you would hear: "*Si, madre, ce n'ho tre.*" And even across the Adriatic, on the far side of the Balkan peninsula, hardy descendants of the Roman army and Roman colonists will be saying in Rumanian: "*Da, mama mea, eu am trei.*"

The similarities are apparent:

FRENCH:	*Oui, mère, j'en ai trois.*
SPANISH:	*Si, madre, (yo) tengo tres.*

PORTUGUESE: *Sim, mãe, tenho tres.*
ITALIAN: *Si, madre, ce n'ho tre.*
RUMANIAN: *Da, mama mea, eu am trei.*

The situation is comparable to the one which diverted and possibly mystified you in Germanic territory. You have been traversing lands where the people communicate with one another in tongues clearly descended from a single parent. This time the parent language was a form of Latin: not the solemn speech, stilted and formal, which was reserved for polite literature and speeches in the forum, but the popular or "vulgar" Latin spoken by common people throughout the length and breadth of the Roman territory. Plain soldiers, tavern keepers, itinerant merchants, freedmen, small traders, naturalized citizens of all the polyglot Roman provinces, must have used this form of discourse as an international *lingua franca.* In this idiom they bought and sold, exchanged jokes, flirted, lamented, and consoled with one another. We know from late written documents and inscriptions (especially those on the humbler tombstones of poor folk) just how ungrammatical, rapid, informal, and even slangy this Latin was, compared with the intricate and highly mannered periods of a Cicero. People had become impatient with the many case endings required in classical Latin, and were reducing them to two or three. Even these were treated with playful carelessness. The verb was handled in a different way—a more vivid one—to show changes in tense; and the word order was simplified. Moreover, slang words triumphed completely over traditional ones in some provinces. Ordinary people in Gaul (perhaps emulating the jargon of the army) stopped referring to the human head as *caput,* and substituted *testa* or "pot," from which comes modern French *tête.* It is as if all persons speaking English should have fallen into the way of saying "my bean" for the same object, so that it became the accepted word, while "head" was lost entirely.

The popular Roman speech differed from one province to another because popular locutions do tend always to be regional, and because the Romans came in contact with widely differing types of native speech. Thus the pronunciation and even the grammar were affected by the underlying populations. In one place the Latin word *habere* continued to be used for "to have"; in the Spanish peninsula, however, it so happened that *tenere*, meaning "to hold," came to be used in its place in the more general sense of "to have." That is why our imaginary Spanish child says *tengo* instead of any form of the classical *habere*. The number "three," on the other hand, varies only slightly in the series of Romance sentences quoted. The numbers have remained fairly stable in the various daughter languages perpetuated from vulgar Latin. One of the factors tending to preserve a similarity in them throughout the ages has been their similar experience in developing a strong stress accent during the transition to the Middle Ages. This new accentuation caused similar losses in unaccented syllables in a given word in all Mediterranean areas. There were differences, of course, in the forms that emerged; but certainly not enough to make the results unrecognizably alien to one another.

The neo-Latin languages (if the expression may be permitted) give us another example, therefore, of a family which bears its signs of consanguinity very legibly on the external aspect of each of its members. In Roman times, Latin itself could claim cousins (in the ancient *Italic* group) which have since been lost.

The Slavic Family

And here is one further example of language relationship which may metaphorically be called close consanguinity. In eastern Europe a sharp-eared traveler on an international train will also have an opportunity to detect fundamental similarity behind the changing visages of national speech. A farflung territory is occupied by people speaking *Slavic* languages and dialects. It would be possible to pursue the transformation of our key sentence addressed to an imaginary Slavic mother to the east as follows:

CZECHISH:	*Ano, matko, mam tři.*
POLISH:	*Tak, matko, man trzy.*
RUSSIAN:	*Da, matj, u menjá tri.*

When our international train crosses into the Soviet Union, it will pass through various sections of Russia showing distinct dialect colorings. Ukrainian, for instance, shows enough differentiation to be dignified as a national language, with an official spelling of its own. Even an untutored eye, however, can see how close it is to the official language of Great Russia, the classical medium of literature known to the world as "Russian." In the Balkan states, South Slavic languages show these perceptible nuances of our chosen theme. For instance, the Bulgarian version of it would be: *"Da, maika, imom tri."*

Once again, we are justified in assuming that centuries ago there was a single language from which these cousins descended. About the seventh century it was probably still fairly unified. In the ninth century a southern dialect of this early Slavic (Old Bulgarian) was written down in a translation of the Bible made by Saints Cyril and Methodius. The text helps us to get quite a clear picture of parent Slavic, just as runic inscriptions bring us close to Primitive Germanic, and unofficial documents of the Roman Empire tell us much about Vulgar Latin.

Indo-European, Parent of Parents

Slavic, Romance, and Germanic represent three families of languages spoken in Europe today. But surely it must be clear that similarities link these families to one another besides linking the smaller subdivisions within each given family. In *all* the national languages surveyed so far, it will be noticed, the word for "mother" began with the labial nasal [m]; in a considerable number a dental [t], [ð], or [d] appeared in the middle of the word after the first vowel. Likewise in *all* of the languages listed, "three" began with a dental [t], [d], or [θ], followed by an [r]. Why is this?

Clearly, at a still earlier period than the days of early (prehistoric) Germanic and Slavonic, and of Vulgar Latin, there must have been a more ancient and inclusive unity which embraced all three.

The same procedure, if pursued farther, would have revealed

to us other major families belonging to the same larger embracing unity in Europe and parts of Asia.These are:

Celtic, including Irish, Highland Scottish, Welsh, and Breton. (In modern Irish, "mother" is *mathair* and "three" is *tri.*)

Baltic, including Lettish, Lithuanian, and an extinct dialect once spoken in the territory of modern Prussia (Old Prussian). The word for "mother" is *motina,* not closely related to the cognates already cited. *Tris* for "three" is, on the other hand, an obvious cognate.

Hellenic, including modern Greek dialects, some of which go back to very ancient times. (An ancient Greek dialect, Attic, spoken in the city of Athens, produced a body of literature of enduring splendor. Its word for "mother" was *matêr* and for "three," *treîs.* This is the classical language studied in school.)

Albanian, the national language of Albania, with no close relatives outside its own borders. Here "three" is *tre;* but the word for "mother" is not related to the forms in the above languages. A new form, *nona,* has replaced the Indo-European term preserved elsewhere.

Armenian, spoken in Armenia (between Europe and Asia Minor), is, like Albanian, a language with many diverse elements borrowed from outside, but it has an independent history traceable back to the fifth or sixth century A.D. Its word for "mother," *mair,* is easily recognizable as a cognate of the others given; not so, however, is *erek* for "three."

Even in Asia there are languages with venerable histories and rich literary heritage which can be recognized as members of the same linguistic clan:

Indian, including Hindustani, Bengali, Marathi, and Hindi. These dialects are descended from Old Indian, preserved to us in a classical literary form (Sanskrit) which dates back to the fifteenth century B.C. or even several hundred years earlier. Sanskrit, despite its great antiquity, still shows close generic resemblance to its modern European cousins. Its word for "mother" was *mātṛ* and for "three," *tri.*

Iranian, very closely related to Sanskrit, was spoken in the

Persian highlands while Indian was spreading over the interior of India. It produced an early literature in the form of Zoroastrian hymns. Since those ancient times Persian has been subjected to large foreign infiltration, notably Arabic, but its structure still reveals its kinship with the other groups listed.

Hittite, a language spoken by people frequently mentioned in the Bible, is now extinct. Cuneiform inscriptions give us enough material to reveal its fundamental character. Some sort of relationship it surely must have had with the members of the broad family of families now being surveyed, but the precise nature of that relationship is still under discussion.

Tocharian, now extinct, is represented by some fragmentary texts (probably antedating the tenth century), which were discovered in eastern Turkestan in a Buddhist monastery. The material is too scanty to permit of definitive analysis, but it shows relationship to the above subsidiary groups.

Our railroad trip beginning with Germanic territory has taken us far afield, even to the shores of the Indus River in Asia. Even so, and despite the most baffling diversities, skilled comparison of key words has been able to establish that the miniature families surveyed do undoubtedly belong to the same large, inclusive family already postulated to account for likenesses observed among Germanic, Slavonic, and Romance (from Old Italic).

Back of the smaller families lay a single family; attached to this single family it is almost certain there must have been a single language. We call the whole family by the name "Indo-European," a term generally preferred today to "Indo-Germanic" or "Aryan," both of which could easily be misunderstood. That is to say, every language mentioned so far is an Indo-European language, no matter what smaller group it may belong to.

J. N. HOOK AND E. G. MATHEWS

Changes in the English Language

Examples of Old English

At first glance a selection from Old English appears to be in a foreign tongue. More careful scrutiny reveals that some of the words are almost the same as ours, that others have undergone considerable change, and that still others have vanished. Modern English has lost some of the grammatical constructions that formerly existed.

Here is the Lord's Prayer in the Old English (West Saxon) version of approximately a thousand years ago:

> Fæder ūre þū þe eart on heofonum sī þīn nama gehālgod.
> Tō becume þīn rīce. Gewurþe ðīn willa on eorðan swā swā on
> heofonum. Ūrne gedæghwāmlīcan hlāf syle ūs tō dæg. And
> forgyf ūs ūre gyltas swā swā wē forgyfað ūrum gyltendum.
> And ne gelæd þū ūs on costnunge ac ālȳs ūs of yfele. Sōþlīce.

Detailed comment on these few lines would fill many pages; here we shall look at only a few words and constructions. Word order was much less fixed in Old English than it is today: notice the Old English forms of *Father our* and *be thy name hallowed* as examples. Case endings are used with nouns, as in *heofonum* (heaven), *eorðan* (earth), *gyltas* (debts), and *gyltendum* (debtors). Adjectives had to agree in case, number, and gender with their nouns: *ūre, ūrne,* and *ūrum* are today simply *our.* The word *rīce* is now translated as *kingdom,* but it is actually a cognate of *Reich* which survives in German. The symbols þ (thorn) and ð

. . . .

(eth) were both used for *th*. Since Old English times some words have been reduced in the number of syllables: *gehālgod* (hallowed), *gedæghwāmlīcan* (daily), *forgyfað* (forgive). Spelling was much more phonetic than that of today; in general, there were no silent letters. In pronunciation, vowel sounds were more similar to those found in modern continental languages than to those in Modern English; and consonant sounds were not much different from those of Modern English. Punctuation marks other than periods were rare, and even periods were not used very systematically by the scribes.

As a second example consider the following lines from the epic poem *Beowulf*. The manuscript is generally believed to be in the hand of a scribe of the late tenth century. This passage tells of King Hrothgar's sorrow over the killing of his friend and follower by a hideous demon:

Hrothgar spoke	defender of the Scyldings
Hrōðgār maþelode	helm Scyldinga:
Not ask thou about happiness.	Sorrow is renewed
Ne frīn þū æfter sǣlum	Sorh is genīwod
of the Danes for the people	Dead is Aeschere
Denigea lēodum.	Dēad is Æschere
Irmenlaf's	elder brother
Yrmenlāfes	yldra brōþor
my confidant	and my counselor
mīn rūnwita	ond mīn rǣdbora
shoulder-companion	when we in battle
eaxlgestealla	ðonne wē on orlege
head protected	when clashed together troops
hafelan weredon	þonne hniton fēþan
boar-helmets struck	Such should hero be
eoferas cnysedan	Swylc scolde eorl wesan
nobleman good from old times	as Aeschere was.
æþeling ǣrgōd	swylc Æschere wæs.

Even the literal translation of this passage does not seem very clear today. A more free translation might go like this: "Hrothgar, the defender of the Scyldings, spoke: 'Do not ask about happiness, because sorrow has come again to the Danish people. Aeschere is dead. He was Irmenlaf's older brother and my confidant and counselor. He stood at my shoulder when in battle we protected our heads and hewed the boar-helmets as troops clashed. Every hero should be as Aeschere was, a nobleman good to recall from old times.' "

Notice, in comparing these translations, how word order has changed. Observe also how large a proportion of the Old English words have dropped out of the language. Some of them remain, however, in recognizable form: *helm* is a cousin of our *helmets*, *æfter* is *after*, *dēad* has changed only its pronunciation, *yldra broþor* is still recognizable, *þonne* has become *then*, *wē* and *in* are unchanged in spelling, *scolde*, is similar to *should*, *eorl* has altered its meaning and become *earl*, *ǣrgōd* contains the ancestors of *ere* and *good*, and *wæs* is obviously *was*.

Inflectional endings are much more important in Old English than in Modern; for example, *Scyldinga* (genitive plural) requires here a three-word translation, *of the Scyldings;* and *lēodum* also requires either a three-word translation, *for* (or *to*) *the people,* or a revised word order. The endings of such words as *rūnwita*, *fēþan*, and *eoferas* help, along with the context, to show whether the word is to be regarded as a subject or an object. In Modern English we depend more upon word order and upon "function words" such as prepositions than we do upon inflections.

Old English grammar may be made a subject for special study. Here you have seen illustrated only a few of its most obvious characteristics.

Example of Middle English

When we move forward about four hundred years, from the late tenth to the late fourteenth century, we see that the language has changed rather drastically. Here are lines from the Prologue of Chaucer's *Canterbury Tales,* describing the squire, son of the knight:

With him ther was his sone a yong Squyer

(lover)   (aspirant to knighthood)
A lovyere and a lusty bacheler

(curly) (as if)
With lokkes crulle as they were leyd in presse.

Of twenty yeer of age he was I gesse.

. . . . .

(Embroidered)   (meadow)
Embrouded was he, as it were a mede

(flowers)
Al ful of fresshe floures whyte and rede.

(playing the flute)
Singinge he was or floyting al the day.

He was as fresh as is the month of May.

Short was his goune with sleves long and wyde.

(excellently)
Wel coude he sitte on hors and faire ryde.

(compose the words)
He coude songes make and wel endyte

(Joust)   (also)   (draw)
Juste and eek daunce and wel purtreye and wryte.

(hotly)   (in the night-time)
So hote he lovede that by nightertale

He sleep namore than dooth a nightingale.

This passage is closer to Modern English in word order than most
Old English was. Only in two or three places, such as "He coude
songes make," does the order seem very strange to us. Inflectional
endings of Middle English were considerably reduced from Old
English. In a noun an -s or -es usually signified either a genitive
singular or any case of the plural. (The battle between an -s and
an -en plural was almost decided by Chaucer's time, although in
a few words such as oxen the -en plural never surrendered.)
Adjectival forms had in general been reduced to two, one for the
"strong" singular, and a second for the strong plural and the
"weak" singular and plural. Verbs were somewhat simplified also;
in the past tense no distinction was retained between singular
and plural or between first, second, and third person, and the past
tense and past participle were often identical, as they are in
most verbs today.

Of all the things that have happened to English, the reduction
of inflectional endings and the increased inflexibility of word
order have been most important in giving the language its modern
characteristics. Although these changes were not completed in
Middle English and will never be completed while the language
lives, they were far advanced by the year 1500, a date chosen
rather arbitrarily as the beginning of Modern English.

Some of the Developments in Modern English

Since 1500 English word order has become still more fixed, and living inflections have been reduced to seven: an -s or -es plural for nearly all nouns, an -s ending for most third person singular verbs in the present tense, an -ed ending for most verbs in the past tense, an -ing form for verbs, a special past participle for some verbs, an -er ending for the comparative degree of many adjectives and some adverbs, and an -est ending for the superlative degree of the same words.

In other ways grammar has changed only slightly. Representative of the many comparatively small changes are the use of *do* in questions (*Does he consent?* rather than Elizabethan *Consents he?*) and the growth in frequency of the progressive tenses (*He was speaking,* for instance, often replacing *He spoke*). Steadily increasing reliance upon prepositional phrases, greater employment of subordinate clauses, the increase in verb-adverb (or verb-preposition) combinations ("I *ran into* an old friend"), and a tendency to use almost any word as more than one part of speech—these are but a few of the Modern English developments that later will be treated in more detail.

In the eighteenth century some grammarians, failing to recognize the inevitability of linguistic change, strove to stop or at least retard it. They believed that change in a language is undesirable; since Latin was the most highly regarded language, and since Latin had not changed much in fifteen hundred years or so, change must be bad. (Those who held this theory failed to realize that Latin would probably have changed a great deal if it had not become a dead language, and that in monks' Latin it actually did change considerably.) They believed also that the loss of inflections should be stopped to prevent further "deterioration."

The results of the efforts of these few grammarians may be illustrated by referring to a couple of pronouns and a few verbs. The distinction between *who* and *whom,* which is not essential for clarity, was erratically observed during the eighteenth century. But under pressure from prescriptive grammarians, teachers and editors began to insist upon strict maintenance of *whom* as an object. Several verbs, including *blow, know,* and *throw,* were moving toward a "weak" or "regular" past tense and past participle: *blow, blowed, blowed,* and so on. They were thus following other verbs that had made the shift without hurting the language: as examples, *help* once had *healp* as one past form and *holpen* as the past participle; *climb* had *clamb* and *clumben; chew* had *ceaw* and *cowen.* Certainly *blowed* would be no worse than *climbed* or *chewed,* but the prescribers wanted no more "deterioration." As a result of their efforts and those of their intellectual descendants the use of *blowed, knowed,* and *throwed* may even today keep an able person from being employed for a white collar position.

Similarly, in the eighteenth century, a tendency toward identical forms for past tense and past participle was noticeable. The verb *sing* was tending toward *sing, sung, sung; write* toward *write, wrote, wrote.* The original title of Thomas Gray's most famous poem was "Elegy Wrote in a Country Churchyard." But once more the reactionaries went to work, and the schools ever since have insisted upon different forms for the past tense and past participle of *drink, give, ride, shrink, sing, sink, write,* and other verbs. How many million child-hours have been spent on mastering these forms is beyond calculation. Totally false conceptions of "correctness" have resulted from this wasted effort.

Perhaps the most noticeable change that has occurred since 1500 is not in grammar but in vocabulary. Through borrowings from dead Latin, dead Greek, and most of the important living languages of the world, English has multiplied its store of words manyfold. Since no one can precisely define what a word is, no one can say how many words are now in the language. One clue to the number is that unabridged dictionaries have about 600,000 entries. But since no lexicographer would claim that his dictionary lists every existing word in the language, the total may be much larger.

Why the Language Has Changed

A language changes because things happen to people. If we could imagine the impossible—a society in which nothing happened— there would be no changes in language. But except possibly in a cemetery, things are constantly happening to people: they eat, drink, sleep, talk, make love, meet strangers, struggle against natural perils, and fight against one another. They slowly adapt their language to meet the changing conditions of their lives. Although the changes made in one generation may be small, those made in a dozen generations may enormously affect the language. The big and little phases of history—fashions, fads, inventions, the influence of a leader, a war or two, an invasion or two, travel to a foreign land, the demands of business intercourse—may alter a language so much that a Rip Van Winkle who slept two or three hundred years might have trouble in making himself under- stood when he awoke. Even in a relatively quiet society, linguistic change proceeds inexorably.

Think, if you will, of the English language as a river. Its head- waters are the closely interrelated Teutonic languages of the Angles, Saxons, and Jutes, who lived mainly in the northern part of what is now Germany. They provided the basic grammatical structure of the language that we call English; they provided most of its linguistic heritage; they provided its basic words, the common everyday words that still are the most important in our simple communications. But to the basic elements brought in by these Teutonic peoples many additions have been made.

When the Teutons began invading and settling in the British Isles in 449 A.D., they found in possession the Celts, who previ- ously had been pushed about by Roman soldiers for several cen- turies. The Teutons pushed the Celts about some more, finally tending to localize them in what we now call Ireland, Wales, and parts of Scotland. But the Teutonic language was influenced somewhat by the Celtic and indirectly by the Latin which the Celts had fragmentarily learned. So in English we have words of Celtic ancestry such as *brat, cairn,* and *crag,* and the place names *Aberdeen* (*Aber =* river mouth), *Avon* (river), *Caerleon,*

Cardiff, Carlyle (*caer* or *car* = fortress), *Dundee, Dunbarton, Dunbar* (*dun* = hill), *Inchcape* (*inch* = island), *Kildare, Kilpatrick* (*kill* = church). And as a result of the early and indirect Latin tributary (which existed on the Continent even before the invasions of Britain) we have *wall* and *street* and *port*, words that give promise of enduring even longer than the Roman constructions that they name; and we have place names: Roman *Londinium* (originally Celtic) is now *London, Eboracum* (also once Celtic) has undergone considerable transformation to appear as *York*, and Latin *castra*, a military camp, appears both in England and the United States in *Lancaster, Worcester, Leicester, Gloucester, Chester, Dorchester, Rochester*. Thus Latin and Celtic are early tributaries of English.

By the end of the sixth century Latin was to renew its influence upon English. In 597 Roman missionaries began coming to the British Isles in an attempt to Christianize the inhabitants. They introduced such church words as *altar, creed, mass,* and *nun* and some homely words such as *beet, pine, cheese,* and *cup*. Some of the words that the priests brought over had been borrowed by Latin from Greek: *bishop, deacon, martyr, church, devil, priest, monk, pope, psalm, dish,* and *plum*. So once more a double tributary entered the river of the English language.

In the seventh and most of the eighth centuries the Anglo-Saxon inhabitants of the British Isles lived a relatively peaceful existence—simple by modern standards, but maybe happier than a more complex society can be. But starting in about 790, "Northmen" or Danes began to invade the islands. They were rough and vigorous; in 793, "the heathen men miserably destroyed God's church at Lindisfarne with rapine and slaughter," a contemporary account says. The forays grew into expeditions; the Danes began to colonize; Alfred the Great for a while paid them tribute but then organized military forces and compelled the invaders to sign a peace treaty. One of the terms of the treaty was that the Danes accept Christianity. Since the chief difference between the Danes and the Anglo-Saxons had been in religion, this concession meant that the two groups, already speaking kindred and often mutually intelligible languages, would merge. However, attacks by new groups of Danes, not covered by the treaty, continued, and early in the eleventh century a Danish king, Cnut, ruled in England.

It is often difficult to separate the linguistic contributions of the Danes from the closely related Anglo-Saxon, but apparently we owe to Danish such words as *fellow, husband, law, wrong,* and a number of words with an *sk* sound, as *skill, scale, scare, skirt* (*shirt,* a cognate form, is from Anglo-Saxon), *skin, sky, score,* and *bask.* Numerous English place names are Danish in origin. Danish *thwaite* (piece of ground) appears in many names such as *Stonethwaite, Hallthwaite; thorp* (village) is in names like *Lowthorpe* and *Northorpe; by* (town) is in *Derby, Kirkby, Selby, Whitby,* etc.; *toft* (a clearing) is in *Lowestoft.*

The next big tributary came from north via east. Northmen, later called Normans, had begun moving into France at about the time that the Danes invaded England. They were flexible people who adopted French as their language, changing it somewhat in the process. They made of Normandy one of the most vigorous and ambitious states of Europe. In 1066, after the death of England's Edward the Confessor, the Duke of Normandy decided that he would attempt to gain the crown of his late cousin, and at Hastings he earned the more glorious title of William the Conqueror. His people moved into the British Isles, relegated natives to the rank of second-class citizens, and eventually concentrated their grip upon England as they lost their continental footholds.

Now began the period of greatest linguistic turmoil that English has known. England was a country of two languages: the Norman French of the ruling classes and the English of the conquered. The Bishop of Worcester was deposed in 1095 because he was "an idiot who did not know French." French was used in the churches, in the courts, in important business transactions, and in the schools. But inevitably the two groups had to meet. A French landowner had to give instructions to his tenants; an English farmer or smith had to try to sell his goods or his skills; intermarriage became frequent. Each group picked up words from the other. However, just as American occupation troops learned only the rudiments of German, Italian, and Japanese after World War II, the Normans did not learn the intricacies of English nor did the English learn the intricacies of Norman French. Each group learned only the fundamentals.

Before the Norman conquest there had been signs that grammatical inflections were being reduced—the dative and accusative cases, for instance, were blending their forms. But the coming of the Normans seems to have expedited such change. At any rate, after the Normans had been in England for about three centuries, English inflections were not nearly so numerous.

The two groups gradually blended. So did their vocabularies, and to a much smaller extent their grammar, although the impact of Norman French upon English was less than one might think. But partly as a result of that impact, and more largely as a result of other, less tangible causes, grammatical gender was replaced by natural gender, word order became less free as inflections were reduced, pronunciations changed, and many words from Norman French, French, and Latin entered the language.

Chaucer's contemporary, John Gower, in the fourteenth century wrote three major works—one in English, one in French, and one in Latin. He chose three languages because he was not sure which language would become standard in England, and he wanted one of his works to be in the language that endured. Had he lived fifty years later, he would have had no difficulty in seeing that English was going to be the winner.

During the Renaissance two more large tributaries entered English. These, of course, were in the form of additional Latin and Greek contributions. Thousands of words came into the English vocabulary during this period, including huge numbers of relatively useless terms that lived briefly and were then buried in soon-to-be-forgotten graves. English spellings were also influenced by the new interest in the Classical languages. Learned men perhaps foolishly proclaimed that the orthography of English words should reveal their Latin backgrounds. They therefore recommended the spellings *debt* and *doubt*, even though the *b*'s in these words were not pronounced, and even though the

French, from whom the English had borrowed both words, had already dropped the *b*'s that existed in Latin. A number of words with *tio*, like *nation*, had also been taken from the French, which often used a phonetically accurate *c* instead of *t;* in English the sound in question was pronounced as *s* or *sh*, but Renaissance scholars insisted that the Latin *t* be retained. Many other of our present illogical spellings may be attributed to the scholars of the Renaissance.

During the Renaissance period and later, the feeling grew that English grammar should be described in the terminology of Latin grammar. Sometimes that procedure was not objectionable, for many elements of the two languages were similar. But when the grammarians insisted upon finding in English everything that existed in Latin, when they made of Latin a procrustean bed into which English must be in some way fitted, and when they ignored the fact that English was basically a Teutonic and not an Italic language, they did irreparable harm to many generations of persons who wanted to acquire a clear understanding of the structure and peculiarities of the language.

Since the Renaissance, many small tributaries have enlarged the stream of English. These cannot be listed in chronological order. Latin has kept appearing, as have French and Greek. Italian has contributed many of the technical terms of music. Dutch has given sailing terms like *ahoy, boom, deck, hoist, skipper, sloop,* and *yacht.* Spanish has given, directly or indirectly, miscellaneous words like *matador, vanilla, armada, alligator,* and *mosquito.* North American Indian has contributed such words as *hominy, Mississippi* (an Algonquin word meaning "big river," not "Father of Waters"), *moccasin, moose, opossum, papoose, pemmican, raccoon, skunk, squaw, toboggan, tomahawk, wampum,* and *wigwam.* Among other contributing languages, with one or two representative words from each, have been Bengali, (*bungalow*); Persian (*azure*); Slavic (*polka, vampire, mammoth*); Hebrew (*amen, hallelujah, behemoth*); Hungarian (*goulash*); Tartar (*khan*); Malay (*amuck, gong, cockatoo*); Indian (*rajah, nabob, khaki, yogi*); Australian (*boomerang, kangaroo*); South American Indian (*alpaca, condor, jaguar, quinine*); Polynesian (*taboo, tattoo*); African (*gumbo, mumbo jumbo, okra*). Even Chinese has given us some words (*tea, typhoon, chop suey,* and *chow mein*); Chinese Pidgin English has contributed the familiar *chopstick;* Japanese has given us *tycoon, kimono, judo,* and *ju-jitsu.*

The borrowing has of course gone the other way, also, although the details need not concern us here. English and American gastronomic and athletic terms, for instance, have been incorporated in many European languages. An American can use the terms *cocktail* and *beefsteak* with satisfactory results in almost any European restaurant.

Why did English change? Simply because many things happened to many people in many countries. Had the Angles, Saxons, and Jutes moved southeast instead of southwest, the language of the British Isles might never have been Teutonic. Had Harold defeated William the Conqueror at Hastings in 1066, the language of today might have been considerably different, perhaps more complicated in morphology, more simple in syntax. Had the English been stay-at-homes, their language might have lacked some of the versatility, the expressiveness, and the color that we believe it now has.

ALBERT H. MARCKWARDT

The Language of the Colonists

In considering the history and development of American English
we must remember that the courageous bands who ventured
westward into the unknown with Captain John Smith or on board
the *Mayflower*, as well as those who followed them later in the
seventeenth century, were speaking and writing the English language as it was currently employed in England. Consequently,
whatever linguistic processes operated to produce the differences
between American and British English which exist today must
either have taken place in American English after the colonists
settled on this continent or have occurred in British English after
the emigrants left their homeland. Or, as a third possibility, there
may have been changes in both divisions of the language after
the period of settlement. We cannot, however, escape the conclusion of original identity and subsequent change.

Our first concern, therefore, is with the kind of English spoken
by Smith's Virginians, Calvert's Marylanders, the Plymouth
Fathers, the Bostonians of the Massachusetts Bay Colony, Roger
Williams' Rhode Islanders, and Penn's Quakers. What was the
state of the language at the time they left the shores of their
native England?

The answer to this entails making a comparison between the
memorable dates of our early colonial history with those pertinent to the English literary scene throughout the seventeenth
century. It shows, for example, that Jonson was at the height of
his career and that Shakespeare was still writing when James-
. . . .

town was settled. Plymouth Colony was founded before the publication of Shakespeare's First Folio and less than a decade after the completion of the Authorized Version of the Bible.

Dryden, who is often called the father of modern prose, was not born until after the settlement of the second colony in New England. His *Essay of Dramatic Poesy* was not written until the capture of New York by the English, nor were the essays of Cowley, equally modern in style and temper. The publication date of *Paradise Lost* is somewhat later, and that of *Pilgrim's Progress* actually follows King Philip's War in point of time. I mention these in particular because we often think of these last two works as indicative of the same kind of dissent against the Anglican Church as that which is reflected in the colonial settlement, particularly in the north. Yet Massachusetts, Connecticut, and Rhode Island were all established and flourishing by the time these books appeared. Even such late prose representative of Elizabethan exuberance, complication, involution, and to some extent lack of discipline as Burton's *Anatomy of Melancholy* and Browne's *Religio Medici* postdate the establishment of the early New England settlements.

The émigrés who accompanied Smith and Bradford had learned their native language long before the years 1607 and 1620 respectively. Many of them were mature; some were old. Even a man of forty on the Jamestown expedition would presumably have learned to speak English about 1570; John Rolfe, the future husband of Pocahontas, acquired his native tongue probably in 1587. A young man of twenty-one, John Alden for example, in the Mayflower company must have learned English at the height of Shakespeare's career; Miles Standish, when Shakespeare was beginning to write. In short, the earliest English colonists in the New World were speaking Elizabethan English, the language of Shakespeare, Lyly, Marlowe, Lodge, and Green, when they came to America—not the measurably different English of Dryden, Defoe, and Bunyan. This is important and necessary for our understanding of some of the distinctive features which American English was to develop later on.

Next, what was the general state of Elizabethan English? How many people spoke it? The population of England, excluding Ireland and Scotland, in Shakespeare's time has been estimated at 4,460,000. This is a little more than the present population of Massachusetts, somewhat less than that of Michigan. Of these, probably 200,000 lived in London in 1600; the population in 1605 is given as 224,275. This is approximately the population of Syracuse, New York, or of Oklahoma City. These people and possibly 25,000 more in the immediate vicinity spoke London English, the regional variety which was in the process of becoming a standard for the English-speaking world as a whole.

Naturally the language sounded somewhat different from its twentieth-century counterpart. Certain though not all of these differences provide us with a partial explanation of the current variations in pronunciation between British and American English. For one thing, many words which are now pronounced with the vowel of *meat* had, at the time of the earliest settlements in America, the quality of present-day English *mate*. In fact, Londoners were accustomed to hear both the *ee* and the *ay* sounds in such words as *meat, teach, sea, tea, lean,* and *beard.* The conservative *ay* pronunciation continued in the language as late as the time of Pope. On occasion Shakespeare was capable of rhyming *please* with *knees* and at other times with *grace.* Without this double pronunciation a speech such as that by Dromio, "Marry sir, she's the Kitchin wench, & al *grease (grace)*" would have lost its punning effect.

It is quite possible that words which today have the vowel of *mate* were also pronounced at times with the vowel of *sand.* In addition to the play on the words *grease* and *grace* cited in the foregoing paragraph, there is in *All's Well* another punning passage involving a common or highly similar pronunciation of *grace* and *grass:*

> CLOWN.   Indeed sir she was the sweete margerom of the sallet or rather the hearbe of grace.
> LAFEW.   They are not hearbes you knave, they are nose-hearbes.
> CLOWN.   I am no great Nevuchadnezar sir, I have not much skill in grace.

A rhyme such as the following from *Venus and Adonis* suggests the same conclusion:

> Even so poor birds, deceived with painted grapes . . .
> Even so she languisheth in her mishaps.

There was undoubtedly quite as much fluctuation in words which are generally spelled with *oo;* those of the *food, good,* and *flood* classes respectively. It is only recently that the pronunciation of many of these words has become standardized. All three of these words constitute one of Shakespeare's rhymes, and a half-century later Dryden rhymed *flood* with *mood* and *good.* Even today certain words of this class (*roof, room, root, hoof, coop, soot,* etc.) are pronounced variously in different parts of the United States.

At the time of which we are writing, the vowel of *cut* had but recently developed in London speech and was not yet a feature of all the English dialects. Combinations of *ir, er,* and *ur* in words like *bird, learn,* and *turn* had not long before coalesced into a vowel which was more like the sound to be heard over most of the United States today than that which is characteristic of southern British English. Contemporary pronunciation was far from settled in words like *clerk,* which seemed to be classed part of the time with the sound of *dark* and at other times with the vowel of *jerk.* Moreover, this variation affected many more words than it does now. Shakespeare rhymed *convert* with *art, serve* with *carve, heard* with *regard.*

In addition, the language at that time had no sound like the stressed vowel of present-day *father* or *calm.* The diphthongs characteristic of such words as *house* and *loud* had, instead of the *ah* first element commonly employed today, a sound something like the final vowel of *Cuba.* The whole diphthong was pronounced in a manner quite similar to that which may be heard at the present time in tidewater Virginia or in the Toronto area. The diphthong in words like *bite* and *bide* began with this same neutral element. The so-called short *o* sound of *cot* and *fog* was always pronounced with the lips somewhat rounded, as in Modern English *fall.*

Nor were the stress patterns of Shakespeare's English absolutely identical with those of the modern period. A line such as "The light will show, character'd in my brow," indicates clearly that in such a trisyllabic word as *character'd,* the stress had not yet shifted to the first syllable. A good many two-syllable words which now stress the first, at that time had the accent on the second. Note, "And there I'll rest, as after much *turmoil.*" Many derivatives in *-able* had a distinct stress, at least secondary in value, on the suffix. A line such as "What *acceptable* audit canst thou leave?" can scarcely be read in any other fashion.

Many words show a double stress pattern: *sincere* with stress at times on the first and at times on the second syllable; *confiscate* on occasion has initial stress, and elsewhere on the second syllable. It is probably fair to say that just as with vowel quality, the language during the Elizabethan period permitted somewhat more latitude than it does today.

It must be kept in mind, moreover, that the pronunciations which have just been discussed reflect only the language practices of the inhabitants of London and its environs, constituting approximately 5 per cent of the five million who spoke English at that time. The remaining 95 per cent spoke the regional or provincial dialects. Those who live in the United States find it hard to conceive of the extent to which regional dialects may differ even today within an area no larger than one of our moderate-size states.

At the present time, to select just a single instance, a word such as *about* will be pronounced with the stressed vowel of *bite* in Devon, with the vowel of *boot* along the Scottish border, with the vowel of *father* and a final consonant more like *d* than *t* in London Cockney, and with a pronunciation something like *abaeut* in Norfolk.

To anyone who has grown up in a tradition of relative linguistic uniformity over a territory virtually three million square miles in area, such differences in speech present in a country only one-sixtieth as large are startling, to say the least. But in the England of today, regional dialects are confined to a relatively small portion of the population as compared with three centuries ago. There can be little question about the wide prevalence of dialect and the general lack of uniformity of speech among the vast majority of the settlers of the seventeenth century.

Seventeenth-century English differed from its modern counterpart in other aspects of speech as well. Although the language had in general developed most of the inflections which are used in present-day English—the noun plurals, the object form *them* in the plural pronoun, the past tense and past participle forms of the weak verb—a few interesting earlier features still remained. Among these were the double forms of the pronoun of address: *thou* and *ye* or *you*. Because the distribution of these was governed partly by considerations of social rank and in part on the basis of emotional overtones, their very presence in the language made for a subtlety which today must be achieved through quite different means. Note, for example, in the following well-known passage from the first part of *Henry IV*, how the choice of pronouns reflects Hotspur's shift of mood from jesting concealment to stern warning, concluding with a gentler and more intimate tone:

> Come, wilt *thou* see me ride?
> And when I am o'horseback, I will swear
> I love *thee* infinitely. But hark *you*, Kate;
> I must not have *you* henceforth question me
> Whither I go, nor reason whereabout.
> Whither I must, I must; and, to conclude,
> This evening must I leave *you*, gentle Kate.
> I know *you* wise; but yet no farther wise
> Than Harry Percy's wife. Constant *you* are,
> But yet a woman; and for secrecy,
> No lady closer; for I well believe
> *Thou* wilt not utter what *thou* dost not know;
> And so far will I trust *thee*, gentle Kate.

And again in Kate's preceding speech but one, her change from exaggeration to gentle entreaty is indicated in precisely the same manner.

> Come, come, *you* paraquito, answer me
> Directly unto this question that I ask.
> In faith, I'll break *thy* little finger, Harry,
> An if *thou* wilt not tell me all things true.

Actually, at one point slightly later than Shakespeare's time, this matter of the second personal pronoun became a politico-religious issue. The Quakers, committed to a belief in the innate equality of all men, interpreted the duality of the pronoun of address as a negation of that equality and argued, quite intemperately at times, for a return to an older state of the language where the two forms were differentiated solely on the basis of number. In the following passage, George Fox, the founder and leader of the sect, set forth his views in no uncertain terms.

> Do not they speak false English, false Latine, false Greek . . . and false to the other Tongues, . . . that doth not speak *thou* to *one*, what ever he be, Father, Mother, King, or Judge; is he not a Novice and Unmannerly, and an Ideot and a Fool, that speaks *You* to *one*, which is not to be spoken to a *singular*, but to many? O Vulgar Professors and Teachers, that speaks Plural when they should Singular . . . Come you Priests and Professors, have you not learnt your Accidence?

It is worth noting that the English language did eventually go along with Fox's democratic notions by giving up the pronoun differentiation based upon social status, but in so doing, ironically selected the form which he considered inappropriate for the task.

This double supply of pronouns also carried with it an accompanying difference in verb structure, for *thou* as subject regularly demanded a verb ending in *-est*. *Ye* or *you* as subjects were accompanied merely by the simple or root form of the verb. Thus we would have had at this time *thou teachest* but *ye* or *you teach*, *thou knowest* but *you know*. After the *thou* forms fell into disfavor, so too did the verb inflections in *-est*, leaving the second person singular of the verb identical with the first person and with all forms of the plural.

In addition Elizabethan English represents a period of change from an earlier *-eth* inflection for the third person singular of the verb to the *-s* forms characteristic of the language today. There is an interesting difference here between the practice of Shakespeare and that of the contemporary King James Version of the Bible. The latter regularly uses *-eth*: "He maketh me to lie down in green pastures." In his ordinary dramatic prose, Shakespeare employs *-s* regularly for all verbs except *have* and *do,* which retain the archaic *hath* and *doth* (the latter only occasionally) presumably because these were learned as individual forms early in life by the average speaker instead of as part of an over-all pattern.

Even here, however, one must exercise due caution in interpreting the *-eth* spellings. In the middle of the seventeenth century one Richard Hodges wrote *A Special Help to Orthographie,* which consisted chiefly in listing words "alike in sound but unlike both in their signification and writing." Among the homophonic pairs which appear in this treatise are *roweth* and *rose, wrights,* and *righteth, Mr. Knox* and *knocketh.* He goes on to say in explanation:

> Therefore, whensoever *eth* cometh in the end of any word, wee may pronounce it sometimes as *s,* and sometimes like *z,* as in these words, namely, in *bolteth it,* and *boldeth it,* which are commonly pronounc't, as if they were writen thus, *bolts* it, and *bolds* it: save onely in such words, where either *c, s, sh, ch, g,* or *x* went before it: as in *graceth, pleaseth, washeth, matcheth, rageth, taxeth:* for these must still remaine as two syllables. Howbeit, if men did take notice, how they use to speak, in their ordinary speech to one another, they might plainly perceive, that in stead of *graceth,* they say *graces,* and so they pronounce al other words of this kinde, accordingly.

Unquestionably the best way to acquire a feeling for many of the differences between the language of today and that of the age of Elizabeth is to observe with some care a selection of one of the earliest examples of what might be called American English. The following selection from William Bradford's *History of Plimmoth Plantation* will serve the purpose:

> In these hard and difficulte beginnings they found some discontents and murmurings arise amongst some, and mutinous speeches and carriages in other; but they were soone quelled and overcome by the wisdome, patience, and just and equall carrage of things by the Gov[erno]r and better part, which clave faithfully togeather in the maine. But that which was most sadd and lamentable was, that in 2 or 3 moneths time halfe of their company dyed, espetialy in Jan: and February,

being the depth of winter, and wanting houses and other comforts; being infected with the scurvie and other diseases, which this long voiage and their inacomodate condition had brought upon them; so as ther dyed some times 2 or 3 of a day, in the aforesaid time; that of 100 and odd persons, scarce 50 remained. And of these in the time of most distres, ther was but 6 or 7 sound persons, who, to their great comendations be it spoken, spared no pains, night nor day, but with abundance of toil and hazard of their owne health, fetched them woode, made them fires, drest them meat, made their beads, washed their lothsome cloaths, cloathed and uncloathed them; in a word, did all the homly and necessarye offices for them which dainty and quesie stomacks cannot endure to hear named; and all this willingly and cherfully, without any grudging in the least, shewing herin their true love unto their freinds and bretheren. A rare example and worthy to be remembered. Tow of these 7 were Mr. William Brewster, ther reverend Elder, and Myles Standish, ther Captein and Military comander, unto whom my selfe, and many others, were much beholden in our low and sicke condition. And yet the Lord so upheld these persons, as in this generall calamity they were not at all infected either with sickness, or lamnes. And what I have said of these, I may say of many others who dyed in this generall visitation, and others yet living, that whilst they had health, yea, or any strength continuing, they were not wanting to any that had need of them. And I doute not but their recompence is with the Lord.

But I may not hear pass by an other remarkable passage not to be forgotten. As this calamitie fell among the passengers that were to be left here to plant, and were hasted a shore and made to drinke water, that the sea-men might have the more bear, and one in his sickness desiring but a small can of beere, it was answered, that if he were their owne father he should have none; the disease begane to fall amongst them also, so as allmost halfe of their company dyed before they went away, and many of their officers and lustyest men, as the boatson, gunner, 3 quarter-maisters, the cooke, and others. At which the m[aste]r was something strucken and sent to the sick a shore and tould the Gov[erno]r he should send for beer for them that had need of it, though he drunke water homward bound.

Most noticeable, perhaps, in the passage just quoted are a number of words no longer current in the language. Among them are *inacomodate* and *hasted. Yea, unto,* and *beholden* are rarely employed except in certain set phrases and at times in religious connections. Other words have come to be used in contexts quite unlike those in which they appear in this passage. For instance, *carriages* no longer signifies behavior in the abstract sense; *clothed,* here meaning the specific act of dressing, has become more general in its use. *Offices* is used here in the sense of services; *lustiest* to mean healthiest. Though by no means inclusive, these examples suggest the changes which have taken place in the English vocabulary during the last three centuries, both with respect to the words it comprises and the meanings of these words.

Likewise, certain changes in the forms of words have taken place. Almost at the beginning of the passage, *other* was used as a plural pronoun, although the modern form *others* appears later on. *Scarce,* in an adverbial use, indicates that the fetish of the *-ly* ending was somewhat less strong at that time than it is at present. As might be expected, the most pronounced differences are in the verb forms, where *clave* and *drunke* appear as past tenses and *strucken* as a past participle.

Differences in syntax are even more numerous. The plural form of the abstractions *discontents* and *murmurings* would be unlikely to appear in present-day usage, as would *commendations.* Closely connected with this same problem of number is the lack of agreement between subject and verb in, "There was but 6 or 7 sound persons." The word *as* in constructions like, "so as ther dyed," and "as in this generall calamity," would today be replaced by *that.* At the same time, certain pronominal uses of *that* in this selection would unquestionably call for *who* in the language of today.

Even more striking than any of these features is the sentence structure. In general the sentences lack unity and are replete with dangling phrases and clauses. The first sentence in the selection contains fifty-three words, the second eighty-three, and the third attains a total of one hundred and six. These are all long according to modern standards. Ironically enough, the third sentence is followed by an eight word fragment that does not fit the modern pattern of the conventional sentence at all. In the second sentence the parallelism of the phrases introduced by *being* and *wanting* is faulty. The majority of the sentences are without coherence and direction in the present sense of these terms.

The proper conclusion, however, is not that Bradford was a bad writer—in fact he was not—but that there were differences between seventeenth-century prose and our own. Some of these differences are purely a matter of historical development. The roots of our modern forms and practices were already in the language. It is even more important to recognize this as a period prior to a certain codification, settlement, one might almost say a jelling, of English written prose. A man's spelling was still his own concern, as is clearly evident, and so too, to some extent, were his sentences. If this codification or jelling took place after the two speech areas, England and America, were already separated, it is more than possible that the settling processes might not work out in the same way in both places.

Consequently, since the earliest American settlers employed Elizabethan English, it is the highly variable and complex character of that medium that provides us with an explanation of the beginning of the divergence in the two great streams of our language. It remains to be seen how, and through what means, this divergence developed throughout the course of the intervening centuries.

CHARLES C. FRIES

What Language Matters To Teach

Anxiety concerning the kind of English spoken and written by
English people seems to have had its most vigorous early expressions in the eighteenth century as an outgrowth of the striving
for "elegance," and especially attending the rise of the commercial middle classes into more prominence socially.[1] Several quotations from eighteenth century publications will reveal clearly
enough the important aspects of the attitude of this time.

a. From Swift's letter to the Lord Treasurer in 1712.

"My lord, I do here, in the name of all the learned and polite
persons of the nation complain to your lordship, as first minister,
that our language is extremely imperfect; that its daily improvements are by no means in proportion to its daily corruptions;
that the pretenders to polish and refine it, have chiefly multiplied
abuses and absurdities: and that in many instances it offends
against every part of grammar . . . and these corruptions very
few of the best authors in our age have wholly escaped. . . .
Besides the grammar part, wherein we are allowed to be very
defective, they will observe many gross improprieties, which,
however authorized by practice, and grown familiar, ought to be
discarded."

b. From the preface of Robert Lowth's *Grammar* in 1762, referring to Swift's letter.

"But let us consider how, and in what extent, we are to under-

. . . .

stand this charge brought against the English Language. . . . Does it mean that the English Language, as it is spoken by the politest part of the nation, and as it stands in the writing of our most approved authors, often offends against every part of grammar? Thus far, I am afraid, the charge is true. Or does it further imply, that our Language is in its nature irregular and capricious; not hitherto subject, nor easily reducible to a System of rules? In this respect, I am persuaded, the charge is wholly without foundation."

c. From the preface of Thomas Sheridan's *Dictionary* in 1780.

". . . Yet so little regard has been paid to it [the English language] . . . that out of our most numerous array of authors, very few can be selected who write with accuracy; . . . nay it has lately been proved by a learned prelate in an essay upon our grammar, that some of our most celebrated writers, and such as have hitherto passed for our English classics, have been guilty of great solecisms, inaccuracies, and even grammatical improprieties, in many places of their most finished works."

d. From William Ward's *Grammar* in 1765.

"This piece is excellent [referring to the work of Lowth] on account of the notes, in which are shown the grammatic Inaccuracies that have escaped the Pens of our most distinguised Writers . . . If your Scholars are Natives of England, . . . false English pointed out to them may be of the greatest use. For they are apt to follow Custom and example, even when it is faulty, till they are apprized of their Mistake. And therefore by shewing where Custom is erroneous, his Lordship has well deserved the Thanks of everyone who values the English Language and Literature . . . In short a very blameable Neglect of grammatic Propriety has prevailed amongst the English Writers, and at length we seem to be growing generally sensible of it; as likewise of the Use which may be made of a Knowledge of the English Grammar, towards assisting children to comprehend the general Import and Advantage of Rules concerning Language."

e. From Richard Johnson's *Grammatical Commentaries*, 1706.

"I cannot but think it would be of great Advantage, both for the Improvement of Reason in general . . . and also for the exact use of our own Language; which for want of Rule is subject to Uncertainty and the Occasion of frequent Contentions. And upon this account, it has been the Practice of several wise Nations, such of them, I mean, as have a thorough Education, to avoid that Confusion, that must needs follow from leaving it wholly to vulgar Use."

f. From James Buchanan's *Syntax* of 1767.

"Considering the many grammatical Improprieties to be found in our best Writers, such as Swift, Addison, Pope, etc., a Systematical English syntax is not beneath the Notice of the Learned themselves. Should it be urged, that in the Time of these Writers, English was but a very little subjected to Grammar, that they had scarcely a single Rule to direct them, a question readily occurs. Had they not the Rules of Latin Syntax to direct them?"

g. From J. Newberry's *Grammar Made Easy*, 1745.

"This [English Grammar] ought to be taught children as soon as they have a Capacity for it, which is generally very early: for 'tis a Shame we should be ignorant of our own Tongue: . . . For want of an early Acquaintance with *English* Grammar, there are many grown Persons, and those of good natural Abilities, who not only express themselves very improperly in common Discourse, but who cannot so much as write a Letter of a moderate Length to a Friend or Correspondent, without trespassing a hundred times either against the Rules of Orthography or Syntax."

The point of view revealed in these quotations from the eighteenth century may be briefly described in the two statements following:

a. The *English* used by most English people, even by the learned and the best authors, is deplorable because of its grammatical incorrectness and inaccuracy.

b. The only remedy for this deplorable use of English will be for English people, young and old, to set out to learn *correct* English by means of a study of grammar rules.

The first attempts, therefore, to determine what English language matters to teach in the schools grew out of this eighteenth century point of view and naturally resulted in the great stress that was laid upon the study of systematic or formal grammar.

This emphasis upon formal grammar as the necessary material in an effective program of teaching good English lasted well through the nineteenth century.[2] Even today many schools continue the former practice and its advocates are by no means few.

Throughout more than half of the nineteenth century, however, the opponents of formal grammar insisted that there was no necessary connection between a knowledge of systematic grammar and a practical control of good English; but the study of grammar was not only deeply intrenched in the traditional prejudices of the public, it was also supported by the "mental discipline" theory of psychology as well as by the teachers of Latin and of the modern foreign languages.

Formal or systematic grammar continued to provide most important material of the English language program until the coming of the measurement movement in education brought the first really effective challenge of the asserted connection between grammar and good English. The results of the tests administered seemed to demonstrate "the absence of any relation between knowledge of English grammar and the ability either to write or to interpret language." [3] Then too, repudiation of the older "faculty" psychology with its grosser conception of the "transfer of training" and the acceptance of a psychology of learning which emphasized the need of specific training for each specific ability in every activity helped to make necessary a new approach to the problem of teaching good English. The second attempts, therefore, to determine what English language matters to teach in the schools grew out of this emphasis put upon specific training and showed itself in the many efforts to discover the particular items of English forms and structure which should furnish the materials of drill in the various school grades. These attempts led to the demand for "functional" grammar as distinct from "formal" grammar. The following quotation provides a statement of this particular point of view:

"The reaction against English grammar arose from the knowledge that the formal work in the subject that was being done was of small practical value. A further influence resulted from investigations tending to show that grammar provides little mental discipline of a general character. The movement in favor of simplifying the school course and concentrating on essentials did the rest. . . . A sane attitude toward the teaching of grammar would seem to be to find out what parts and aspects of the subject have actual value to children in enabling them to improve their speaking, writing, and reading, to teach these parts according to modern scientific methods, and to ignore any and all portions of the conventional school grammar that fall outside these categories." [4]

Many methods were employed in the effort to determine just what aspects of the material taught as English language would adequately serve the needs of both children and adults. Language error counts became popular under the assumption that the details of a grammar curriculum should be selected "upon the basis of the errors of school children" and therefore, "that the first step is to ascertain the rules which are broken." [5] In most of these studies the investigation took for granted that frequency of occurrence meant importance for teaching. In a few there was some attempt to evaluate the items selected in relation to the frequency of their use in contemporary writing. [6] Others have depended on the opinions of teachers, or on opinions of the general public, or on opinions of the members of the various professions; all gathered by questionnaire and statistically summarized. [7] All these efforts, however, assumed as the infallible measure of good English the conventional rules of the common school grammars. They have been concerned solely with *selecting* the particular items out of the mass of traditional material which has all along constituted the English language program, but they have emphasized mastery by drill upon these items rather than knowledge of rules as the end of teaching. In the higher grades they have been responsible for the appearance and wide-spread use of "handbooks" of usage. Most of the programs in English language in the more progressive schools of today are in accord with the point of view just outlined.

The attempts to challenge the traditional material and the conventional rules as valid measures of correctness, can be set off as the third group of efforts to determine what English language matters to teach. These attempts start from the knowledge that many of the rules inherited in our grammars are either the result of striving to apply to the English language formulas of Latin or those which were products of eighteenth century reasoning concerning what English people ought to say,[8] and they assume that usage is the sole criterion of correctness. They have grown out of the attempt to interpret, for practical teaching, the more scientific approach to language. On the whole, however, most of the stress here has been directed toward eliminating from the teaching program those matters which have not a validity based upon usage,[9] but very little attention has been given to the problem of a constructive program of English language teaching. Two important examples of this particular kind of effort are J. Leslie Hall's *English Usage* and S. A. Leonard's *Current English Usage*.[10] The former bases its challenge of the handbooks upon the actual usage of eminent and reputable authors in literary works that are above question.[11] The latter depends primarily upon a summary of the opinions expressed by some thirty of the recognized scholars in English language. These opinions were also compared with the opinions expressed by six other groups of judges.[12] The opinions asked for in S. A. Leonard's study were not the opinions of "what usage *should* be," but the judgments arising from an "observation of what *is* actual usage." Both studies should be helpful in eliminating from the teaching program the drill upon many language practices that have no validity outside the classroom. Unfortunately, however, the items that make up the traditional material of the drills and the formal tests most frequently given are so firmly supported by the textbooks and practice pads, to say nothing of the inertia of much teaching routine, that these efforts to challenge the handbooks, rhetorics, and grammars have thus far had but little effect.

The various attempts to determine the material of an effective English language program for the schools can thus be roughly arranged in three groups. The first used the study of systematic or formal grammar, aimed at a knowledge of rules, and demanded much practice in classification, analysis, and parsing. The second used the rules of the conventional grammars as the criteria of good or correct English and set out to determine the common errors of language used by school children and adults. Adopting the psychology of specific training for each specific ability and assuming that frequency of error argued importance for teaching, they built up an English language program of teaching and tests made up of a large number of items for drill. The third group has tried to sift the items for drill and center attention in teaching upon driving out of the language of pupils, practices which are not *used* by "educated" people. They refuse to adopt the rules of the conventional grammars as the necessary standard of good English, and assume that only usage by the writers of literature or usage in the speech of those whose education is above question guarantees the satisfactory correctness of any item. They also assume the psychology of specific training, and their program consists therefore of a large number of items for drill and mastery.

The study here presented in this report, in its attempt to arrive at the details of a sound program for the teaching of the English language, differs fundamentally from any of those described above, in three respects.

a. It assumes that the only method to attain really good English-effective language nicely adapted in both denotation and connotation to the circumstances of the occasion and the needs of both the speaker and the hearer—demands constant observation of the actual practice of the users of the language together with *a sensitiveness to the suggestions inevitably attached to words and constructions.* Any procedure, therefore, which makes one conscious of the "rules of grammar" or which centers attention solely on particular facts to be learned as such, rather than on actual observation of usage, serves to deaden this sensitiveness to one's speech environment and to turn the student away from the only path to real knowledge.

b. This study, therefore, does not attempt to set forth a closed handbook or authority of usage. It does not aim at a series of details judged to be "established" or "disputed" or "illiterate" which can be mastered by drill. It strives to present the material so organized as to provide the tools for further observation, classification, and interpretation; to show certain tendencies and patterns with the details that deviate from them; to provide a method and outline for *continual* filling in on the part of the reader and the student.

c. It assumes that the most important facts concerning any words, forms, or constructions of language are the circumstances in which they are usually used, because these words, forms, or constructions will inevitably suggest these circumstances.[13] As indicated in the preceding chapter, there are language forms and constructions that are somewhat limited in their constant use to particular social groups. To use any such forms seriously, whether they be those customary to the "vulgar" or those customary only to precise "school mistresses," helps to give the impression that the common social contacts of the user are with that particular group. This study, therefore, has attempted to find the important matters of American English that thus have distinct social class connotations. Unlike any of the former studies it has not been limited to an examination of the so-called "disputed" constructions and phrases; it has been concerned with a first-hand examination of the grammatical matters that appeared in a large number of carefully selected specimens of the language of several social groups.

NOTES

1. See H. C. Wyld, *History of Modern Colloquial English* (New York, E. P. Dutton and Co., 1920), p. 18.
   C. C. Fries, "Rules of the Common School Grammars," *Publications of the Modern Language Association*, Vol. 42, March, 1927, pp. 232–236.
   S. A. Leonard, *The Doctrine of Correctness in English Usage, 1700–1800*, University of Wisconsin Studies in Language and Literature, Vol. 25, 1929.
2. In the United States especially, with its great middle class gaining control of affairs and striving for social acceptability, the speller and the school grammar became the most important instruments of the accepted marks of culture, so that in this country the study of systematic grammar received an additional emphasis. This fact probably accounts for the present attitude toward grammar in our schools, an attitude phrased by Professor J. H. Grattan, of the University of London, as follows:
   "Now the attitude of the American schools is, so far as the English

language is concerned, ultra-conservative. Eighteenth-century ideals of 'correctness' are not yet dead in the United States.

"Indeed, by American standards, many idiomatic usages long sanctioned in Great Britain are still 'bad grammar.' Such are the construction of the collective noun with plural verb, the use of *their* referring back to *every one*, the compound pronoun *these kind of*, the employment of *who* as object and of *me* as predicative. Without attempting to justify this rigid formalism, we can recognize in it a sign of the strength of tradition in the United States."—"On Anglo-American Cultivation of Standard English," *Review of English Studies*, October, 1927, p. 437.

3. See especially the study by Franklin S. Hoyt in *Teachers College Record*, Vol. 7, November, 1906, pp. 467–500. Other such studies are indicated in R. L. Lyman's *Summary of Investigations Relating to Grammar, Language, and Composition*, Chicago, 1929.

4. *Reorganization of English in the Secondary Schools*, Department of Interior, Bureau of Education, Bulletin, Vol. 2, p. 37.

5. Summaries of the studies of language errors appear in the *Sixteenth Yearbook* of the National Society for the Study of Education, Part I, pp. 85–110; R. L. Lyman, *Summary of Investigations Relating to Grammar, Language, and Composition*, pp. 71–133; Henry Harap, "The Most Common Grammatical Errors," *English Journal*, Vol. 19, June, 1930, pp. 440–446.

6. See Stormzand and O'Shea, *How Much English Grammar?* Baltimore, 1924.

E. L. Thorndike and others, "An Inventory of English Constructions with Measures of Their Importance," *Teachers College Record*, Vol. 17, February, 1927, pp. 580–610.

7. See Bibliography in Lyman, *op. cit.*, pp. 256–292.

8. C. C. Fries, "Rules of the Common School Grammars," *Publications of the Modern Language Association*, Vol. 42, March, 1927.

S. A. Leonard, *Doctrine of Correctness in English Usage, 1700–1800*, University of Wisconsin Studies in Language and Literature, Vol. 25, 1929.

9. "It should hardly need to be said that if we really intend getting down to fundamentals it is necessary first to stop teaching a great mass of valueless distinctions and untrue dicta about usage: the usual distinctions between *shall* and *will;* the arbitrary condemnation of *was* in all *if* and *as if* clauses, or *have got*, and of *get* for *receive, have, become, grow;* . . ."—"Report of the Committee on Economy of Time," *English Journal*, Vol. 8, March, 1919, p. 185.

10. *Current English Usage*, a monograph published by the National Council of Teachers of English in 1932, is a development of an earlier study by Leonard and Moffett reported in the *English Journal*, Vol. 16, May, 1927, pp. 345–359, under the title "Current Definition of Levels in English Usage."

Another presentation of similar material from these sources and from the *Oxford Dictionary* which has much the same purpose is R. C. Pooley's "Handbook of Current English Usage," *Colorado State Teachers College Bulletin*, Series 30, June, 1930, No. 3.

11. "In the ensuing sections, the author will take up a number of locutions at issue in our language, most of them burning questions in the best grammars and rhetorics. Evidence *pro* and *con* will be given, the opinions of the best grammars, rhetorics, and dictionaries cited, and the reader left to

draw his own conclusions. In many cases the word or phrase will be traced through the literature for centuries. . . . About two hundred authors, either 'reputable' or eminent, will be cited or quoted. Those who believe in the authority of a few supreme writers will find that these have been emphasized. Those who prefer to find their authority in a majority or a large number of reputable authors will no doubt be satisfied. . . . One prime object of this volume is to show the continuous use of certain words and phrases in the literature. If a locution can be so traced from early periods down to recent or present days, there is every reason to regard it as good English. On the other hand, a new word, or phrase, if found in enough standard writers, ought to be given a fair chance to spread through the language. . . . The tables, or lists, in the ensuing pages are, of course, not exhaustive: they simply show how often the various locutions have been found in over 75,000 pages of English and American literature. If a statement such as 'Found in 65 reputable authors 453 times' does not carry conviction to the reader, it might at least entitle the word to a fair chance and help to mitigate any attacks made upon it by purists and pedants. . . . The author of this volume relies mainly upon usage to establish a locution. . . . 'Custom is the most certain mistress of language.' "–J. Leslie Hall, *English Usage* (Chicago, Scott, Foresman and Co., 1917), pp. 23, 25, 26.

12. "The conclusions arrived at in the following pages were derived from a study of the results of two ballots. The first contained 102 expressions . . . of whose standing there might be some question. This ballot was submitted to a number of groups of judges whose standing qualified them to indicate what seemed to them to be the norm of usage among educated people generally. . . . The first group of judges comprised a number of the foremost linguistic experts in the world-lexicographers, philologists, and grammarians. As trained observers of language ways, they were naturally qualified above all others to estimate the standing in actual cultivated use of the various items on the ballot. Therefore, in the following discussion of the separate items, their comments are given special prominence. . . . Where the other groups show any significant divergence from the judgment of the linguists, the fact is noted. The second group consisted of active members of the National Council of Teachers of English. A third group was composed of well-known authors; a fourth, of the editors of influential publications; a fifth, of leading business men; a sixth, of members of the Modern Language Association; and a seventh, of teachers of speech. Returns were received from 229 judges altogether. They should constitute a significant sampling of cultivated usage. . . . Ballot II consisted of 130 additional expressions of the same nature as those in Ballot I."–S. A. Leonard, *Current English Usage* (Chicago, National Council of Teachers of English, 1932), pp. 95, 96, 97.

13. "A part of a complex stimulus, recurring by itself or in some foreign context provokes a complete reaction previously made to the total situation of which this detail was a part. . . . The fundamental fact underlying all these associative processes is perhaps a tendency for brain patterns to be reinstated more or less completely when any of their parts are excited."–H. L. Hollingworth, *The Psychology of Thought* (New York, D. Appleton-Century Co., 1926), pp. 92, 94.

ALBERT H. MARCKWARDT

The Future of English

It is neither exaggeration nor idle chauvinism to say that the English language, with an exceptional past behind it, appears to be on the threshold of a still greater future. Moreover, this future is to a considerable extent in the hands of those who regularly speak and write the language. What can they do to insure and even to further the development which lies ahead?

This basic question may best be answered by considering the dangers which may conceivably beset a language in the particular situation in which English finds itself today. There would seem to be two such perils, diametrically opposed to each other. On the one hand there are some who have seen, even in certain of the developments which have been mentioned earlier in this chapter —for example, the disappearance of the inflected subjunctive, the establishment of *who* in pre-verbal position, the use of *have got* to indicate possession—indications of a too great liberty, if not license. The unchecked development of tendencies such as these, it is argued, could lead to developments so divergent that the English language would lose its unity, and consequently its utility as a medium of communication. Opposed to this is the view that highly restrictive rules and conservative attitudes springing from a fear of solecism and leading to a denial of what is actual usage will exert such a confining influence upon the language that its flexibility will be lost and its ultimate potentialities remain unrealized.

. . . .

Although there may be some danger from the first of these, the present social and cultural situation, in the United States especially, would seem to indicate that the greater of the two perils is the second. A number of factors enter into this situation. We have seen that from the beginning until late in the nineteenth century there was always a frontier, an area where unlettered pioneers toiled to secure cultural advantages for their children—including the mastery of Standard English. Moreover, the children of foreign-speaking immigrants felt the sting of social disapproval if their language betrayed their origin. The spread of higher education to social groups who in Europe would have remained comfortably within the confines of a regional or class dialect, also brought with it an emphasis upon correctness of speech and writing.

In learning a language, whether it be a different form of our native tongue or a totally foreign idiom, we operate inductively. We learn specific facts and usages first. When we have absorbed enough of these, we begin to synthesize—we form patterns, general behavior traits, upon which we then rely when a new situation faces us. The more uncertain we are of ourselves, culturally or in any other way, the more insistent we are upon guidance in specific facts and instances, and the more reluctant we are to rely upon an instinctive grasp of these general patterns. As far as raising the level of English is concerned, American textbooks and teaching practices have too seldom taken the students beyond the level of instruction in specific matters. As a consequence, most people in the United States carry about with them a strange assortment of linguistic taboos. The feeling against *ain't*, even as a first person interrogative, is very widespread. Some react against *like* for *as*. For many the pronunciation *ice cream* with primary stress on the first syllable is taboo; for others the taboo against *John and me* is so powerful that it prompts them to use *John and I* even when it is structurally objective and *me* would normally be demanded.

It may be reasonably argued that these taboos, which are after all the results of a primarily negative approach to language, or to expression, have performed their function and outlived their usefulness. They should be replaced with something positive. We are at a point where the doctrine of original sin, linguistically speaking, must be replaced by a faith in intuition, by dependence upon the established, unconsciously known patterns of the language. Such an instinct can be developed only by giving attention to the broader aspects of structure and the evolving tendencies of the language.

The history of English during the last two centuries demonstrates that highly restrictive and unrealistic rules of grammar do not have a lasting effect upon the language as a whole. The more incredible portions of the body of rules developed by Nathaniel Ward, Dr. Johnson, Lindley Murray, and their followers have generally disappeared. In the present situation, however, the attitude behind the creation of a mass of non-pertinent and unscientific linguistic legislation can still do positive harm. It can create and preserve taboos, which ought never to have been created, against certain expressions and constructions. It can develop anxiety neuroses in many of the people who employ the language. Both of these are undesirable conditions for the future development of the English language. We cannot expect a medium of communication to develop in advance of the courage and resourcefulness of the people who employ it.

It is our responsibility to realize whither the language is tending, and the duty of our schools and teachers to promulgate healthy linguistic attitudes. If this is done, we may be certain that some individuals can and will attain greatness in the use of the language, which in turn will make of it a more flexible and sensitive medium for the rest of us. In this sense, a new era lies before all the English-speaking peoples.

III.

THE STRUCTURE OF ENGLISH

To acquire confidence and judgment in the use of our language, we need to know not only how English developed but also what it actually looks like today. The description of a spoken language is the linguist's first step toward objective mastery of its structure. It is hard to look accurately and dispassionately at anything so much a part of us as our own language. The technique of observation is easier to manage when it is applied to someone else's language. That technique is explained in the first essay in this section by Professor H. A. Gleason, Jr., who prepares missionaries to deal with languages for which there are no interpreters, dictionaries, or grammars. One of the necessary tools in the objective description of a language is a system of symbols for reporting spoken sounds, and such a system is illustrated here through the G. & C. Merriam Company's chart of the International Phonetic Alphabet, with an accompanying sample transcription. The sounds of a language, which strike a foreigner as disorganized noise, are in fact patterned by stress, pitch, and pauses or juncture (sly twitch or slight witch)—terms explained in the third selection by Professor Paul A. Roberts of San José State College. How precise linguistic description can be, and how much we are unconsciously influenced in our thinking as well as in our speaking by such deep-seated linguistic patterns as the structure of one-syllable words, are points explained by Benjamin Lee Whorf. Winchell may coin "thrub" but he will never coin "srub." How the grammar as well as the sounds of a living language may be discovered and described objectively is illustrated by Charles C.

Fries in an essay taken from his influential *American English Grammar*. An introductory outline of a grammar based on such an objective description of our language is presented in the following essay by Dudley Bailey, Dona W. Brown, and Wallace C. Brown, professor of English at the University of Kansas City.

Other essays in this section deal with the relations between spoken and written English. Punctuation, as Harold Whitehall shows, is largely one of the often crude devices by which we try to translate the meaningful tones of the speaking voice into writing and print. (Was he mad? Was he mad!) A far cruder device is spelling. How our spelling got that way is explained by the late distinguished Danish linguist, Otto Jespersen, who gives "if not rational at any rate historical reasons" for the differences between our sounds and our spellings. Our surprising anxiety about spelling and its effect on our attitude toward language in general are problems critically examined in the following essay by Professor Robert A. Hall, Jr., of Cornell University. The notion that one should simply write as one speaks is discussed by Harold Whitehall, who reminds us that "to speak with a local accent is not disadvantageous; to write serious prose with a local accent definitely is." Written English, Whitehall adds, "must be more carefully organized than speech in order to overcome its communicative deficiencies as compared with speech." The organization of the English sentence, its grammar and style, is the subject of the essay by Professor Simeon Potter of the University of Liverpool.

H. A. GLEASON, JR.

Language

As you listen to an unfamiliar language you get the impression of a torrent of disorganized noises carrying no sense whatever. To the native speaker it is quite otherwise. He pays little attention to the sounds, but concerns himself instead with some situation which lies behind the act of speech and is, for him, somehow reflected in it. Both you and he have failed to grasp the nature of the phenomenon. Neither the casual observer nor the usual native speaker can give any real information about a language. To be sure, some people, Americans perhaps more than most others, have decided notions about language. But the ideas held and discussed come far short of giving a complete picture of the language and sometimes have very little relationship to the facts. Even people with considerable education are often wholly unable to answer certain quite simple questions about their language. For most people language is primarily a tool to be used, rather than a subject for close and critical attention.

It is probably well that it is so. Yet there are important human problems into which language enters intimately and on which it exerts such a profound influence that an understanding of its mechanism would contribute materially to their solutions. Moreover, every phase of human activity is worthy of study. Thus, for practical reasons, as well as to satisfy man's innate curiosity, language deserves careful and intelligent study.

Language has so many interrelationships with various aspects
. . . .

of human life that it can be studied from numerous points of view. All are valid and useful, as well as interesting in themselves. Linguistics is the science which attempts to understand language from the point of view of its internal structure. It is not, of course, isolated and wholly autonomous, but it does have a clearly and sharply delimited field of inquiry, and has developed its own highly effective and quite characteristic method. It must draw upon such sciences as physical acoustics, communications theory, human physiology, psychology, and anthropology for certain basic concepts and necessary data. In return, linguistics makes its own essential contributions to these disciplines. But however closely it may be related to other sciences, it is clearly separate by reason of its own primary concern with the structure of language.

What then is this structure? Language operates with two kinds of material. One of these is sound. Almost any sort of noise that the human vocal apparatus can produce is used in some way in some language. The other is ideas, social situations, meanings— English lacks any really acceptable term to cover the whole range —the facts or fantasies about man's existence, the things man reacts to and tries to convey to his fellows. These two, insofar as they concern linguists, may conveniently be labeled *expression* and *content*.

The foreigner who hears merely a jumble of sounds has not really heard the language, not even the part of it which we have called *expression*. All that he has heard is sounds, the material which language uses to carry its message. This is not the domain of the linguist, but that of the physicist. The latter can analyze the stream of speech as sound and learn many things about it. His findings have both theoretical and practical importance; the designs of telephones, radios, and much other electronic equipment depends in an essential way upon such findings. They also contribute basic data to linguistics, and to numerous other sciences, including psychology and physiology, as well as to physics itself.

The linguist is concerned with sound as the medium by which information is conveyed. To serve in this way, speech must be something quite different from the jumble of sound apparent to the foreigner. It is, in fact, an organized system or structure, and it is this structure that lies within the subject field of linguistics. The linguist analyzes speech as an orderly sequence of specific kinds of sounds and of sequences of sounds. It is orderly in terms of a very complex set of patterns which repeatedly recur and which are at least partially predictable. These patterns form the structure of *expression*, one major component of language in the sense that the linguist uses the term.

The native speaker has his attention focused on something else, the subject of the discourse. This may be a situation which is being described, some ideas which are being presented, or some social formula which is being repeated. None of these things are language, any more than are the sounds which convey speech. The subject of the discourse stands on the opposite side and in much the same relationship to speech as do the sounds. The speaker comprehends what he is talking about in terms of an organizing structure. This structure causes him to select certain features for description and determines the ways in which he will interrelate them. It also cuts the situation up into portions in a characteristic way. These selected features, like the sounds mentioned above, also form patterns which recur, and which are at least partially predictable. These recurrent patterns are the structure of *content*, a second major component of language as the linguist treats it.

Finally, these two structures are intimately related and interacting. Parts of the structure of expression are associated in definite ways with parts of the structure of content. The relations between these two complex structures are themselves quite complex. In every language they are different from what is found in every other language. The differences may be profound and extensive, or they may be relatively slight. But in every instance, the two structures are intricate and their relationships quite characteristic.

The native speaker uses this complex apparatus easily and without conscious thought of the process. It seems to him simple and natural. But to a speaker of another of the world's three thousand languages it may present quite a different picture. It may give an impression of being cumbersome, illogical, or even ridiculous. Actually, of course, the strange language is merely different. A true picture of language can only be had by seeing languages more objectively. Such a view will emphasize the immense complexity, the arbitrariness, and the high degree of adequacy for their purposes—features which are shared by all languages in spite of their divergencies.

The dual structure of language can best be made clear by an example. . . .

Consider a rainbow or a spectrum from a prism. There is a continuous gradation of color from one end to the other. That is, at any point there is only a small difference in the colors immediately adjacent at either side. Yet an American describing it will list the hues as *red, orange, yellow, green, blue, purple,* or something of the kind. The continuous gradation of color which exists in nature is represented in language by a series of discrete categories. This is an instance of structuring of content. There is nothing inherent either in the spectrum or the human perception of it which would compel its division in this way. The specific method of division is part of the structure of English.

By contrast, speakers of other languages classify colors in much different ways. In the accompanying diagram, a rough indication is given of the way in which the spectral colors are divided by speakers of English, Shona (a language of Rhodesia), and Bassa (a language of Liberia).

English:

purple	blue	green	yel-low	orange	red

Shona:

cips^{w}uka	citema	cicena	cips^{w}uka

Bassa:

hui	ziza

The Shona speaker divides the spectrum into three major portions. *Cips^wuka* occurs twice, but only because the red and purple ends, which he classifies as similar, are separated in the diagram. Interestingly enough, *citema* also includes black, and *cicena* white. In addition to these three terms, there are, of course, a large number of terms for more specific colors. These terms are comparable to English *crimson, scarlet, vermilion,* which are all varieties of *red.* The convention of dividing the spectrum into three parts instead of into six does not indicate any difference in visual ability to perceive colors, but only a difference in the way they are classified or structured by the language.

The Bassa speaker divides the spectrum in a radically different way: into only two major categories. In Bassa there are numerous terms for specific colors, but only these two for general classes of colors. It is easy for an American to conclude that the English division into six major colors is superior. For some purposes it probably is. But for others it may present real difficulties. Botanists have discovered that it does not allow sufficient generalization for discussion of flower colors. Yellows, oranges, and many reds are found to constitute one series. Blues, purples, and purplish reds constitute another. These two exhibit fundamental differences that must be treated as basic to any botanical description. In order to state the facts succinctly it has been necessary to coin two new and more general color terms, *xanthic* and *cyanic,* for these two groups. A Bassa-speaking botanist would be under no such necessity. He would find *zĩza* and *hui* quite adequate for the purpose, since they happen to divide the spectrum in approximately the way necessary for this purpose.

Now for a simple statement of structure in the expression part of language: The sounds used by English are grouped into consonants and vowels (and some other categories). These are organized into syllables in a quite definite and systematic way. Each syllable must have one and only one vowel sound. It may have one or more consonants before the vowel, and one or more after the vowel. There are quite intricate restrictions on the sequences that may occur. Of all the mathematically possible combinations of English sounds, only a small portion are admitted as complying with the patterns of English structure. Not all of these are actually used, though the unused ones stand ready in case they should ever be needed. Perhaps some day a word like *ving* may appear in response to a new need. *Shmoo* was drawn out of this stock of unused possibilities only a few years ago. But *ngvi* would be most unlikely: it simply is not available as a potential English word, though it contains only English sounds.

Six of these permissable sequences of sounds are somehow associated with the six portions into which English language-habits structure the spectrum. These are the familiar *red, orange, yellow, green, blue, purple*. This association of expression and content is merely conventional. There is no reason why six others could not be used, or why these six could not be associated with different parts of the spectrum. No reason, that is, except that this is the English-language way of doing it, and these are conventions to which we must adhere reasonably closely if we are to be understood. Sometime in the past history of the language, these conventions became established and have persisted with only gradual changes since. In their ultimate origins, all such conventions are the results of more or less accidental choices. It is largely fortuitous that the spectrum came to be so divided, that the specific words were attached to the colors so distinguished, or, indeed, that the sounds from which they were formed were so organized that these words were possible. These irrational facts, with many others like them, constitute the English language. Each language is a similarly arbitrary system.

The three major components of language, as far as language lies within the scope of linguistics, are the structure of expression, the structure of content, and vocabulary. The latter comprises all the specific relations between expression and content—in the familiar terminology, words and their meanings.

Vocabulary comes and goes. It is the least stable and even the least characteristic of the three components of language. That portion of the vocabulary which changes most freely is sometimes referred to as "slang." But even staid and dignified words are constantly being created and continually passing out of active use, to be preserved only in literature which is dated by their very presence. While certain types of words are more transient than others, none are absolutely immortal. Even the most familiar and commonly used words, which might be expected to be most stable, have a mortality rate of about twenty percent in a thousand years.

Moreover, in the life history of an individual speaker the birth and death of words is very much more frequent than in the language community as a whole. Every normal person probably learns at least three words every day, over a thousand a year, and forgets old ones at an appreciable but lower rate. This figure must be a minimum, because most people have total vocabularies which could only be reached through even more rapid acquisition of vocabulary during at least part of their life.

We have no comparable method by which the rate of change of content structure can be estimated. The learning of new vocabulary, particulary technical terms associated with the learning of new concepts, does of course imply certain minor changes. But it is quite evident that change rarely touches the most basic features in any given language. With regard to the structure of expression the facts are clearer. Few, unless they learn a second language, will add, substract, or change any of their basic sound patterns after they reach adolescence. Grammatical constructions may increase, but at a rate much slower than the increase of vocabulary. Vocabulary is indeed the transient feature of language.

In learning a second language, you will find that vocabulary is comparatively easy, in spite of the fact that it is vocabulary that students fear most. The harder part is mastering new structures in both content and expression. You may have to free yourself from the bondage of thinking of everything as either singular or plural. Perhaps the new language will organize content into singular, dual, and plural (here meaning "three or more"). Or perhaps the new language will not give routine consideration to the matter. English speakers can never make a statement without saying something about the number of every object mentioned. This is compulsory, whether it is relevant or not. In Chinese, objects are noted as singular or plural only when the speaker judges the information to be relevant. The Chinese experience suggests that it actually seldom is, for that language operates with only occasional references to number.

You will have to make similar changes in habits of thought and of description of situations in many other instances. You may, for example, have to learn to think of every action as either completed or incomplete, and to disregard the time of the action unless it has special relevance. The reorganization of thinking and perception may extend much deeper than such changes. In some languages, situations are not analyzed, as they are in English, in terms of an actor and an action. Instead the fundamental cleavage runs in a different direction and cannot be easily stated in English. Some of these divergencies between languages have been described by Benjamin L. Whorf in a series of papers which have been reprinted under the title *Four Articles on Metalinguistics*. Every student of linguistics or languages can profit from the reading of these articles.

You will also have to reorganize your habits of making and hearing sounds. You will have to discriminate between sounds that you have learned to consider the same. You will find that others, in clear contrast in English, function as one, and you will have to learn to respond to them as to one sound. Patterns which seem impossible will have to become facile, and you will have to learn to avoid some English patterns that seem to be second nature.

The most difficult thing of all, however, is that these profound changes will have to become completely automatic. You will have to learn to use them without effort or conscious attention. In this learning process constant disciplined practice is essential. Special ability may be helpful, but probably much less so than is popularly supposed. An understanding of the basic principles of language structure—that is, the results of modern linguistic research—while not indispensable, can contribute in many ways.

As we listen to a person speaking our native language we hear not only what is said, but also certain things about the speaker. If he is an acquaintance, we recognize him. If not, we identify him as male or female and perhaps obtain some idea of his age, his education, and his social background. A person's voice serves at least two functions in communication. One is linguistic, in that it serves as the vehicle of the expression system of language. The other is non-linguistic, in that it carries information of a quite different sort about the speaker.

This distinction is made, at least roughly, even by the unsophisticated. If we are told to REPEAT exactly what another says, we will duplicate (provided our memory serves us adequately) every feature which is included in the language expression system. We can do that, if it is our own language, even without understanding the content. In repeating we will make no effort to reproduce anything beyond the linguistically pertinent features. If, however, we are asked to MIMIC another, we attempt to reproduce not only the linguistic features, but every discernible characteristic. Few can mimic with any degree of success, whereas every normal native speaker can, perhaps with a little practice, repeat exactly up to the limit imposed by his memory span.

The most basic elements in the expression system are the **phonemes.** These are the sound features which are common to all speakers of a given speech form and which are exactly reproduced in repetition. In any language, there is a definite and usually small number of phonemes. In English there are forty-six. Out of this limited inventory of units, the whole expression system is built up. In many respects the phonemes are analogous to the elements of chemistry, ninety-odd in number, out of which all substances are constructed.

The phoneme is one of those basic concepts, such as may be found in all sciences, which defy exact definition. Yet some sort of working characterization is necessary before we go on. The following is hardly adequate beyond a first introduction to the subject, but will make it possible to proceed with the analysis and enumeration of the phonemes of English. . . .

With this in mind, we may define a **phoneme** as a minimum feature of the expression system of a spoken language by which one thing that may be said is distinguished from any other thing which might have been said. Thus, if two utterances are different in such a way that they suggest to the hearer different contents, it must be because there are differences in the expressions. The difference may be small or extensive. The smallest difference which can differentiate utterances with different contents is a difference of a single phoneme. This description is best illustrated by a full-scale application in the presentation of the phonemic system of a language. . . .

There are two things about phonemes that must be explicitly pointed out in anticipation of any such presentation:

Phonemes are part of the system of one specific language. The phonemes of different languages are different, frequently incommensurable. It is for this reason that a foreigner hears only a jumble which he cannot repeat. The sounds of the unfamiliar language do not fit into his phonemic system, and so he can comprehend no order in a simple utterance. If anything which is said about the phonemes of one language happens to apply to those of another, we must regard it as fortuitous.

Phonemes are features of the spoken language. Written language has its own basic unit, the grapheme. Something will be said about this later. If, of necessity, written words are cited as illustrations, it must be constantly borne in mind that the written form is not, and cannot be, an illustration of a phoneme. Instead, it is the spoken form which the written form is expected to elicit which illustrates the phoneme under discussion. This inevitably introduces a major difficulty into the presentation. The illustrative words have been selected with the intention that they should be as generally as possible pronounced by all Americans in the same way. Undoubtedly this principle of selection fails in some instances because of dialect and individual peculiarities of the writer and the reader. Such instances will not vitiate the argument. For some Americans other examples might be needed, but examples can be found which will lead to the same results.

The thinking that most Americans do about language is almost exclusively concerned with written English. A written language is, of course, a valid and important object of linguistic investigation. It can, however, easily mislead the unwary. Most of the misunderstandings which Americans have about language arise from a failure to keep clearly in mind the nature and limitations of a written language.

A written language is typically a reflection, independent in only limited ways, of spoken language. As a picture of actual speech, it is inevitably imperfect and incomplete. To understand the structure of a written language one must constantly resort either to comparison with the spoken language or to conjecture. Unfortunately, recourse has been too largely to the latter. Moreover, conjecture has been based not so much upon an intimate knowledge of the ways of languages in general (the results of descriptive linguistics) as to a priori considerations of supposed logic, to metaphysics, and to simple prejudice. While logic and metaphysics are important disciplines and can make significant contributions to an understanding of language, the customary manner of applying them has redounded neither to their credit nor to the elucidation of language structure. Linguistics must start with thorough investigation of spoken language before it proceeds to study written language. This is true of languages with long histories of written literature, such as English, no less than those of isolated tribes which have never known of the possibility of writing.

The second basic unit in the expression system is the **morpheme**. This again cannot be exactly defined . . . For the present, however, let us characterize a **morpheme** as follows: It is the unit on the expression side of language which enters into relationship with the content side. A morpheme is typically composed of one to several phonemes. The morpheme differs fundamentally from the phoneme, which has no such relationship with content. That is, phonemes have no meanings; morphemes have meanings.

The simpler words of English are morphemes. Other words consist of two or more morphemes. Like the phonemes, the morphemes enter into combinations in accordance with definite and intricate patterns. The expression structure is merely the sum of the patterns of arrangement of these two basic units.

Using the phoneme and the morpheme as their basic units, linguists have been able to build a comprehensive theory of the expression side of language, and to make detailed and comprehensive statements about the expression systems of specific languages. This is what is ordinarily called **descriptive linguistics**. It is the basic branch of linguistic science. Others are **historical linguistics**, dealing with the changes of languages in time, and **comparative linguistics**, dealing with the relationships between languages of common origin. Descriptive linguistics is conventionally divided into two parts. **Phonology** deals with the phonemes and sequences of phonemes. **Grammar** deals with the morphemes and their combinations.

In some respects linguistics has developed more precise and rigorous methods and attained more definitive results than any other science dealing with human behavior. Linguists have been favored with the most obviously structured material with which to work, so this attainment is by no means due to any scientific superiority of linguists over other social scientists. It is also the direct result of the discovery of the phoneme, a discovery which allows the data to be described in terms of a small set of discrete units. Within a given language, a given sound is either a certain phoneme or it is not; there can be no intergradation. This fact eliminates from linguistics a large measure of the vagueness and lack of precision characteristic of most studies of human behavior. It would be presumptuous to claim that this advantage has been thoroughly exploited by linguists, but it is certainly fair to say that in some places, linguistics has achieved an appreciable measure of scientific rigor and has the foundations for further development in this regard.

The chief evidence for the high order of development of linguistics as a science lies in the reproducibility of its results. If two linguists work independently on the same language, they will come out with very similar statements. There may be differences. Some of these differences will be predictable. Very seldom will any of the differences be deep-seated. Usually it will be quite possible to harmonize the two statements and show that by simple restatements one result can be converted into the other. That is, the two results will have differed largely in inconsequential ways, often only in external form.

The content side of linguistics has developed much less rapidly and to a very much less impressive extent than the study of expression. Indeed, it cannot as yet justifiably be called a science. Undoubtedly this has been a source of frustration in linguistics as a whole. One of the greatest shortcomings of descriptive work with the expression aspect of language has been a lack of understanding of the relationships between expression and content, and the inability to use the analysis of content in attacking related problems in expression. Here is the great frontier in linguistic knowledge on which we may look for progress in the next decades.

There have been three reasons for this neglect of the content side. First, linguists have been late in comprehending the real significance of the two-sided nature of language. Their attention has been diverted from this basic problem by the great advances being made within the analysis of expression.

Second, there has been no way to gain access to the content structure except through the expression structure. This requires an inferential method which has not appealed to linguists busy with building a highly rigorous method for the handling of more directly observed data. Content has therefore had an inferior status in the eyes of linguists.

Third, the content, apart from its structure, has not been amenable to any unified study. The substance of content is, of course, the whole of human experience. Thousands of scientists have labored, each in some one of numerous disciplines, in elucidating this mass of material. But there is no one approach which can comprehend the whole and so serve as a starting point for comparison of the different structures which can be imposed upon it. Only isolated portions of the content system can as yet be studied as structure imposed on a measurable continuum of experience. The examples of structuring of color concepts discussed above suggest the possibilities and make the lack of further opportunities for comparison the more tantalizing.

In contrast, the expression plane starts with much simpler materials. The sounds producible by the human voice can be studied comprehensively by several approaches. Two of these have reached the degree of precision which makes them useful to linguistics: **articulatory phonetics,** a branch of human physiology, and **acoustic phonetics,** a branch of physics. . . . It is hard to imagine the scientific study of the expression aspect of speech attaining anywhere near the present degree of development without the aid of phonetics. The structure can be systematically described only because the underlying sounds can be accurately described and measured.

THE EDITORS, G. & C. MERRIAM CO.

A transcription illustrating use of the International Phonetic Alphabet

Passage from Rip van Winkle

The great error in Rip's composition was an insuperable aversion to all kinds of profitable labor. It couldn't be from the want of assiduity or perseverance, for he would sit on a wet rock, with a rod as long and heavy as a Tartar's lance, and fish all day without a murmur, even though he should not be encouraged by a single nibble. He would carry a fowling-piece on his shoulder for hours together, trudging through woods and swamps, and up hill and down dale, to shoot a few squirrels or wild pigeons. He would never refuse to assist a neighbor even in the roughest toil, and was a foremost man at all country frolics for husking Indian corn or building stone fences; the women of the village, too, used to employ him to run their errands, and to do such little odd jobs as their less obliging husbands would not do for them. In a word, Rip was ready to attend to anybody's business but his own; but as to doing family duty, and keeping his farm in order, he found it impossible.

In fact, he declared it was of no use to work on his farm; it was the most pestilent little piece of ground in the whole country; everything about it went wrong, and would go wrong, in spite of him. His fences were continually falling to pieces; his cows would either go astray, or get among the cabbages: he couldn't keep 'em at home; weeds were sure to grow quicker in his fields than anywhere else; the rain always made a point of setting in just as he had some out-of-door work to do; so that though his patrimonial estate had dwindled

· · · · · · · · ·

> away under his management, acre by acre, until there was little more left than a mere patch of Indian corn and potatoes, yet it was the worst-conditioned farm in the neighborhood.

The passage from *Rip van Winkle* (with one slight addition) contains all the speech sounds shown in the key at the bottom of the pages in the Kenyon-Knott *Pronouncing Dictionary of American English*. It is transcribed in the three principal types of the everyday speech of cultivated Americans. The types are here numbered according to the proportion of Americans using them. Type I, spoken by the largest number, was designated by the late Professor George P. Krapp as "General American," in this dictionary called Northern (N). It is also sometimes called "Mid-western," though it extends from the Connecticut River to the Pacific Ocean. Type II, the next most frequent, is commonly called Southern (S), and is heard most typically (though not exclusively) in the southeastern and southern coastal regions. Type III, called Eastern (E), is heard principally in eastern New England and New York City.

The transcriptions are primarily intended to familiarize the reader with the method of representing pronunciation in the International Phonetic Alphabet; not to present an exclusively "correct" pronunciation, but rather a normalized one for each of the three types. One or more variant pronunciations of the words here shown are commonly used by cultured Americans. Some of these variants are shown in the vocabulary of this dictionary, and others are described in the Introduction, §§90–119; both places should be consulted whenever a question of pronunciation arises.

In these passages, which are intended to represent cultivated colloquial English, in order to give a normal pronunciation to the numerous small connecting and relational words—conjunctions, prepositions, pronouns, etc.—which constantly vary in normal speech, it is necessary to speak whole phrases or clauses without pause, instead of pronouncing each word separately, as might be done in reading aloud a list of unconnected words.

When accent marks are occasionally used on one-syllable words, they are intended to show sense stress, the stress of the monosyllable among the surrounding words (§49). When a secondary accent mark (ˌ) is the only one shown on a word, that is intended to show a subordinate sense stress; if the word is a plurisyllable, the primary accent has in that case been reduced by sense stress.

The passage from *Rip van Winkle* may be heard on a phonograph record as spoken by John S. Kenyon (with slight differences from this transcription). The record, called "American English," may be obtained from W. C. Garwick, Rye, N. Y.

The Phonetic Alphabet

VOWELS

Symbol	Spelling	Spoken Form	Symbol	Spelling	Spoken Form
i	bee	bi	ɝ	further	ˈfɝðɚ *accented*
ɪ	pity	ˈpɪtɪ			*syllable*
e	rate	ret			*only, r's*
ɛ	yet	jɛt			*sounded*
æ	sang	sæŋ	ɜ	further	ˈfɜðə *accented syl-*
a	bath	baθ *as heard in the*			*lable only,*
		East, be-			*r's silent*
		tween æ	ɚ	further	ˈfɝðɚ *unaccented*
		(sang) *and*			*syllable*
		ɑ (ah)			*only, r's*
ɑ	ah	ɑ			*sounded*
	far	fɑr	ə	further	ˈfɜðə *unaccented*
ɒ	watch	wɒtʃ *between* ɑ			*syllable*
		(ah) *and* ɔ			*only, r's*
		(jaw)			*silent*
ɔ	jaw	dʒɔ		custom	ˈkʌstəm *unac-*
	gorge	gɔrdʒ		above	əˈbʌv *cented*
o	go	go			*syllable*
ʊ	full	fʊl	ʌ	custom	ˈkʌstəm *accented*
u	tooth	tuθ		above	əˈbʌv *syllable*

DIPHTHONGS

aɪ	while	hwaɪl	ju	using	ˈjuzɪŋ
aʊ	how	haʊ		fuse	fjuz
ɔɪ	toy	tɔɪ	ɪu	fuse	fɪuz

CONSONANTS

Symbol	Spelling	Spoken Form	Symbol	Spelling	Spoken Form
p	pity	'pɪtɪ	dʒ	jaw	dʒɔ
b	bee	bi		edge	ɛdʒ
t	tooth	tuθ	m	custom	'kʌstəm
d	dish	dɪʃ	m̩	keep 'em	'kipm̩
k	custom	'kʌstəm	n	vision	'vɪʒən
g	go	go	ṇ	Eden	'idṇ
f	full	fʊl	ŋ	sang	sæŋ
v	vision	'vɪʒən		angry	'æŋ·grɪ
θ	tooth	tuθ	l	full	fʊl
ð	further	'fɝðɚ	l̩	cradle	'kredl̩
s	sang	sæŋ	w	watch	wɒtʃ
z	using	'juzɪŋ	hw	while	hwaɪl
ʃ	dish	dɪʃ	j	yet	jɛt
ʒ	vision	'vɪʒən	r	rate	ret
h	how	haʊ		very	'vɛrɪ
tʃ	watch	wɒtʃ		far	fɑr
	chest	tʃɛst		gorge	gɔrdʒ

This alphabet is reprinted from *A Pronouncing Dictionary of American English*.

Type I—Northern

ˌpæsɪdʒ frəm ˌrɪpvæn'wɪŋkl̩

ðə gret 'ɛrɚ ɪn rɪps ˌkampə'zɪʃən wəz ən ɪn'supərəbl̩ ə'vɝʒən tu ɔl kaɪndz əv 'prafɪtəbl̩ 'lebɚ. ɪt 'kudn̩t bi frəm ðə want əv ˌæsə'djuɛtɪ ɚ ˌpɝsə'vɪrəns, fɚ i wəd sɪt an ə wet rak, wɪð ə rad əz lɔŋ ən 'hɛvɪ əz ə 'tartɚz læns, ən fɪʃ ɔl de wɪð'aʊt ə 'mɝmɚ, 'ivən ðo i 'ʃudn̩t bi ɪn'kɝdʒd baɪ ə 'sɪŋgl̩ 'nɪbl̩. hid 'kærɪ ə 'faʊlɪŋˌpis an ɪz 'ʃoldɚ fɚ aʊrz tə'gɛðɚ, 'trʌdʒɪŋ θru wudz n̩ swamps, ənd ʌp hɪl ən daʊn del, tə ʃut ə fju 'skwɝəlz ɚ waɪld 'pɪdʒənz. hi wəd 'nɛvɚ rɪ'fɪuz tu ə'sɪst ə 'nebɚ, 'ivən ɪn ðə 'rʌfɪst tɔɪl, ənd wəz ə 'forˌmost mæn ət ɔl 'kʌntrɪ 'fralɪks fɚ 'hʌskɪŋ 'ɪndiən kɔrn ɚ 'bɪldɪŋ ston 'fɛnsɪz; ðə 'wɪmɪn əv ðə 'vɪlɪdʒ, tu, jus tu ɪm'plɔɪ ɪm tə rʌn ðer 'erəndz, ən tə du sʌtʃ 'lɪtl̩ ad dʒabz əz ðer les ə'blaɪdʒɪŋ 'oʌzbəndz 'wudn̩t du for ðəm. ɪn ə wɝd, rɪp wəz 'redɪ tu ə'tɛnd tu 'ɛnɪˌbadɪz 'bɪznɪs bət ɪz on; bət æz tə 'duɪŋ 'fæmlɪ ˌdjutɪ, ən 'kipɪŋ ɪz farm ɪn 'ordɚ, hi faʊnd ɪt ɪm'pasəbl̩.

ɪn fækt, hi dɪ'klerd ɪt wəz əv no 'jus tə wɝk an ɪz farm; ɪt wəz ðə most 'pɛstlənt 'lɪtl̩ pis əv graʊnd ɪn ðə hol 'kʌntrɪ; 'ɛvrɪˌθɪŋ ə'baʊt ɪt wɛnt rɔŋ, ən 'wud go rɔŋ, ɪn spaɪt av ɪm. hɪz 'fɛnsɪz wɚ kən'tɪnjʊəlɪ 'fɔlɪŋ tə 'pisɪz; hɪz kaʊz wəd 'iðɚ go ə'stre, ɚ get ə'mʌŋ ðə 'kæbɪdʒɪz: hi 'kudn̩t 'kipm̩ ət hom; wɪdz wɚ ʃur tə gro 'kwɪkɚ ɪn 'hɪz fildz ðən 'ɛnɪˌhwer'ɛls; ðə ren 'ɔlwɪz med ə pɔɪnt əv 'sɛtɪŋ 'ɪn dʒʌst əz i hæd səm 'aʊtəvˌdor 'wɝk tə du; so ðət ðo ɪz

ˌpætrəˈmonɪəl əˈstet əd ˈdwɪndļd əˈwe ˈʌndɚ ɪz ˈmænɪdӡmənt, ˈekɚ baɪ ˈekɚ, ən̩ˈtɪl ðɚ wəz ˈlɪtļ mor lɛft ðən ə mɪr pætʃ əv ˈɪndɪən kɔrn ən pəˈtetoz, jɛt ɪt wəz ðə ˈwɝstkənˈdɪʃənd farm ɪn ðə ˈnebɚˌhud.

Type II—Southern

ˈpæsɪdӡ frəm ˈrɪpvænˈwɪŋkļ

ðə gret ˈɛrər ɪn rɪps ˌkampəˈzɪʃən wəz ən ɪnˈsupərəbļ əˈvӡӡən tu ɔl kaɪndz əv ˈprɑfɪtəbļ ˈlebə. ɪt ˈkudņt bi frəm ðə wɒnt əv ˌæɛsəˈdjuətɪ ə ˌpɜsəˈvɪrəns, fər i wəd sɪt ɒn ə wɛt rɑk, wɪð ə rad əz lɒŋ ən ˈhɛvɪ əz ə ˈtɑːtəz læns, ən fɪʃ ɔl de wɪðˈaut ə ˈmɜmə, ˈivən ðo i ˈʃudņt bi ɪnˈkӡrɪdӡd baɪ ə ˈsɪŋgļ ˈnɪbļ. hid ˈkærɪ ə ˈfaulɪŋˌpis ɒn ɪz ˈʃoldə fər auəz təˈgɛðə, ˈtrʌdӡɪŋ θru wudz ņ swɒmps, ənd ʌp hɪl ən daun del, tə ʃut ə fju ˈskwɝrəlz ə waɪld ˈpɪdӡənz. hi wəd ˈnevə rɪˈfjuz tu əˈsɪst ə ˈnebə, ˈivən ɪn ðə ˈrʌfɪst tɔɪl, ənd wəz ə ˈfoəˌmost mæn ət ɔl ˈkʌntrɪ ˈfralɪks fə ˈhaskɪŋ ˈɪndɪən kɔən ə ˈbɪldɪŋ ston ˈfensɪz; ðə ˈwɪmɪn əv ðə ˈvɪlɪdӡ, tu, jus tu ɪmˈplɔɪ ɪm tə rʌn ðɛr ˈɛrəndz, ən tə du sʌtʃ ˈlɪtļ ad dӡɑbz əz ðɛə lɛs əˈblaɪdӡɪŋ ˈhʌzbəndz ˈwudņt du fɔə ðəm. ɪn ə wɝd, rɪp wəz ˈredɪ tu əˈtɛnd tu ˈɛnɪˌbadɪz ˈbɪznɪs bət ɪz on; bət æz tə ˈduɪŋ ˈfæmlɪ ˌdjutɪ, ən ˈkipɪŋ ɪz ˈfɑːm ɪn ˈɔədə, hi faund ɪt ɪmˈpɑsəbļ.

ɪn fækt, hi dɪˈklææd ɪt wəz əv no ˈjus tə wɝk ɒn ɪz fɑːm; ɪt wəz ðə most ˈpestļənt ˈlɪtļ pis əv graund ɪn ðə hol ˈkʌntrɪ; ˈɛvrɪˌθɪŋ əˈbaut ɪt wɛnt rɒŋ, ən ˈwud go rɒŋ, ɪn spaɪt ɑv ɪm. hɪz ˈfensɪz wə kənˈtɪnjuəlɪ ˈfɔlɪŋ tə ˈpɪsɪz; hɪz kauz wəd ˈiðə go əˈstre, ə gɛt əˈmʌŋ ðə ˈkæbɪdӡɪz: hi ˈkudņt ˈkipm̩ ət hom; wɪdz wə ʃuə tə gro ˈkwɪkər ɪn ˈhɪz fɪldz ðən ˈɛnɪˌhwærˈɛls; ðə rɛn ˈɔlwɪz med ə pɔɪnt əv ˈsɛtɪŋ ˈɪn dӡʌst əz i hæd səm ˈautəvˌdoə ˈwɝk tə du; so ðət ðo ɪz ˌpætrəˈmonɪəl əˈstet əd ˈdwɪndļd əˈwe ˈʌndər ɪz ˈmænɪdӡmənt, ˈekə baɪ ˈekə, ən̩ˈtɪl ðə wəz ˈlɪtļ moə lɛft ðən ə mɪə pætʃ əv ˈɪndɪən kɔən ən pəˈtetoz, jɛt ɪt wəz ðə ˈwɝstkənˈdɪʃənd fɑːm ɪn ðə ˈnebəˌhud.

Type III—Eastern

ˈpæsɪdӡ frəm ˌrɪpvænˈwɪŋkļ

ðə gret ˈɛrər ɪn rɪps ˌkɒmpəˈzɪʃən wəz ən ɪnˈsupərəbļ əˈvӡӡən tu ɔl kaɪndz əv ˈprɒfɪtəbļ ˈlebə. ɪt ˈkudņt bi frəm ðə wɒnt əv ˌæɛsəˈdjuətɪ ə ˌpɜsəˈvɪrəns, fər i wəd sɪt ɒn ə wɛt rɒk, wɪð ə rɒd əz lɒŋ ən ˈhɛvɪ əz ə ˈtɑːtəz lans, ən fɪʃ ɔl de wɪðˈaut ə ˈmɜmə, ˈivən ðo i ˈʃudņt bi ɪnˈkӡrɪdӡd baɪ ə ˈsɪŋgļ ˈnɪbļ. hid ˈkærɪ ə ˈfaulɪŋpis ɒn ɪz ˈʃoldə fər auəz təˈgɛðə, ˈtrʌdӡɪŋ θru wudz ņ swɒmps, ənd ʌp hɪl ən daun del, tə ʃut ə fju ˈskwɝrəlz ə waɪld ˈpɪdӡənz. hi wəd ˈnevə rɪˈfjuz tu əˈsɪst ə ˈnebə, ˈivən ɪn ðə ˈrʌfɪst tɔɪl, ənd wəz ə ˈfoəˌmost mæn ət ɔl ˈkʌntrɪ ˈfrɒlɪks fə ˈhaskɪŋ ˈɪndɪən kɔən ə ˈbɪldɪŋ ston ˈfensɪz; ðə ˈwɪmɪn əv ðə ˈvɪlɪdӡ, tu, jus tu ɪmˈplɔɪ ɪm tə rʌn ðɛr ˈɛrəndz, ən tə du sʌtʃ ˈlɪtļ ɒd dӡɒbz əz ðɛə lɛs əˈblaɪdӡɪŋ ˈhʌzbəndz ˈwudņt du fɔə ðəm. ɪn ə wɝd, rɪp wəz ˈredɪ tu əˈtɛnd tu ˈɛnɪˌbɒdɪz ˌbɪznɪs bət ɪz on; bət æz tə ˈduɪŋ ˈfæmlɪ ˌdjutɪ, ən ˈkipɪŋ ɪz ˈfɑːm ɪn ˈɔədə, hi faund ɪt ɪmˈpɒsəbļ.

ɪn fækt, hi dɪˈkleəd ɪt wəz əv no ˈjus tə wɝk ɒn ɪz fɑːm; ɪt wəz ðə most ˈpestļənt ˈlɪtļ pis əv graund ɪn ðə hol ˈkʌntrɪ; ˈɛvrɪˌθɪŋ əˈbaut ɪt wɛnt rɒŋ, ən ˈwud go rɒŋ, ɪn spaɪt ɒv ɪm. hɪz ˈfensɪz wə kənˈtɪnjuəlɪ ˈfɔlɪŋ tə ˈpɪsɪz; hɪz kauz wəd ˈiðə go əˈstre, ə gɛt əˈmʌŋ ðə ˈkæbɪdӡɪz: hi ˈkudņt ˈkipm̩ ət hom; wɪdz wə ʃuə tə gro ˈkwɪkər ɪn ˈhɪz fɪldz ðən ˈɛnɪˌhwərˈɛls; ðə rɛn ˈɔlwɪz med ə pɔɪnt əv ˈsɛtɪŋ ˈɪn dӡʌst əz i hæd səm ˈautəvˌdoə ˈwɝk tə du; so ðət ðo ɪz ˌpætrəˈmonɪəl əˈstet əd ˈdwɪndļd əˈwe ˈʌndər ɪz ˈmænɪdӡmənt, ˈekə baɪ ˈekə, ən̩ˈtɪl ðə wəz ˈlɪtļ moə lɛft ðən ə mɪə pætʃ əv ˈɪndɪən kɔən ən pəˈtetoz, jɛt ɪt wez ðə ˈwɝstkənˈdɪʃənd fɑːm ɪn ðə ˈnebəˌhud.

PAUL M. ROBERTS

Intonation

The Punctuation of Speech

In recent years it has become increasingly clear that any discussion of English punctuation that takes no account of the intonation in speech patterns is, if not meaningless, at least highly artificial. Intonation is to punctuation what vowels and consonants are to letters of the alphabet. There is, to be sure, no exact relationship in either case. We do not spell words just as we pronounce them, and our punctuation marks do not come near showing all the intonation that occurs in our sentences. But ultimately we get our letters from the vowels and consonants of speech, and so do we ultimately get our commas and periods and semicolons from the intonation of speech. Therefore, before we go on to examine the punctuation habits of American writers, we need to get a rough idea of the intonation of American speech.

The idea will necessarily be rough because intonation is not an easy thing to study. It is in one sense obvious and plain and in another obscure and difficult. We all of us react accurately to the intonation signals of the language. If we didn't, we would constantly misunderstand and be misunderstood. Gross differences are easy to see. Anyone can perceive a difference between "Was he mad?" and "Was he mad!" and can perceive further that the difference subsists not in vowels and consonants but in something we call "tone of voice." But to understand just what this

....

"tone of voice" consists of, what physical features make one sentence different from the other, is another matter.

The difficulty of studying intonation can be seen in the fact that, although mankind has been studying language for thousands of years, it is only in the last decade or so that linguists have achieved a useful grasp of the features of intonation. Indeed, much still remains obscure, and many details are still being debated. But enough has been done that we can now see the main structure of intonation, or at least of English intonation.

Intonation consists of three features, which are called *stress*, *pitch*, and *juncture*. Stress is simply the loudness or softness with which sounds are uttered. Pitch is the frequency with which voiced sounds vibrate as they issue from the glottis. If they vibrate relatively fast, we have what we call high pitch; if they vibrate relatively slowly, we have low pitch. Juncture, which is closely related to both pitch and stress, is a way of marking division points in speech by lengthening out the sounds adjacent to the break.

Presumably all languages have intonation. One cannot speak without speaking softly or loudly or without vibration of voiced sounds, and presumably in all languages there is some variation, the discourse being not all on one level of loudness or at one vibration frequency. But languages differ markedly in the use they make of vibration features. Some languages use intonation lexically, to distinguish between different words, much as speakers of English use vowels and consonants. The best known of such languages is Chinese. In Chinese the sounds [ma], for instance, produce any of four different words, depending on the pitch pattern with which they are uttered.

English, like many other languages, uses intonation chiefly for syntactical purposes or for discriminating between different emotional states. We have had the examples "Was he mad?" and "Was he mad!" where one intonation pattern signals a question and the other an exclamation. Consider also the many different attitudes or emotions that can be signaled by the intonation used on the word "well" or on the word "oh."

We shall have various other examples as we examine the three intonation features one by one.

Stress

Stress has been defined as the loudness or softness with which sounds are uttered. We can see it working in many pairs of words in which one member is a noun and the other a verb; the noun in such pairs has a loud stress on the first syllable and the verb the loud stress on the root syllable. For instance, if I say, "What's your object?" I pronounce *ob* more loudly than *ject*. But if I say, "I object" the *ject* is louder than the *ob*. If one were to reverse the stresses in these sentences, the sentences would sound un-English.

Other such pairs are *súbject* and *subjéct, cóntrast* and *contrást, próduce* and *prodúce, réwrite* (*a rewrite man*) and *rewríte, invíte* and the dialectal *ínvite*. Stress is thus a signal distinguishing between members of different form classes, though sometimes it is only one of the signals. For instance *refúse* and *réfuse* are distinguished by stress and also by contrasting final consonants. *Anticipate* and *anticipation* are distinguised by stress and also by the suffix on the noun.

But there are more than two contrasting stresses in English speech as can be seen by contrasting the pronunciations of *separate* in "I'll separate them" and "They are separate." In both sentences *separate* has the heaviest stress on the first syllable. In the adjective, the second and third syllables have about equal stress. But in the verb the third syllable has a weaker stress than the first but a heavier stress than the second.

Using such and more complicated methods of comparison, linguists have arrived at the conclusion that English speech has four contrasting levels of stress. Since the contrasts are used to distinguish between different meanings, they are phonemic, and the four stress levels are four different phonemes, just as vowels and consonants are phonemes.

The four stress phonemes are named and symbolized as follows:

Primary Stress (the loudest): / ´ /
Secondary Stress (next to loudest): / ^ /
Tertiary Stress (next to softest): / ` /
Weak Stress (the softest): / ˘ /

These stress levels are relative, not absolute. That means that primary stresses, for instance, do not all have the same volume. I may generally speak more loudly than you do, so that my typical tertiary stresses are louder than your typical primary stresses. Nevertheless we would each have the four contrasting stress levels in our respective sentences.

Or I may speak more loudly at some times than at others. I can say the sentence "I'll separate them" twice, once very loudly and once very softly. But both times there would be clear stress contrasts between *sep* and *ar* and *ate*.

The four stress contrasts do not appear in every utterance we make. If we speak a two-word sentence, like "Shut up," obviously only two stresses can appear. It is only when we examine longer stretches of speech that the four-stress pattern of English emerges.

The four can be seen in the following sentences. All might be spoken in other ways, but they would frequently be uttered as marked:

Jôhn's òn thĕ sófă.

Whêre's thĕ stréetcàr?

Hê's ă fôolĭsh wísemàn.

Functions of Stress in English

It is not our purpose to learn to analyze accurately the intonation of English sentences. This is a task for the expert. We can content ourselves with noting some of the obvious contrasts that distinguish meanings.

For instance, if the sentence "He is my brother" is pronounced with the primary stress on the first syllable of *brother*, we have a simple statement of fact. You wanted to know who he was, and I told you. But if we shift the primary stress, we get different meanings:

He is my brother. (not the other fellow)

He is my brother. (Why do you deny it?)

He is my brother. (not Sam's)

Or consider these:

That's a nice mess.

That's a nice mess.

That's a nice mess.

Stress is used extensively to signal different kinds of modification. We had the sentence "This is an orderly room," which we called ambiguous. But it is ambiguous in writing only, not in speech:

This is an orderly room. (a room for orderlies)

This is an orderly room. (in good order)

Or

He's a fine clerk. (a good one)

He's a fine clerk. (collects fines)

Thus we see that, in general, when an adjective modifies a noun, we have primary stress on the noun and secondary on the adjective:

a handsome man

a strange story

an old streetcar

But when a noun modifies another noun, we generally have primary stress on the modifier and tertiary stress on the head-word:

a city man

a bottle plant

a used-car dealer

Stress also distinguishes the two kinds of V-ing * words that modify nouns. V-ing modifiers like the one in "reading room" take the primary stress on the modifier with tertiary on the headword:

> a réadǐng ròom
> a dáncǐng schòol
> a wáitǐng lìst

But V-ing modifiers like that in "burning room" have secondary stress on the modifier and primary on the noun:

> a bûrnǐng roóm
> a laûghǐng gírl
> a soârǐng pláne

Consequently, constructions like "a smoking room" can be ambiguous only in writing, never in speech:

> a smôkǐng roóm (a room on fire)
> a smókǐng ròom (a room for smoking)

Native speakers of English manage these pitch structures so automatically that they seldom think of them. It is only when someone, accidentally or intentionally, does violence to the patterns that the patterns become obvious. It is nothing special to see "a dáncǐng schòol," but "a dâncǐng schoól" would be quite a sight. So would "a rêadǐng roóm" or "a laûghǐng gìrl" (girl who makes her living laughing, like "a dáncǐng gìrl"?). On the other hand, "câllǐng cárds" are fairly common; they're just visiting humorists. And "Frênch teáchěrs" are nearly as plentiful as "Frénch teàchěrs."

* Verb in the -ing form.

Pitch

Pitch we have defined as the frequency of vibration of voiced sounds coming from the glottis. The glottis, you may remember, is the opening in the larynx through which the breath passes on its way to the mouth. If the glottis is wide open, there is no vibration, and we get unvoiced sounds, like /s/. If the glottis is partly closed, a tension resulting in vibration is set up, and we get voiced sounds, like /z/. All the vowels and more than half the consonants in English are voiced.

Pitch is of course important to music. In music variation in pitch produces what we call melody. (Notice that you can "sing" the sound z-z-z- but that you can't sing s-s-s-.) But it is important also in ordinary language. We use it in English not only to convey various states of emotion but also as an integral part of our syntax.

English has four pitch phonemes, as it has four stress phonemes. These are usually given numbers, rather than names. The number 4 indicates the highest pitch and 1 the lowest, thus:

HIGH PITCH: /4/
NEXT TO HIGH: /3/
NEXT TO LOW: /2/
LOWEST PITCH: /1/

Like the stress phonemes, these four pitches are relative, not absolute. They cannot be defined as so many vibrations per second. They are simply points of contrast set up in the speech of individuals as they speak particular sentences. In general, children have higher pitch than adults, and women have higher pitch than men. Thus a child's low pitch may be higher than an adult's high pitch. But the child will have the four pitch contrasts within his register, and the adult will have them in his.

In scientific work, pitch is usually written with the numbers only, thus:

2   3   1
Where are you going?

This would indicate that the sentence begins on the second pitch level, rises to the third on the first syllable of *going*, and falls to the first on the second syllable of *going*.

For general purposes, however, it is a little easier to show pitch with lines rather than numbers. A line just under the letters indicates pitch 2; a line well under indicates pitch 1; a line just above the letters indicates pitch 3; and a line well above indicates pitch 4. Thus:

$$4 \underline{\qquad}$$
$$3 \underline{\qquad}$$

Where   2 Where   Where   Where

1 $\underline{\qquad}$

Then we can show the pitch in "Where are you going?" in this way:

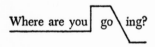

Functions of Pitch

Let us see, then, some of the uses made of pitch in English. The example already given shows a very common pitch pattern for ordinary statements and for questions introduced by interrogatives. It is a 2–3–1 pattern. We begin on the second pitch, rise to the third on the stressed syllable, and fall to the first at the end. In American English (not so commonly in British) the third pitch level frequently coincides with the primary stress.

But many variations are possible. We can put a bit of panic into the question by rising to the highest (fourth) pitch on the primary stress:

Where are you | go \ ing?

Thus a mother might address a child tottering toward the **brink** of a precipice.

We put in exasperation by rising twice to the third level:

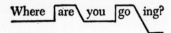

Where are you go ing?

This suggests that we've had trouble with you before and are getting tired of it.

If we want to insist on the *where*, we get the third level at the beginning:

Where are you going?

Don't tell me you're going; I know that; now I want to know *where*.

A double rise will often come after persistent questioning:

Where are you go ing?

I've asked you several times without getting an answer; now I want one.

Thus considerable meaning of one kind and another can be added to the simple question by variation in the pitch.

There is a widely spread notion that we regularly signal questions by a rise in pitch. The voice rises, it is said, at the end of a question, and falls at the end of a statement. This is only partially true. To be sure, most statements in American English end in a fall to the lowest pitch:

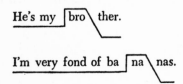

He's my bro ther.

I'm very fond of ba na nas.

But, as we have seen, questions may have the same pitch pattern. Indeed, this is the regular pattern for questions beginning with an interrogative—*who, where, whose, what, why,* etc.:

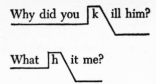

Why did you ⌐k\ ill him?

What ⌐h\ it me?

However, we have another type of question which does not usually end with a fall in pitch. This is the *yes/no* question— i.e., a question that can be answered by *yes* or *no*. Such questions are signaled not by interrogatives but by a reversal of subject and verb or of subject and auxiliary, as well as by the different pitch pattern:

Did you ⌐kill him?

Are you fond of ba⌐nanas?

Is he ⌐going somewhere?

These sentences can also be uttered with the 2–3–1 pattern, but this will add a note of insistence. Compare these:

Did you ⌐kill him?

Did you ⌐k\ ill him?

In the first I am simply making a polite inquiry. In the second, I am attempting to brush aside your evasions and get at the essential fact.

Thus a rising pitch at the end could scarcely be described as *the* question signal in English. A great many questions end in falling pitch, and in the others there are usually more obvious question signals present. Sometimes, however, pitch contrast will be the only signal of a question. Compare these:

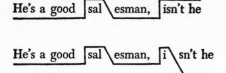

The first is a question; it calls for an answer—yes or no. But the second isn't really a question. The person spoken to is not expected to answer but to agree.

We also use rising pitch when we repeat a question, either because we haven't understood it or because we are surprised at its being asked. Thus:

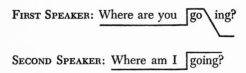

This indicates that the second speaker didn't quite catch the question and wants it repeated.

Or consider this colloquy:

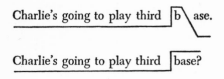

The repetition of the question without the fall indicates the second speaker's surprise at the assignment. He could show that he is simply stunned by it by saying it this way:

Charlie's going to play third ⌐base?

Such words as *who, when, where, how* can signal two entirely different kinds of questions, depending on the pitch:

We need to appoint a secretary.

Okay. W̅\ho?

Let's appoint Ed secretary.

W̲/ho?

The first *who* is an ordinary question. The second *who* indicates either that the speaker didn't catch the name or is surprised at it. And similarly:

I'm going to Europe next summer.

H̅\ow?

I'm going to Europe in a canoe.

H̲/ow?

Thus the variations in English pitch are manifold. But they all carry clear meaning to which we react effortlessly.

Juncture

The third feature of English intonation is juncture. This is at once the hardest to understand and, for us, the most important, since it is the part of intonation most directly related to punctuation.

Juncture may be very roughly described as various kinds of breaks or division points in the flow of speech. As there are four stress phonemes and four pitch phonemes, so there are four juncture phonemes, though one of these is quite different from the other three. The juncture phonemes are generally named after the symbols used to indicate them, thus:

PLUS JUNCTURE:	/+/
SINGLE-BAR JUNCTURE:	/│/
DOUBLE-BAR JUNCTURE:	/‖/
DOUBLE-CROSS JUNCTURE:	/#/

Plus Juncture

Plus juncture, so called because linguists indicate it with a plus sign when they transcribe speech, is the difference between "gray train" and "great rain." These expressions are uttered with exactly the same vowel and consonant phonemes: /greytreyn/. They are pronounced with the same pitch and stress. There is no pause, in the usual sense, in either. Yet, if one were to read the utterances say fifty times, in mixed up order, to a native speaker of English, he would be able to tell which was which most if not all of the time. The only inference is that he must hear a distinguishing difference. What is it?

What he hears is a different variety in the phonemes. . . A phoneme is not a single sound but a bundle of similar sounds called allophones. We have one allophone of /t/ occurring in the final position, as in /set/; another allophone occurs when /t/ is followed by /r/ as in /trip/. Similarly one allophone of /r/ occurs when the sound is initial, as in /rip/; quite a different allophone occurs when /r/ follows /t/, as in /trip/. In "gray train" the hearer hears the allophone of /t/ that precedes /r/ and the allophone of /r/ that follows /t/; in "great rain" he hears the allophone of /t/ that occurs at the end of words and the allophone of /r/ that occurs at the beginning of words. This is indicated in phonemic transcription by writing the sign of plus juncture at one place or the other: /grey+treyn/ or /greyt+reyn/.

Other examples of the operation of plus juncture can be noted in the pronunciation differences between "seem able" and "see Mabel," "another directed person" and "an other-directed person," "fly trap" and "flight wrap," "dough pad" and "dope ad." Often, of course, such similar structures are distinguished by other signals in addition to plus juncture. Thus "neat owl" and "knee towel" would have different allophones of the /t/ phoneme but also a different position for the primary stress.

Single-Bar Juncture

Plus juncture is for us of mostly academic interest. Obvious writing problems are not closely bound to the occurrence or nonoccurrence of plus juncture. The other three junctures, however, connect in one way or another with the punctuation marks of writing.

Single-bar juncture is linked to the occurrence of primary stresses in an utterance. Let us take this sentence:

The men of the family milked the goats.

A sentence of this sort is most commonly spoken with just one primary stress; the primary stress falls toward the end of the sentence:

The men of the family milked the góats.

But it could also be uttered with two primary stresses.

The men of the fámily milked the góats.

Now if we say it this way there is a kind of break between *family* and *milked*. This is not so much a pause as a lengthening out of the final syllable of *family*. The pitch stays the same. That is, we go into the word *milked* at about the same pitch that we left off on the last syllable of *family*, like this:

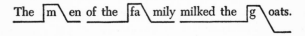

Now this break or division in the utterance is called single-bar juncture. It can occur only between primary stresses, and it consists of a lengthening out of the phonemes before the break with a sustension of the pitch level across the break.

The sentence could have three primary stresses. In that case, there would be two single-bar junctures:

The ⌐m\en of the ⌐fa\mily milked the ⌐g\oats.

Or we could write it thus, showing just the junctures:

The men | of the family | milked the goats.

This would be a very slow and emphatic way of speaking the sentence.

A hundred years or so ago it was conventional to mark most single-bar junctures with commas. In recent times, however, the tendency has been toward less punctuation, and modern writers are less likely to use commas where these junctures occur. Learners, who overpunctuate as often as they under-punctuate, often do put commas in such positions. They may write, for example, "The men of the family, milked the goats." If they are challenged by a teacher, they will very likely say, "I put a comma there because there would be a pause there if the sentence were spoken." Presumably what they mean by "pause" is single-bar juncture. As we have seen, there could be such a juncture in this position, a primary stress on family, followed by a lengthening out of the last syllable of the word with the sentence continuing on the same pitch level. But whether there is or not, the experienced writer would not use a comma. Single-bar junctures in such constructions are not ordinarily shown by punctuation.

Double-Bar Juncture

Double-bar juncture, however, is usually indicated by punctuation, and it will be useful to understand the difference. Let us compare these two sentences:

> The people who were sick didn't go.
> My friend Al who was sick didn't go.

The first sentence could be spoken with no internal juncture or with one or two single-bar junctures:

> The people who were sick didn't go.
> The people who were sick | didn't go.
> The people | who were sick | didn't go.

These vary principally in emphasis and speed of delivery. None would normally have any punctuation.

But the second sentence is quite different. In the first place, it would normally have three primary stresses, not just one or two:

> My friend Aĺ who was sićk didn't gó.

Secondly, the pitch would go something like this:

My friend ⌐A⟍1⟋   who was ⌐s⟍ick⟋   didn't ⌐g⟍o.

Note the upturn in the pitch after *Al* and after *sick*. This is double-bar juncture. As in single-bar juncture, there is a lengthening out of the phonemes before the break. But the pitch, instead of continuing level across the break, rises toward, but not to, the next higher pitch.

Many American speakers would use single-bar junctures in this sentence in place of double-bar. But all speakers would use junctures, two of them, in the places indicated. In this sentence type we do not sometimes use the junctures and sometimes not, as in the type, "the people who were sick didn't go."

Double-bar juncture is frequently marked in writing by a comma, though sometimes dashes or other marks are used. Our sentences would of course be punctuated this way:

> The people who were sick didn't go.
> My friend Al, who was sick, didn't go.

This contrast in junctures reflects a contrast in the structure of the sentences. In the first sentence, *who were sick* is part of the noun cluster *the people who were sick*. The S-group modifies the headword *people*. But in the second sentence *who was sick* is not part of a cluster. There is no unit *my friend Al who was sick* in this sentence. *Who was sick* is here really a sentence modifier, another idea applying against the main idea of the sentence. One idea is that Al didn't go, another that Al was sick. But we would not say that the first sentence is separable in this way. In the first sentence *who were sick* is an integral part of the noun cluster. The meaning is not that people were sick and people didn't go but that those particular people who were sick didn't go.

The marking off of sentence modifiers from the sentences they modify is an important function of double-bar juncture. Here are some further examples. If you say them aloud, you may be able to hear the slight upturn of the pitch. Many speakers will normally employ the sustained pitch of single-bar instead. Commas, of course, would replace the juncture signs in conventional writing:

> Ordinarily ‖ we stayed home.
> (Cf. "We ordinarily stayed home" in which *ordinarily* is part of the verb cluster and there is no juncture.)
> When he fell on his face ‖ we laughed heartily.
> (Cf. "We laughed heartily when he fell on his face.")
> Charlie ‖ having a guilty conscience ‖ consulted the chaplain.
> (Cf. "Anyone having a guilty conscience should consult the chaplain.")
> We knew ‖ nevertheless ‖ that there would be trouble.
> (Cf. "We nevertheless expected trouble.")
> The teacher shook my hand ‖ smiling at me warmly.
> (Cf. "The teacher frowned at the girl who was smiling at me warmly.")

Sometimes double-bar juncture will be the only signal distinguishing meanings. Compare these:

> Mr. Simkin hired me because I had an honest face.
> Mr. Simkin hired me ‖ because I had an honest face.

The first sentence would be a response to the question "Why did Mr. Simkin hire you?" The second would be a response to the question "What did Mr. Simkin do?" In the first sentence, the S-group is a verb modifier. In the second it is a sentence modifier.

Double-bar juncture also occurs between units in a series. If we count aloud—*one, two, three, four*—we have double-bar juncture after each unit but the last one: one ‖ two ‖ three ‖ four. After *one, two,* and *three* there will be a prolongation of the sound accompanied by an upturn in the pitch. If we put a double-bar juncture after *four* in this series, it will signal that we are not done counting, and the hearer will wait for us to say "five."

The same juncture occurs in series of units other than numbers:

> We bagged a lion ‖ an antelope ‖ and a giraffe.
> He worked all day ‖ danced all night ‖ and died young.
> He made his way through the woods ‖ across the stream ‖ and up the mountain.
> He was young ‖ courageous ‖ and optimistic.

Commas would indicate these junctures in most American writing.

Double-bar juncture occurs also at the end of certain questions, particularly those of the *yes/no* variety. If we speak the sentence "Is he ready" we will probably rise to the third pitch level on the syllable with primary stress:

Is he | ready

But the sentence will end not on a level third pitch but with the upturn of double-bar juncture, something like this:

Is he | ready

This is normal in questions or other sentences ending on the third pitch.

Double-Cross Juncture

The last of the junctures—double-cross juncture—is a falling off into silence, usually from the low pitch. We have seen that the pitch pattern 2–3–1 is most common for statements and some questions in American English:

He's | re \ ady.

But the pitch doesn't end with level pitch but falls at the very end:

He's | re \ ady.

This fall is double-cross juncture, so called because linguists use a double cross (#) to mark it in transcribing speech. Double-cross juncture is the most important of the features dividing our speech into sentences. It is presumably the feature which gave early writers the idea of using periods. . . .

BENJAMIN LEE WHORF

Linguistics as an Exact Science

The revolutionary changes that have occurred since 1890 in the
world of science—especially in physics but also in chemistry,
biology, and the sciences of man—have been due not so much
to new facts as to new ways of thinking about facts. The new
facts themselves of course have been many and weighty; but
more important still, the realms of research where they appear
—relativity, quantum theory, electronics, catalysis, colloid chemistry, theory of the gene, Gestalt psychology, psychoanalysis,
unbiased cultural anthropology, and so on—have been marked
to an unprecedented degree by radically new concepts, by a failure to fit the world view that passed unchallenged in the great
classical period of science, and by a groping for explanations,
reconciliations, and restatements.

I say new ways of *thinking* about facts, but a more nearly accurate statement would say new ways of *talking* about facts.
It is this *use of language upon data* that is central to scientific
progress. Of course, we have to free ourselves from that vague
innuendo of inferiority which clings about the word "talk," as
in the phrase "just talk"; that false opposition which the English-
speaking world likes to fancy between talk and action. There is
no need to apologize for speech, the most human of all actions.
The beasts may think, but they do not talk. "Talk" *ought to be*
a more noble and dignified word than "think." Also we must face
the fact that science begins and ends in talk; this is the reverse

. . . .

From *Language, Thought, and Reality: Selected Writings of Benjamin Lee
Whorf*, ed. John B. Carroll, 1956. By permission of John Wiley & Sons and
The Technology Press.

of anything ignoble. Such words as "analyze," "compare," "deduce," "reason," "infer," "postulate," "theorize," "test," and "demonstrate," mean that whenever a scientist does something, he talks about this thing that he does. As Leonard Bloomfield has shown, scientific research begins with a set of sentences which point the way to certain observations and experiments, the results of which do not become fully scientific until they have been turned back into language, yielding again a set of sentences which then become the basis of further exploration into the unknown. This scientific use of language is subject to the principles or the laws of the science that studies all speech— linguistics.

As I was concerned to point out in a previous article, "Science and Linguistics," we all hold an illusion about talking, an illusion that talking is quite untrammeled and spontaneous and merely "expresses" whatever we wish to have it express. This illusory appearance results from the fact that the obligatory phenomena within the apparently free flow of talk are so completely autocratic that speaker and listener are bound unconsciously as though in the grip of a law of nature. The phenomena of language are background phenomena, of which the talkers are unaware or, at the most, very dimly aware—as they are of the motes of dust in the air of a room, though the linguistic phenomena govern the talkers more as gravitation than as dust would. These automatic, involuntary patterns of language are not the same for all men but are specific for each language and constitute the formalized side of the language, or its "grammar" —a term that includes much more than the grammar we learned in the textbooks of our school days.

From this fact proceeds what I have called the "linguistic relativity principle," which means, in informal terms, that users of markedly different grammars are pointed by their grammars toward different types of observations and different evaluations of externally similar acts of observation, and hence are not equivalent as observers but must arrive at somewhat different views of the world. From each such unformulated and naïve world view, an explicit scientific world view may arise by a higher specializa-

tion of the same basic grammatical patterns that fathered the
naive and implicit view. Thus the world view of modern science
arises by higher specialization of the basic grammar of the western
Indo-European languages. Science of course was not *caused* by
this grammar; it was simply colored by it. It appeared in this
group of languages because of a train of historical events that
stimulated commerce, measurement, manufacture, and technical
invention in a quarter of the world where these languages were
dominant.

The participants in a given world view are not aware of the
idiomatic nature of the channels in which their talking and thinking run, and are perfectly satisfied with them, regarding them
as logical inevitables. But take an outsider, a person accustomed
to widely different language and culture, or even a scientist of
a later era using somewhat different language of the same basic
type, and not all that seems logical and inevitable to the participants in the given world view seems so to him. The reasons
that officially pass current may strike him as consisting chiefly
of highly idiomatic *façons de parler*. Consider the answers that
were at one time given even by learned men to questions about
nature: Why does water rise in a pump? Because nature abhors
a vacuum. Why does water quench fire? Because water is wet
or because the fiery principle and the watery principle are anti-
thetical. Why do flames rise? Because of the lightness of the
element fire. Why can one lift a stone with a leather sucker?
Because the suction draws the stone up. Why does a moth fly
toward a light? Because the moth is curious or because light
attracts it. If once these sentences seemed satisfying logic but
today seem idiosyncrasies of a peculiar jargon, the change is not
because science has discovered new facts. Science has adopted
new linguistic formulations of the old facts, and now that we
have become at home in the new dialect, certain traits of the
old one are no longer binding upon us.

We moderns are not yet in a position to poke fun at the wise-
acres of old who explained various properties of water by its
wetness. The terminology which we apply to language and
cultural phenomena is often of a piece with the wetness of water

and nature's abhorrence of a vacuum. The researches of linguists into the ways of languages many and diverse are needed if we are to think straight and escape the errors which unconscious acceptance of our language background otherwise engenders. An increasing contribution from linguistics to the general philosophy of science is demanded by the new ways of thinking implied by those new realms of science cited at the beginning of this essay. It is needed for science's next great march into the unknown.

The situation is not likely to be aided by the philosophical and mathematical analyst who may try to exploit the field of higher linguistic symbolism with little knowledge of linguistics itself. Unfortunately the essays of most modern writers in this field suffer from this lack of apprenticeship training. To strive at higher mathematical formulas for linguistic meaning while knowing nothing correctly of the shirt-sleeve rudiments of language is to court disaster. Physics does not begin with atomic structures and cosmic rays, but with motions of ordinary gross physical objects and symbolic (mathematical) expressions for these movements. Linguistics likewise does not begin with meaning nor with the structure of logical propositions, but with the obligatory patterns made by the gross audible sounds of a given language and with certain symbolic expressions of its own for these patterns. Out of these relatively simple terms dealing with gross sound patterning are evolved the higher analytical procedures of the science, just as out of the simple experiments and mathematics concerning falling and sliding blocks of wood is evolved all the higher mathematics of physics up into quantum theory. Even the facts of sound patterning are none too simple, but they illustrate the unconscious, obligatory, background phenomena of talking as nothing else can.

For instance, the structural formula for words of one syllable in the English language (Fig. 1) looks rather complicated; yet for a linguistic pattern it is rather simple. In the English-speaking world, every child between the ages of two and five is engaged in learning the pattern expressed by this formula, among many other formulas. By the time the child is six, the formula has

```
                                                                                        C₁C₁ > C₁
        g─l   h     h                  k                        l─b,m,f  k
        k─l   k     k                  t                        m        ks
        s̨     g     g           k─w    l                   w─   s        n          t/d
0, C-n, d  r,  f    f    y(u),s±t  r,s  n   f +V+(ᵃₒ)0,±r, C—h, s─ k l|c  t     θ,± s/z
        e      t    v           p─l    p                   y—o    n j.   d          st/zd
        f─l    d    p                  m                        l,n g    l
        b─l    e    b                  w                        s─  t    n              (over-
                    m                                               d    f               riding
                                                                    s    p               restric-
                                                                          m─pf           tion)

(1) (2)   (3)  (4)  (5)      (6)   (7)      (8)      (9) (10) (11) (12)  (13)  (14)    (15)
```

Figure 1

become ingrained and automatic; even the little nonsense words the child makes up conform to it, exploring its possibilities but venturing not a jot beyond them. At an early age the formula becomes for the child what it is for the adult; no sequence of sounds that deviates from it can even be articulated without the greatest difficulty. New words like "blurb," nonsense words like Lewis Carroll's "mome raths," combinations intended to suggest languages of savages or animal cries, like "glub" and "squonk"—all come out of the mold of this formula. When the youth begins to learn a foreign language, he unconsciously tries to construct the syllables according to his formula. Of course it won't work; the foreign words are built to a formula of their own. Usually the student has a terrible time. Not even knowing that a formula is back of all the trouble, he thinks his difficulty is his own fault. The frustrations and inhibitions thus set up at the start constantly block his attempts to use foreign tongues. Or else he even *hears* by the formula, so that the English combinations that he makes sound to him like real French, for instance. Then he suffers less inhibition and may become what is called a "fluent" speaker of French—bad French!

If, however, he is so fortunate as to have his elementary French taught by a theoretic linguist, he first has the patterns of the English formula explained in such a way that they become semi-conscious, with the result that they lose the binding power over him which custom has given them, though they remain automatic as far as English is concerned. Then he acquires the French patterns without inner opposition, and the time for attaining command of the language is cut to a fraction. To be sure, probably no elementary French is ever taught in this way—at least not in public institutions. Years of time and millions of dollars' worth of wasted educational effort could be saved by the adoption of such methods, but men with the grounding in theoretic linguistics are as yet far too few and are chiefly in the higher institutions.

Let us examine the formula for the English monosyllabic word. It looks mathematical, but it isn't. It is an expression of pattern symbolics, an analytical method that grows out of linguistics and bears to linguistics a relation not unlike that of higher mathematics to physics. With such pattern formulas various operations can be performed, just as mathematical expressions can be added, multiplied, and otherwise operated with; only the operations here are not addition, multiplication, and so on, but are meanings that apply to linguistic contexts. From these operations conclusions can be drawn and experimental attacks directed intelligently at the really crucial points in the welter of data presented by the language under investigation. Usually the linguist does not need to manipulate the formulas on paper but simply performs the symbolic operations in his mind and then says: "The paradigm of Class A verbs can't have been reported right by the previous investigator"; or "Well, well, this language must have alternating stresses, though I couldn't hear them at first"; or "Funny, but *d* and *l* must be variants of the same sound in this language," and so on. Then he investigates by experimenting on a native informant and finds that the conclusion is justified. Pattern-symbolic expressions are exact, as mathematics is, but are not quantitative. They do not refer ultimately to number and dimension, as mathematics does, but to pattern and structure. Nor are they to be confused with theory of groups or with symbolic logic, though they may be in some ways akin.

Returning to the formula, the simplest part of it is the eighth term (the terms are numbered underneath), consisting of a V between plus signs. This means that every English word contains a vowel (not true of all languages). As the V is unqualified by other symbols, any one of the English vowels can occur in the monosyllabic word (not true of all syllables of the polysyllabic

English word). Next we turn to the first term, which is a zero and which means that the vowel may be preceded by nothing; the word may begin with a vowel—a structure impossible in many languages. The commas between the terms mean "or." The second term is *C* minus a long-tailed *n*. This means that a word can begin with any single English consonant except one—the one linguists designate by a long-tailed *n*, which is the sound we commonly write *ng*, as in "hang." This *ng* sound is common at the ends of English words but never occurs at the beginnings. In many languages, such as Hopi, Eskimo, or Samoan, it is a common beginning for a word. Our patterns set up a terrific resistance to articulation of these foreign words beginning with *ng*, but as soon as the mechanism of producing *ng* has been explained and we learn that our inability has been due to a habitual pattern, we can place the *ng* wherever we will and can pronounce these words with the greatest of ease. The letters in the formula thus are not always equivalent to the letters by which we express our words in ordinary spelling but are unequivocal symbols such as a linguist would assign to the sounds in a regular and scientific system of spelling.

According to the third term, which consists of two columns, the word can begin with any consonant of the first column followed by *r*, or with *g*, *k*, *f*, or *b* followed by *l*. The *s* with a wedge over it means *sh*. Thus we have "shred," but not "shled." The formula represents the fact that "shled" is un-English, that it will suggest a Chinese's pronunciation of "shred" or a German's of "sled" (*sl* is permitted by term 7). The Greek theta means *th*; so we have "thread" but not "thled," which latter suggests either a Chinese saying "thread" or a child lisping "sled." But why aren't *tr*, *pr*, and *pl* in this third term? Because they can be preceded by *s* and so belong in term 6. The fourth term similarly means that the word can begin with a consonant of the first column followed by *w*. *Hw* does not occur in all dialects of English; in ordinary spelling it is written backward, *wh*. If the dialect does not have *hw*, it pronounces the spelled *wh* simply as *w*. *Thw* occurs in a few words, like "thwack" and "thwart," and *gw*, oddly enough, only in proper names, like

Gwen or Gwynn. *Kw,* ordinarily spelled *qu,* can have *s* before it and therefore belongs in term 6.

The fifth term indicates that the word may begin with one of the first-column consonants followed by *y,* but only when the vowel of the word is *u;* thus we have words like "hue" (*hyuw*), "cue," "few," "muse." Some dialects have also *tyu, dyu,* and *nyu* (e.g., in "tune," "due," and "new"), but I have set up the formula for the typical dialects of the northern United States which have simple *tu, du, nu* in these words. The sixth term indicates pairs that can commence a word either alone or preceded by *s,* that is, *k, t,* or *p* followed by *r,* also *kw* and *pl* (think of "train," "strain"; "crew," "screw"; "quash," "squash"; "play," "splay"). The seventh term, which means the word can begin with *s* followed by any one of the consonants of the second column, completes the part of the word that can precede its vowel.

The terms beyond the eighth show what comes after the vowel. This portion is rather more complex than the beginning of the word, and it would take too long to explain everything in detail. The general principles of the symbolism will be clear from the preceding explanations. The ninth term, with its zero, denotes that a vowel can end the word if the vowel is *a*—which means (1) the vowel of the article "a" and the exclamation "huh?" and (2) the vowel of "pa," "ma," and the exclamations "ah!" and "bah!"—or the vowel can end the word if it is the *aw* sound, as in "paw," "thaw." In some dialects (eastern New England, southern United States, South British) the vowel ending occurs in words which are *spelled* with *ar,* like "car," "star" (*ka, sta,* in these dialects), but in most of the United States' dialects and in those of Ireland and Scotland these words end in an actual *r.* In eastern New England and South British dialects, but not in southern United States, these words cause a linking *r* to appear before a vowel beginning a following word. Thus for "far off" your Southerner says *fa of;* your Bostonian and your Britisher say *fa rof,* with a liquid initial *r;* but most of the United States says *far of,* with a rolled-back *r.* For some dialects, term 9 would be different, showing another possible final vowel, namely, the peculiar sound which the Middle Westerner may notice in the Bostonian's pronunciation of "fur," "cur," (*fe, ke*) and no doubt may find very queer. This funny sound is common in Welsh, Gaelic, Turkish, Ute, and Hopi, but I am sure Boston did not get it from any of these sources.

Can one-syllable words end in *e, i, o,* or *u*? No, not in English. The words so spelled end in a consonant sound, *y* or *w*. Thus "I," when expressed in formula pattern, is *ay,* "we" is *wiy,* "you" is *yuw,* "how" is *haw,* and so on. A comparison of the Spanish *no* with the English "No!" shows that whereas the Spanish word actually ends with its *o* sound trailing in the air, the English equivalent closes upon a *w* sound. The patterns to which we are habituated compel us to close upon a consonant after most vowels. Hence when we learn Spanish, instead of saying *como no,* we are apt to say *kowmow now;* instead of *si,* we say our own word "see" (*siy*). In French, instead of *si beau,* we are apt to say "see bow."

Term 10 means that *r, w,* or *y* may be interpolated at this point except when the interpolation would result in joining *w* and *y* with each other. Term 11 means that the word may end in any single English consonant except *h;* this exception is most unlike some languages, e.g., Sanskrit, Arabic, Navaho, and Maya, in which many words end in *h.* The reader can figure out terms 12, 13, and 14 if he has stuck so far. A small *c* means *ch* as in "child"; *j* is as in "joy." Term 13, which contains these letters, expresses the possibility of words like "gulch," "bulge," "lunch," and "lounge." Term 14 represents the pattern of words like "health," "width," "eighth," (*eytθ*), "sixth," "xth" (*eksθ*). Although we can say "nth" power or "fth" power, it takes effort to say the unpermitted "sth" power or "hth" power. "Hth" would be symbolized *$*eycθ$, the star meaning that the form does not occur. Term 14, however, allows both *mθ* and *mpf,* the latter in words like "humph" or the recent "oomph" (*umpf*). The elements of term 15 may be added after anything—the *t* and *s* forms after voiceless sounds, the *d* and *z* after voiced sounds. Thus "towns" is *tawnz,* with *wnz* attained by term 10 plus 11 plus 15; whereas "bounce" is *bawns,* with *wns* by 10 plus 12. Some of the combinations resulting in this way are common; others are very rare but still are possible English forms. If Charlie McCarthy should pipe up in his coy way, "Thou oomphst, dost thou not?" or a Shakespearean actor should thunder out, "Thou triumphst!" the reason would be that the formula yields that weird sputter *mpfst* by term 14 plus term 15. Neither Mr. Bergen nor Mr. Shakespeare has any power to vary the formula.

The overriding factor applicable to the whole expression is a prohibition of doubling. Notwithstanding whatever the formula says, the same two consonants cannot be juxtaposed. While by term 15 we can add *t* to "flip" and get "flipt" ("flipped"), we can't add *t* to "hit" and get "hitt." Instead, at the point in the patterns where "hitt" might be expected we find simply "hit" (I hit it yesterday, I flipt it yesterday). Some languages, such as Arabic, have words like "hitt," "fadd," and so on, with both paired consonants distinct. The Creek Indian language permits three, e.g., nnn.

The way the patterns summarized in this formula control the forms of English words is really extraordinary. A new monosyllable turned out, say, by Walter Winchell or by a plugging ad man concocting a name for a new breakfast mush, is struck from this mold as surely as if I pulled the lever and the stamp came down on his brain. Thus linguistics, like the physical sciences, confers the power of prediction. I can predict, within limits, what Winchell will or won't do. He may coin a word "thrub," but he will not coin a word "srub," for the formula cannot produce an *sr*. A different formula indicates that if Winchell invents any word beginning with *th*, like "thell," or "therg," the *th* will have the sound it has in "thin," not the sound it has in "this" or "there." Winchell will not invent a word beginning with this latter sound.

We can wheeze forth the harshest successions of consonants if they are only according to the patterns producing the formula. We easily say "thirds" and "sixths," though "sixth" has the very rough sequence of four consonants, $ks\theta s$. But the simpler "sisths" is against the patterns and so is harder to say. "Glimpst" (glimpsed) has *gl* by term 3, *i* by 8, *mpst* by 12 plus 15. But "dlinpfk" is elminated on several counts: Term 3 allows for no *dl,* and by no possible combination of terms can one get *npfk.* Yet the linguist can say "dlinpfk" as easily as he can say "glimpsed." The formula allows for no final *mb;* so we do not say "lamb" as it is spelled, but as *lam.* "Land," quite parallel but allowed by the formula, trips off our tongues as spelled. It is not hard to see why the "explanation," still found in some serious textbooks, that a language does this or that "for the sake of euphony" is on a par with nature's reputed abhorrence of a vacuum.

The exactness of this formula, typical of hundreds of others, shows that while linguistic formulations are not those of mathematics, they are nevertheless precise. We might bear in mind that this formula, compared with the formulation of some of the English (or other) grammatical patterns that deal with meaning, would appear like a simple sum in addition compared with a page of calculus. It is usually more convenient to treat very complex patterns by successive paragraphs of precise sentences and simpler formulas so arranged that each additional paragraph presupposes the previous ones, than to try to embrace all in one very complex formula.

Linguistics is also an experimental science. Its data result from long series of observations under controlled conditions, which, as they are systematically altered, call out definite, different responses. The experiments are directed by the theoretic body of knowledge, just as with physics or chemistry. They usually do not require mechanical apparatus. In place of apparatus, linguistics uses and develops *techniques.* Experimental need not mean quantitative. Measuring, weighing, and pointer-reading devices are seldom needed in linguistics, for quantity and number play little part in the realm of pattern, where there are no variables but, instead, abrupt alternations from one configuration to another. The mathematical sciences require exact measurement, but what linguistics require is, rather exact "patternment" —an exactness of relation irrespective of dimensions. Quantity, dimension, magnitude, are metaphors since they do not properly belong in this spaceless, relational world. I might use this simile:

Exact measurement of lines and angles will be needed to draw exact squares or other regular polygons, but measurement, however precise, will not help us to draw an exact circle. Yet it is necessary only to discover the principle of the compass to reach by a leap the ability to draw perfect circles. Similarly, linguistics has developed techniques which, like compasses, enable it without any true measurement at all to specify *exactly* the patterns with which it is concerned. Or I might perhaps liken the case to the state of affairs within the atom, where also entities appear to alternate from configuration to configuration rather than to move in terms of measurable positions. As alternants, quantum phenomena must be treated by a method of analysis that substitutes a point in a pattern under a set of conditions for a point in a pattern under another set of conditions—a method similar to that used in analysis of linguistic phenomena.

Physics and chemistry, dealing with inanimate matter, require chiefly inanimate apparatus and substances for their experiments. As conducted today upon a large scale, they require highly wrought physical equipment at every step, immense investments in physical plant. Their experiments are costly to conduct, both absolutely and relatively to the number of scientists. Experimental biology uses much inanimate apparatus, too, but its fundamental apparatus is its experimental animals and plants and their food, housing, and growth facilities. These also are expensive in the quantities needed. No one grudges the expense, either here or in the physical sciences, so long as an increase in human knowledge and welfare is promised.

The apparatus of linguistics is much less expensive than that of these sciences, but it, too, costs money. The experimental linguist, like the biologist, uses and must have experimental animals. Only, his "animals" are human. They are his informants and must be paid for working with him. Sometimes he must make trips to Indian reservations or African villages where his informants live; at other times it is more economical to transport them to him. They provide the field for experimental investigation. They are apparatus, not teachers. It is as important to study in this way languages of Indians, Africans, and other aborigines as it is to study the English dialects of Brooklyn, Boston, Richmond, or London.

While informants are the basic apparatus, the linguist can improve and speed up his work with the aid of mechanical tools, just as the biologist studies his animals and plants with the aid of microscopes, x-ray machines, and other costly instruments. The linguist is aided by judicious use of good phonographic reproducing devices. Much could also be done with the help of business machines.

Although linguistics is a very old science, its modern experimental phase, which stresses the analysis of unwritten speech, could be called one of the newest. So far as our knowledge goes, the science of linguistics was founded, or put on its present basis, by one Panini in India several centuries before Christ. Its earliest form anticipated its most recent one. Panini was highly algebraic, i.e., pattern symbolic, in his treatment; he used formulas in a very modern way for expressing the obligatory patterns of Sanskrit. It was the Greeks who debased the science. They showed how infinitely inferior they were to the Hindus as scientific thinkers, and the effect of their muddling lasted two thousand years. Modern scientific linguistics dates from the rediscovery of Panini by the Western world in the early Nineteenth Century.

Yet linguistics is still in its infancy so far as concerns wherewithal for its needed equipment, its supply of informants, and the minimum of tools, books, and the like. Money for mechanical aids, such as I referred to above, is at present only a happy dream. Perhaps this condition results from lack of the publicity the other sciences receive and, after all, fairly earn. We all know now that the forces studied by physics, chemistry, and biology are powerful and important. People generally do not yet know that the forces studied by linguistics are powerful and important, that its principles control every sort of agreement and understanding among human beings, and that sooner or later it will have to sit as judge while the other sciences bring their results to its court to inquire into what they mean. When this time comes, there will be great and well-equipped laboratories of linguistics as there are of other exact sciences.

CHARLES C. FRIES

A Classification of Grammatical Phenomena

In the attempt to gather, analyze, and record the significant facts from any such mass of material as the specimens here examined, one cannot depend upon general impressions and note only the special forms that attract attention. If he does, the unusual forms and constructions or those that differ from his own practice will inevitably impress him as bulking much larger in the total than they really are. Those forms and constructions that are in harmony with the great mass of English usage will escape his notice. This seems to me to be a fundamental difficulty with the earlier editions of Mencken's *The American Language* and accounts in part for the difference between his representations of "The Common Speech" and the results given here. Mencken, for example, prints in the 1924 edition of his book the "Declaration of Independence in American," as one of his "Specimens of the American Vulgate" or, as he says, "translated into the language they use every day." [1]

> When things get so balled up that the people of a country have to cut loose from some other country, and go it on their own hook, without asking no permission from nobody, excepting maybe God Almighty, then they ought to let everybody know why they done it, so that everybody can see they are on the level, and not trying to put nothing over on nobody.
>
> All we got to say on this proposition is this: first, you and

. . . .

me is as good as anybody else, and maybe a damn sight better; second, nobody ain't got no right to take away none of our rights; every man has got a right to live, to come and go as he pleases, and to have a good time however he likes, so long as he don't interfere with nobody else. That any government that don't give a man these rights ain't worth a damn; also, people ought to choose the kind of government they want themselves, and nobody else ought to have no say in the matter.

In the 176 words here quoted there are, for example, five uses of the multiple negative. Every negative statement except one has two or three negative particles. This excessive use of the multiple negative construction cannot be found in any actual specimens of Vulgar English. Even in Old English, where the use of the double negative was normal, less than 35 per cent of the total negative statements occur with multiple negative particles. Such a complete use of the multiple negative construction as Mencken displays will only be heard from those who consciously attempt to caricature Vulgar English. Most of the comic writers produce their language effects in similar fashion by seizing upon a few such especially noticeable or spectacular forms and expressions of Vulgar English and then working them excessively. Such representations of Vulgar English become grossly inaccurate both because the amount of deviation from the standard forms is greatly exaggerated and also because many of the forms characteristic of Vulgar English that are not sufficiently picturesque to be funny are completely ignored.[2]

In order to avoid errors of this kind we have in the study of this material tried first to record *all* the facts in each category examined. For example, every preterit and past participle form was copied on a separate slip of paper in order that we might determine not only the kind of variety that existed in actual usage but also something of the relative amounts of that variation. In similar fashion all instances with forms expressing number in verbs and in demonstratives used attributively as well as in substantives were gathered to form the basis of the summaries we offer concerning concord in number. We do not assume that the absolute frequency of occurrence of particular forms in the limited material here examined is in itself significant; we have simply tried to make sure of the *relative* frequency of the language usages appearing here in order to give proportion to our picture of actual practice and to prevent a false emphasis upon unusual or picturesquely interesting items.

This approach to the gathering and analysis of the language facts to be observed in our material made necessary some system of classification by which those facts of essentially similar nature should be inevitably brought together. We were seeking to record as completely as possible the methods used by the English language to express grammatical ideas and to discover the precise differences in these methods as employed by the various social dialects. The outlines of our grouping quite naturally settled themselves. The facts gathered in an early preliminary study of our material all fitted into a classification made up of three general types of devices to express grammatical ideas.

First of all there were the *forms* of words. The way in which the word *tables* differs from the word *table* indicates one grammatical idea; the way in which *roasted* differs from *roast*, or *grew* from *grow* expresses another; and the way in which *harder* differs from *hard* shows another. These examples illustrate the expression of grammatical ideas by the *forms* of words. Other ideas, however, are also shown by word forms as *truth* differing from *true*, or *kindness* from *kind*, or *rapidly* from *rapid*, or *stigmatize* from *stigma*, or *national* from *nation*, or *writer* from *write*. These latter derivational forms will not be included here although it is difficult to draw an exact line between them and the grammatical forms with which we are especially concerned. It is enough for our purpose to point out that most of these derivational forms are, in Present-day English, chiefly vocabulary or word-formation matters rather than inflectional matters and that we have limited our study to grammatical structure and have excluded vocabulary. But these "forms of words" as we shall use them are interpreted broadly to include even entirely different words as *we* or *me* or *us* in relation to *I*, *went* in relation to *go*, and *worse* in relation to *bad*.[3]

Second, there were the uses of *function* words. These words frequently have very little meaning apart from the grammatical relationship they express. Examples are *of* in "A house *of* stone," or *with* in "He struck the animal *with* a rod," or *more* in "A *more* important battle," or *have* in "They *have* had their reward," or *going* in "He is *going* to go to New York." Many of the grammatical ideas formerly expressed by the *forms* of words are now expressed by such function words.

Third, there were the uses of *word order*. Word order is often an important item of the idiom of a language, but it is not always a grammatical device as it is in English. In Latin, for example, the periodic structure with the verb at the end occurs very frequently, but the word order in such a sentence as "Nero hominem interfecit" has nothing whatever to do with indicating the so-called "subject" and "object." The basic meaning of the Latin sentence remains unchanged with every possible order of these three words. In English, however, "Nero killed the man" and "The man killed Nero" express very different ideas and that difference comes to us solely through the order in which the words are placed. Some of the grammatical ideas formerly expressed in English by the forms of words are now expressed by *word order*.

All the language facts gathered from the letters here examined were classified in one of these three groups—the uses of the forms of words, the uses of function words, or the uses of word order—and there studied. In respect to each group the description will first set forth the practice of Group I or "standard" English and then indicate the deviations from that practice, characteristic of Group III, or of Group II and Group III combined. Some of the significance of these language facts will, however, be best revealed by showing them in relation to similar situations as they appeared in older stages of the English language, for even complete statistics of the relative frequency of two alternative forms in any single period of language history can never give us a guide as to the relative importance of those forms or the direction of change. For such purposes the statistics must be viewed in relation to the situation in a previous or in a later period. For example, if we were living at the close of the first quarter of the fifteenth century, the bare fact that the alternative pronoun forms *them* and *hem* were used with a relative frequency of approximately 20 per cent of *them* to 80 per cent of *hem* would tell us little without the knowledge that *hem* was the form that was being superseded and that the tendency to use *them* in its place had already progressed one fifth of the way along which the forms *they* and *their* had already gone much farther. In the effort therefore to make clear the significance of the records of contemporary English which formed the basis of this study it will frequently be necessary to picture the present usage against the background of the practice in older stages of the language. We shall try always to deal with the patterns of the language to which particular forms belong and to show the path along which these patterns have developed.

It will be clearly evident as we proceed that the three general types of grammatical processes in accord with which our language material has been classified and are not now and have not been in the history of the English language thoroughly coordinate or of equal value. As a matter of fact any one of the three could have served quite adequately all necessary grammatical needs. Instead, they overlap in the expression of grammatical ideas and in some respects may be said to compete for the expression of the same ideas. The function-word method and the word-order method of expressing dative and accusative relationships have, for example, almost entirely displaced the inflectional method. In the early stages of the language there is no doubt that the use of the forms of words as a grammatical process was much more important than the grammatical uses of either word order or of function words. Some of the problems of usage in Present-day English arise where there is such a so-called conflict between two types of grammatical processes for the expression of a single grammatical idea. While, therefore, we shall classify and describe our language details in accord with the demands of each of the three types of grammatical processes indicated above, it will be necessary to discuss them in relation to the historical patterns with which they are connected and sometimes to refer to the use of a competing type of grammatical process for the expression of the same idea. . . .

NOTES

1. H. L. Mencken, *The American Language* (New York, Alfred A. Knopf, 3rd ed., 1924), p. 398. See, however, the following quotation from the 4th edition, 1936, Preface, p. vii: "I have also omitted a few illustrative oddities appearing in that edition [the 3rd edition]—for example, specimens of vulgar American by Ring W. Lardner and John V. A. Weaver and my own translations of the Declaration of Independence and Lincoln's Gettysburg Address. The latter two, I am sorry to say, were mistaken by a number of outraged English critics for examples of Standard American, or of what I proposed that Standard American should be. Omitting them will get rid of that misapprension. . . ."

2. See also Professor Robert J. Menner's comments in his article "The Verbs of the Vulgate," *American Speech*, January, 1926, pp. 230–231. Concerning *The American Language* he says, "but Mencken seems to have gathered his forms from all kinds of sources, oral and written; it is impossible to distinguish those he has observed personally from those he has found in contemporary writers of comic stories. Furthermore, he gives the impression of preferring to record as characteristic of the common speech whatever is furthest removed from the language of literature. . . ."

Part of Professor Menner's remarks concerning the accuracy of the writers of comic stories follows: "Ring Lardner . . . employs only forms of the verb which are familiar, or at least conceivable, in colloquial speech. But he besprinkles the conversation of his characters with barbarisms much more plentifully and consistently than they occur in actual life. This is the inevitable exaggeration of comic art. 'He win 10 bucks,' is funnier than 'He won 10 bucks,' and Mr. Lardner now uses the preterite *win* almost consistently, though, according to my observation of oral practice, it is used, even in class D, only once out of ten times."

3. For a thorough analysis of the problem involved here see Leonard Bloomfield, *Language* (New York, Henry Holt and Co., 1933), pp. 207–246. On pages 222 and 223 occur the following statements: ". . . The structure of a complex word reveals first, as to the more immediate constituents, an outer layer of *inflectional* constructions, and then an inner layer of constructions of *word-formation*. In our last example [the word *actresses*], the outer, inflectional layer is represented by the construction of actress with [-ez], and the inner word formational layer by the remaining constructions, of *actor* with -*ess* and of *act* with [-r]. . . . Another peculiarity of inflection, in contrast with word-formation, is the rigid parallelism of underlying and resultant forms. Thus, nearly all English singular nouns underlie a derived plural noun, and, vice versa, nearly all English plural nouns are derived from a singular noun. Accordingly, English nouns occur, for the most part in parallel *sets of two;* a singular noun (*hat*) and a plural noun derived

from the former (*hats*). Each such set of forms is called a *paradigmatic* set or *paradigm*, and each form in the set is called an *inflected form* or *inflection* . . . It is this parallelism also, which leads us to view entirely different phonetic forms, like *go: went,* as morphologically related (by suppletion): *go* as an infinitive (parallel, say, with *show*) and *went* as a past-tense form (parallel, then, with *showed*)."

DONA WORRALL BROWN, WALLACE C. BROWN,
AND DUDLEY BAILEY

Grammar in a New Key

Probably the most important single fact about ordinary language
is that it also has two kinds of symbols, both of which work
together to express the total meaning of any utterance. This fact
is not widely known; yet, if the basic distinction between these
two ways of expressing meaning is not fully understood, it is
impossible to understand the nature of grammar. These two kinds
of symbols we shall call the "vocabulary" elements and the
"grammatical" elements. The vocabulary elements include the
thousands and thousands of words or parts of words that can be
found, not in sentences, but in random lists, dictionaries, spelling-
books, and the glossary sections of foreign-language textbooks.
Following is a brief list of this kind:

table	happy	soon
walk	throw	mis-
street	apple	un-

This part of the language is often called our vocabulary. The
first kind of language that a child learns is in this area—such
words as: *mamma, bottle, baby,* and *dolly.* As children grow up
and expand this knowledge, they are said to have increased their
vocabulary. And when we do not understand the meaning of
one of these symbols, we usually look it up in a dictionary. There

. . . .

From *Form in Modern English.* © 1958 by Oxford University Press, Inc.
Reprinted by permission.

we find "definitions" of what the symbol stands for in the non-language world. The study of the relationship between these kinds of symbols and their meanings is sometimes called "semantics."

The second kind of symbol—the grammatical symbol—differs basically from the vocabulary symbol, and in describing this difference we shall find the analogy with mathematics most useful. Like the "signs" in mathematics, all grammatical symbols have one thing in common: they do not represent directly the ideas that they stand for. Rather, they operate like a system of shorthand, or like a code, for which the study of grammar provides a cipher or key. For example, when we want to use a grammatical symbol to add the idea of "past time" to a word, such as *walk* in the list above, we do not say or write "walk in the past." Instead, we use the shorthand-like symbol *-ed*, which stands for "earlier than," just as the mathematical symbol $>$ stands for "greater than." Again, we might take the vocabulary symbol *chair*. If we wished to add to this word the idea of "more than one," it is almost certain that we would say *chairs*. When this form of the word is used, the idea of more-than-oneness has not been expressed by vocabulary means (we have not said "more than one"): we have used instead a grammatical symbol, the simple letter *-s*, which is a kind of shorthand for the idea of "more than one."

To illustrate this point in a more complex way, following is a list of vocabulary elements which might appear in a simple sentence:

1. Henry   3. build
2. house   4. old

And let us suppose that we want to express these additional ideas:

5. that *old* qualifies our idea of the man Henry,
6. that *build* expresses an assertion,
7. that the building is continuing at the present time,
8. that Henry is the builder,
9. that the result of the building is the house,
10. that there is a only one house,
11. and that a completed statement is intended.

The resulting sentence would be:

> Old Henry is building a house.

What makes it possible to condense all of these complex ideas into six words? The answer, of course, is grammar: in the sentence above the ideas numbered 5–11 have been translated into the code of grammatical "signs." By using a different set of such signs with the four words which convey the vocabulary meaning —*Henry, house, build,* and *old*—it would be possible to express some very different ideas, such as:

> An old building housed Henry.

The nature of the grammatical symbols can be revealed most dramatically when the vocabulary elements in a sentence are blanked out and only the grammatical symbols are expressed. Following are a few sentences of this kind:

> A——al——will be——en about our——into—s.
> Do——ed——s——ly——at the——ion?
> This——of——'s——s that——are——ing to the——s.

These sentences would probably be "Greek" to most people. Actually, they are full of meaning, but it is a kind of meaning which is mysterious to the uninitiated precisely because of the fact that the grammatical elements are a type of code symbol. Now the question arises: How does one find the key to the meanings in this kind of sentence? As a rule, we do not consult a dictionary, although a few of these symbols are explained there. The only way fully to understand them is, of course, through the study of grammar. This brings us back to the question posed at the beginning of this chapter: What is grammar? After what has been said, the answer must be: GRAMMAR IS THE STUDY OF A SYSTEM OF LANGUAGE CODE SYMBOLS AND THE MEANINGS THAT THESE SYMBOLS EXPRESS. This grammatical apparatus is called the "structure" of the language, and the kind of grammar that describes it is called "structural grammar."

There are three types of grammatical symbols, which both the spoken and written language have in common. These are called the "major grammatical devices." The first, and least well known, is the device of WORD ORDER, which involves the fixed position of the words in a sentence; second, and best known, is the device of INFLECTION, which involves changes in the spelling and pronunciation of a word; the third is the FUNCTION WORD, a kind of grammatical word, which differs basically from the vocabulary words described above.[1] Punctuation, which of course is used only in the written language, may also be considered a grammatical device, but it is a minor one, because the uses of the various marks of punctuation are not completely standardized in modern English, and therefore cannot always be depended on to convey grammatical meaning with complete exactness.

The meanings expressed by these grammatical devices, in contrast to those expressed by any one of the vocabulary symbols, are the most frequently used ideas. A person probably would not mention the vocabulary symbols *chair, house, build,* or *old* more than once or twice a day under ordinary circumstances, and *Henry* would probably get into the conversation even less often unless a gentleman of that name were a close friend or relative. But the ideas of "performer of an action," "time of an action," "result of an action," "qualification," "how many?" and other ideas usually expressed in our language by grammatical symbols are used by everyone hundreds of times a day. Because these symbols are in such frequent use, it is very convenient that they can be expressed by the shorthand-like method of the grammatical devices instead of the more cumbersome longhand of the vocabulary elements. If we did not have grammar, our plight would be almost as ridiculous as that of the Laputians in *Gulliver's Travels,* who, disdaining language altogether, insisted on carrying around with them all the things they expected to talk about during the day!

In other respects, however, these two areas of meaning do not differ significantly. One cannot take a list of ideas and sort them into two distinct columns, one marked "vocabulary" and the other marked "grammatical." Distinctions between them can be made only according to the means by which they are expressed in a given sentence—whether by a vocabulary symbol or a grammatical symbol. This point is borne out by the fact that in any language there is a borderline area in which certain ideas may be expressed by either type of symbol. In English, for example, the idea of something happening in the future may be, and usually is, expressed by a grammatical symbol. When we say, "She will go,' we use a special grammatical word (*will*) to express this idea. But futurity may also be expressed by vocabulary means: we may say, "She goes tomorrow." Here we have expressed the idea by using the word *tomorrow,* an idea which the grammatical form of the verb (*goes*) does not express at all. Again, more-than-oneness is usually expressed grammatically in English: in "We have miles to go," the *-s* added to *mile* is the grammatical sign of more-than-oneness. On the other hand, in the phrase "many a mile" the idea of plurality is expressed not by a grammatical device but by the vocabulary element *many.*

Furthermore, languages vary among themselves as to what meanings should be expressed by grammatical symbols. The Alaskan Eskimo language, for example, has separate grammatical forms to express tense in nouns, as have a number of American Indian languages. One African language is said to have a grammatical method for expressing the idea of "squareness"! And in its earliest period, our own English language (Old English) had a separate grammatical form for expressing the idea of "twoness" (duality) in pronouns as distinct from "oneness" and "more than twoness" (plurality). Modern English, of course, has no way of expressing any of these ideas by means of grammatical devices. *

A surprisingly large number of people raise the question: Why should one study grammar at all? The whole problem of the nature of grammar and the desirability of teaching it was informally and excellently discussed by Mr. E. B. White in a 1957 issue of *The New Yorker* magazine. After remarking that English usage has become "hot news," Mr. White continues:

> Through the turmoil and the whirling waters [of usage] we have reached a couple of opinions of our own about the language. One is that a schoolchild should be taught grammar—for

* I do not understand.

the same reason that a medical student should study anatomy. Having learned about the exciting mysteries of an English sentence, the child can then go forth and speak and write any damn way he pleases. We knew a countryman once who spoke with wonderful vigor and charm, but ungrammatically. In him the absence of grammar made little difference, because his speech was full of juice. But when a dullard speaks in a slovenly way, his speech suffers not merely from dullness but from ignorance, and his whole life, in a sense, suffers— though he may not feel pain.

The living language is like a cowpath: it is the creation of the cows themselves, who, having created it, follow it or depart from it according to their whims or their needs. From daily use, the path undergoes change. A cow is under no obligation to stay in the narrow path she helped make, following the contour of the land, but she often profits by staying with it and she would be handicapped if she didn't know where it was and where it led to. Children obviously do not depend for communication on a knowledge of grammar; they rely on their ear, mostly, which is sharp and quick. But we have yet to see the child who hasn't profited from coming face to face with a relative pronoun at an early age, and from reading books, which follow the paths of centuries.[2]

Actually, everyone agrees that all civilized people have standards of speech and writing and that the teaching of these standards is an important part of education. In the basic college composition course, for example, all students are expected to know and use the acceptable grammatical forms, and anyone would probably feel cheated if he were not helped in these matters. He is also expected to learn a great deal about the intricate business of putting words, phrases, clauses, and marks of punctuation in their proper places in order to form effective and unambiguous structures of communication. And these are all matters of grammar. For the past two hundred years many "rules" have been passed down from generation to generation, which are supposed to solve these problems. Most of these rules are familiar to students even before they come to college. They have been told, for example, that "the form of the verb must agree with its subject in person and number," that "a pronoun must be in the objective case form if it is the object of a verb or preposition," and that "adjective phrases must not dangle." Rules of this kind are important, of course; but it is often not realized that they cannot even be understood unless or until a great deal is first known about "the exciting mysteries of an English sentence" to which the *New Yorker* article refers.

One of the most serious obstacles to good writing is the tendency to compose confusing sentences, especially sentences that have double meanings (ambiguities). Most people know about such problems, but few people realize that they are problems in grammar—that bad sentences of this kind are caused by a misunderstanding of the modern English system of grammar. The following sentences are simple examples of this kind of grammatical confusion:

> He gave her dog biscuits.
> The visitors were drinking in the open air.
> He loved racing horses.
> Ask Mr. Smith who is sitting by the window.
> Clara Schumann was too busy to compose herself.

Unless they are being intentionally humorous, people write sentences like these because they are not aware that they have allowed another meaning, beyond the one they intended, to intrude. And it takes a considerable insight into the subject of grammar to see why this has happened.

In general, these difficulties are caused by a lack of awareness of the fact that the written language, in contrast to the spoken language, has grammatical deficiencies which make written communication difficult and invite ambiguities and confusions. What most people do not realize is that the spoken language has a large battery of very effective grammatical symbols that are lacking in the written language. They include, first, the various kinds of vocal intonations, such as stress and pitch. For example, we usually indicate a declarative sentence by a drop in the voice pitch, whereas at the end of a question the voice usually rises. Running words together without a pause and making an extra long pause are also important grammatical devices. Even gestures and facial expressions may clarify the meaning of a spoken utterance. These devices are usually in a writer's mind as he composes sentences, but he too often forgets that the reader, unlike the listener, cannot hear or see them, and he therefore does not make his meaning clear. The first sentence above—"He gave her dog biscuits"—is a good illustration of this kind of failure on the part of a writer. This sentence would not be ambiguous at all when spoken, for the devices of pitch and stress would make the meaning clear, but in the written language it has two meanings: (1) he gave biscuits to her dog, and (2) he gave dog biscuits to her. The writer of this sentence undoubtedly "heard" a distinct stress and pitch pattern which expressed the meaning he intended—but, alas, his reader could not.

The process of learning to write with clarity and emphasis involves (among other things, of course) knowing how to use the relatively limited number of written devices that must take the place of the missing spoken ones. In the sentence about the dog biscuits, for example, a careful writer could have found several ways to clarify the meaning. For one thing, the words *the* or *some* (both very powerful grammatical symbols) used in the right sentence position, would have eliminated the ambiguity:

> He gave her dog *the* (or *some*) biscuits.
> He gave her *the* (or *some*) dog biscuits.

NOTES

1. For this threefold division of the major grammatical devices, we are indebted to Charles Carpenter Fries, *American English Grammar* (New York, 1940).

2. From an article by E. B. White, © 1957, *The New Yorker*, Inc.

DONA WORRALL BROWN, WALLACE C. BROWN,
AND DUDLEY BAILEY

Grammatical Distribution

. . . In modern English sentences the words tend to fall into
recognizable patterns. We tend to use certain words in certain
places and never in others; we tend to change the forms of some
words in one way and of others in another; and we tend to use
some words with other words and never with still others. Thus
the student of language soon learns to anticipate some combinations of words and to doubt that he will find others. In this
respect he is like the geologist on a prospecting trip, who knows
that certain metals always appear together in the earth. Along
with uranium, he would expect to find lead and a group of rare
and newly discovered metals. He knows that he will likely find
gold and silver together, copper with arsenic and zinc, bromine
with chlorine, sodium with potassium, and magnesium with
calcium. On the other hand, he would be greatly surprised to
find silver or copper with uranium, or platinum with sulphur.

In short, all analysts observe a principle of distribution in their
fields: some of the elements they deal with may be expected only
in certain places and with certain accompaniments; others will be
found in others. When we come to words in sentences, we find
that they have their own kind of distribution. We find that some
words are found only in certain places with a limited group of
other words; and still other words are found only in very different
contexts. Certain words are capable of a set of inflectional changes
which other words cannot undergo. Some words are limited to a
. . . .

From *Form in Modern English*. © 1958 by Oxford University Press, Inc.
Reprinted by permission.

single place or context; others are able to function in various places and to assume various forms.

Some examples makes this clear. Let us consider the two italicized words in the following sentences:

> They *manage* a movie theater.
> The firm changed *management*.

If these words are considered only from the point of view of their vocabulary meaning, it would be natural to group them together, since both have to do with the idea of "managing." But if they are considered from another point of view, it is clear that they are very different and cannot be grouped together at all. First, it is obvious that they have different spellings: the word *management* has a *-ment* suffix, which *manage* does not. Second, their respective positions in the two sentences cannot be interchanged. Third, a *-d* inflection could be added to *manage* in order to change the time of the action, but this could not be done to *management*. On the other hand, an *-s* could be added to *management* to change the number of the word, which could not be done to *manage* to express this same idea. Fourth, *management* may be preceded by the word *the*, but *manage* cannot. By substituting other words for *manage* in this sentence, such as *own*, *operate*, *pass*, or *want*, it can be demonstrated that there are many other words which may use the same set of devices as *manage*, so we may assume that all these words belong to the same kind of group. There is also a large number of words that could be substituted for *management*, such as *foreman*, *director*, or *location*. These, clearly, belong to a second kind of group. These differences and similarities indicate a distinctive way of "distributing" words, and the categories formed by this kind of distribution are called the "parts of speech."

From the examples above, it is clear that words are distributed as one part of speech or another, according to the grammatical devices used with them. In other words, each part of speech has a unique combination, or grouping, of grammatical devices that distinguishes it from other parts of speech. The words "combination" and "grouping" should be emphasized, since each part of speech has a rather large number of grammatical devices which may be associated with it. It is too bad that this is true, for grammar would surely be an easier subject if each part of speech were marked by one special device, such as a circle written over the word, or an *x* written below it. Instead, one part of speech may have as many as a dozen grammatical signs, some of which may be connected with it in one context or another. For example, it is possible for one part of speech to appear in six different positions in the sentence, to have four different inflected forms, and three types of function words. In most instances, it is only by using a combination of these devices that the word may be established as a specific part of speech.

In a given sentence, of course, a word will not be accompanied by all the possible devices that mark it as a certain part of speech, but by a selection from them. Usually two or three will be sufficient. For example, in the sentence

<blockquote>The trumpets will play the finale</blockquote>

trumpets is established as a noun by three devices: one word-order device, one inflection, and one function word; *play* is established as a verb by two devices: one word order and one function word. Sometimes, however, only one device is expressed. This is true of the word *manage* (in the example on page 207), which is established as a verb by word order alone. Since it is possible for a part of speech to be indicated by this one device, some words that belong to different parts-of-speech groups often look confusingly alike. This is true of the word *yellow* in the following sentences:

<blockquote>

Yellow is my favorite color. (noun)

Newspapers *yellow* with age. (verb)

I like my *yellow* dress. (adjective)

</blockquote>

It is often regarded as a grammatical curiosity that there are a few apparently identical words that may appear in sentences as five different parts of speech. *Round* is one of these:

<blockquote>

The last *round* was the best of all.

The *round* package was for George.

We *round* the corner on two wheels.

The carousel went *round* and *round*.

The bandit fled *round* the corner.

</blockquote>

All these *rounds* are spelled and pronounced alike; they all derive from the same word, the Latin *rotundus*, meaning "wheel-shaped." But from the point of view of grammar, these *rounds* are not alike at all. The first one is a noun, the second an adjective, the third a verb, the fourth an adverb, and the last a preposition. These words appear to be alike only because the device of inflection has not been used with them in these sentences. Other types of devices, however, are clearly expressed and it is these devices that establish such words as different parts of speech.

When a word is changed from one part of speech to another by means of a change in one or more of the three major grammatical devices, and by this means alone, this operation is called FUNCTIONAL SHIFT. Modern English uses this method very frequently. Words such as *garden, fear, paper, salt, price, smoke, dawn, wash, contact,* and *base,* to mention only a few, are shifted about freely in ordinary usage from noun to verb to adjective and vice versa, merely by changing the grammatical devices. The three "gardens" in the following sentence illustrate this kind of shift:

We shall *garden* with *garden* tools in the *garden.*

This means that, contrary to what many people think, there is seldom anything in the vocabulary meaning of the word that limits it to one part of speech. Words that have been "defined" for us as "nouns" often turn out to be verbs, and similarly, "verbs" often are really nouns: we read that a man has *authored* a book or *chairmaned* a committee, that his hand has the *trembles,* or that he has been to a *steak fry,* or that he has been given an *assist.* In a sense the vocabulary part of a word is like an all-purpose tool, which has many different uses, depending on the attachments (the grammatical devices) used with it at any special time.

For this reason, there is little use in learning "definitions" of the parts of speech that are based on meaning. Since words shift about from one part of speech to another in such Protean fashion, no definition of this kind can be devised that is not full of holes. For example, the usual definition of a noun is that it "is the name of a person, place, or thing." But *red* is the name of a color, *north* the name of a direction, and *cement* the name of a material; yet an examination of the grammatical devices connected with these words in the following sentences will reveal that none of them are nouns:

> The *red* balloon burst, and my face turned *red*.
> We drove *north* into the *north* end of the city.
> This system of *cement* highways will *cement* friendly relations between the two countries.

Similarly, the definition of a verb—that it expresses action—might lead one to think that the word *walk* in the sentence *We went for a walk,* is a verb; but the grammatical symbols show that this word is not a verb but a noun.

While functional shift is probably the most common method used in modern English for converting a word from one part of speech to another, there is another more traditional method that is also used. This involves the use of a special kind of prefix or suffix. We could, for example, have made *round* into an adjective by using, in addition to one or more of the three major grammatical devices, the suffix *-ish:* "The *roundish* package is for mother." Or we could have used the prefix *a-* to convey the idea that *round* is either an adverb or a preposition.

> The carousel went *around* and *around*.
> The bandit fled *around* the corner.

Similarly, in our sentences on page 207 the suffix *-ment* was used to help convert the verb *manage* into a noun. Also *-er* could have been used for the same purpose. There are literally hundreds of these prefixes and suffixes, but two or three more examples will be enough to show how they operate. Some nouns and adjectives may be changed into verbs by adding the suffixes *-ize* or *-en: standard* to *standardize, rational* to *rationalize, strength* to *strengthen, weak* to *weaken,* etc. A noun may be made into an adjective by using the suffixes *-y* or *-al: dirt* to *dirty, condition* to *conditional.* And most adjectives may be changed into adverbs by adding *-ly: perfect—perfectly, smooth—smoothly, proud—*

proudly, etc. More than one suffix is often used at once. The word *nationalization* contains three of these: *-al, -iza,* and *-tion.*

At first sight, these prefixes and suffixes seem to be very much like the forms which we called inflections earlier; and in one way they are, for, like inflections, they express variations in grammatical ideas by changes in the spelling of words. But there is one very important difference: unlike true inflections, these prefixes and suffixes are not removable. Once added, they become a permanent part of the vocabulary meaning of the word. For this reason we shall call them "permanent" forms. The word *standardize,* a verb form, illustrates this point. This word retains the *-ize* ending under all circumstances, whether it is in the present tense form (*standardizes*), for example, or the past tense form (*standardized*). The regular inflections used in this example are, by contrast, removable elements (the *-s* may be put on or taken off or it may be changed to *-ed*), which are added to the permanent forms, just as they may be added to any other word used as a verb. In a sense, the endings that are used to create the permanent forms are like the plaster that helps to characterize an enclosure as a room; the plaster is a permanent part of the room. The inflections are more like the furnishings which may be added or taken away, depending on whether we want to create the effect of a formal living room, a recreation room, or a study.

As we shall see later, these permanent forms are not an absolute sign that a word is a given part of speech, any more than plaster is an absolute sign that an enclosure is a room. In most instances where prefixes or suffixes are used, at least one of the three major grammatical devices is needed in addition to the permanent ending to establish the function of the word. Furthermore, this method of forming parts of speech is used less frequently today than it was in earlier periods of the language. We are more inclined today to let the major grammatical devices do the work for us. Also the major devices are always more important in establishing grammatical meaning; for, whenever the idea conveyed by them is in conflict with the idea indicated by the permanent form, it is the devices that determine the grammatical meaning of the word. For example, the word *desperation* in the expression *desperation measure* has the permanent form of the noun, but its position before a noun is one of the major grammatical devices that indicates that a word is an adjective, and it is this latter device that determines the part of speech.

All of these things will become much clearer as we progress . . . . It is enough for us to know at this point that there are two ways of marking a given word as a part of speech: first, by the use of the three major grammatical devices; second, by the use of the permanent forms.

About nine hundred years ago an English monk divided the parts of speech into eight groups. These are as follows:

> The verb (from the Latin *verbum,* meaning "the word," which suggests that this part of speech is very important).
> The noun (from the Latin *nomen,* meaning "a name" for something).
> The pronoun (from the Latin *pronomen,* meaning "for a name," that is, a word used in place of a noun).
> The preposition (from the Latin *praepositio, meaning* "place before").
> The adjective (from the Latin *adjectivus,* meaning "added to").
> The adverb (from the Latin *adverbium,* meaning "next to the verb").
> The conjunction (from the Latin *conjunctus,* meaning "joined with").
> The interjection (from the Latin *interjectus,* meaning "thrown between").

This is not the only way words have been divided to indicate differences in their grammatical form and meaning. During the many centuries that English grammar has been studied, many different groupings have been suggested, groupings with as few as three and as many as eighteen parts of speech. Actually, it is impossible to work out a perfect system. Even the traditional one of eight parts has its weaknesses. For one thing, there are many instances of overlapping among the eight different groups: a word may have devices characteristic of more than one part of speech. For example, it may show verb inflection and adjective word order. More than one part of speech may also use the same inflection or pattern of word order. In spite of such weaknesses, this eight-part system, because of its familiarity to everyone, is probably the best one.

Of these eight parts of speech, the verb, the noun, the pronoun, the adjective, the adverb, and the interjection carry the main burden of the vocabulary meaning. Prepositions and conjunctions are mainly function words. . . .

HAROLD WHITEHALL

The System of Punctuation

The traditional purpose of punctuation is to symbolize by means
of visual signs the patterns heard in speech. Grammarians of
the eighteenth century, strongly conscious of pause but little observant of tone and juncture, thought that the comma indicated
pause for a time count of one, the semicolon for a time count
of two, the colon for a time count of three, and the period
for a time count of four. Nowadays, we know that pause is
simply pause, that pause is often optional, and that when present
it combines with preceding junctures to build up what may be
regarded as an audible punctuation of words, word-groups, and
sentences when we are speaking. To these combinations of speech
phenomena, the common punctuation marks of writing (.), (?),
(;), (—), (,) bear a correlation which is at best only approximate.
Moreover, modern English punctuation has become an intricate
system of conventions, some logical, some indicating separations
or connections of context, all of crucial practical importance. Its
most important purpose is "to make grammar graphic." As a
kind of visual configurational feature of grammar, punctuation
cannot be properly understood unless the other grammatical
features of the language are also understood.

Punctuation is employed in the following functions:

a. To *link* sentences and parts of words.
b. To *separate* sentences and parts of sentences.
c. To *enclose* parts of sentences.
d. To *indicate* omissions.

. . . .

We can thus speak of *linking, separating, enclosing,* and *omission* punctuation in the full realization that each function contrasts directly with all the others. It follows, therefore, that when the same marks of punctuation are used in different functions they are very much like words used in different functions: the grammatical meanings of the marks are *different.* The *separating period* (.) is quite distinct in functional use from the *omission period* (.); the *linking dash* (—) is functionally distinct from the *omission dash* (—); the single *separating comma* (,) is functionally distinct from *enclosing commas* (, . . . ,). In an ideal punctuation system, such differences would be clarified by the use of different marks of punctuation. Yet let us be realistic. Man has been speaking for well over 700,000 years. Man has been practicing alphabetic writing only for about 3450 years. Man has punctuated, in the modern sense, for less than 250 years. He has still not mastered an ideal punctuation. In the system as it stands, the distribution of the marks is as follows:

a. For *linking,* use:
 ; the semicolon
 : the colon
 — the linking dash
 - the linking hyphen

b. For *separating,* use:
 . the period
 ? the question mark
 ! the exclamation point
 , the separating comma

c. For *enclosing,* use:
 , . . . , paired commas
 — . . . — paired dashes
 (. . .) paired parentheses
 [. . .] paired brackets
 " . . . " paired quotation marks

d. For *indicating omissions,* use:
 ' the apostrophe
 . the omission period (or dot)
 — the omission dash
 . . .   triple periods (or dots)
 . . . . quadruple periods (or dots)

Linking Punctuation

The semicolon (;), colon (:), and dash (—) are symbolic conjunctions capable of linking subject-predicate constructions without need of conjunctions proper. They differ chiefly in the way they direct emphasis. Semicolons distribute it more or less equally between preceding and following statements; colons throw it forwards towards following statements; dashes throw it backwards towards preceding statements. Since they function as symbolic conjunctions, none of these marks is associated with any distinctive tone pattern of the language. In most cases, indeed, statements preceding any one of them would be read with the final h–l tone-pause pattern characteristic of period punctuation. The hyphen differs from the other linking punctuation marks in that it is used to link parts of the words only. The semicolon, colon, and dash may occur in combination with a final quotation mark, in which case they are always placed *outside* the quotation mark.

The *semicolon* (;) is the symbolic conjunction used to link subject-predicate groups that could otherwise occur as separate sentences, particularly if they are parallel in structure and in emphasis:

> The girl is pretty; you will like her.
> I am out of work; I need financial help.
> I was ill that day; nevertheless, I tried to complete the work.
> He was a close friend of the family; moreover, he had a position open.

It is conventionally used to link word groups containing heavy internal comma punctuation:

> My outfit included a rifle, a shotgun, a water bag, and a bedroll; but I did not forget to include a few good books.
> I liked *The Ordeal of Richard Feverel,* by Meredith; Oliver *Twist,* by Dickens; and Oscar Wilde's fine comedy *The Importance of Being Earnest.*

When the semicolon occurs in conjunction with quotation marks, it is placed *outside* them:

> I was reading Shelley's "Adonais"; I did not wish to be disturbed.

The *colon* (:) is the symbolic conjunction used when emphasis is to be thrown forward upon the word-group or word that follows it:

> It was just as I thought: he had stolen the money.
> My outfit included these necessaries: a rifle, a shotgun, a water bag, and a bedroll.
> I could think of only one word to describe him: cad.

In keeping with its general function of *anticipation,* the colon is conventionally used to introduce the chapter figure of a Bible reference, the page number of a volume reference, the minute figure of a clock reference, and the body of a letter following the salutation:

> Numbers III: 21 (or 3:21)
> American Speech 12: 46–49
> 10:15 A.M.
> Dear Sir:

Like the semicolon, it is always placed *outside* a final quotation mark:

> I found one leading literary tradition in "Adonais": pastoral tone.

The *dash* (—) is the symbolic conjunction to be used when the word-group or word following it is considered to be subsidiary to, a reinforcement or example of, or an unexpected addition to what precedes it. It directs the reader's attention backward:

> A year's work at Harvard—that was what he hoped for.
> A rifle, shotgun, ammunition—these were the essentials of my outfit.
> He comes to dinner, eats your food, smokes your best cigars—then borrows your money.
> He was very crude—crude and utterly crazy.

The dash is conventionally used before the name of the author of a quotation:

> Here lies our sovereign lord, the King.
> Whose word no man relies on;
> Who never spoke a foolish thing,
> And never did a wise one.
>
> —Anonymous

The dash should *not* be used as a kind of coverall punctuation mark for all linking and separating functions.

The *hyphen* (-) links parts of words together. It is most characteristically used to indicate that contiguous words form compounds not marked by stress modification.

> a *well-beloved* woman
> my *commander-in-chief*
> his *better-than-thou* attitude

The conventional uses of the hyphen are these:

a. To indicate that the beginning of a word on one printed line is linked to the rest of the word on the next.

b. To link the elements of compound numbers from twenty-one to ninety-nine:

> *thirty-four* horses
> *sixty-seven* dollars

c. To link the elements of fractions:

> He had a *two-thirds* lead in the election.

Today we tend to write either separately or as single units those words which were formerly hyphenated:

> my *commander in chief*
> a *wellbred* woman

Separating Punctuation

The period separates sentences only. The exclamation mark (!) and the question mark (?), normally used to separate special types of sentences, are also used occasionally to separate parts of sentences. The comma separates *parts* of sentences only. Thus, there is every reason why the period, as sentences separator, should never be confused with the comma, as sentence-part separator, or with the semi-colon, the sentence linker. All the separating punctuation marks are roughly correlated with stress-juncture and tone-pause patterns heard in speech, and it is probable that learning to hear the patterns will direct you towards the appropriate punctuation:

> John was coming(.)
> John was coming(?)
> John was coming(!)
> John was coming(,) and I still had to dress.

When they occur in combination with final quotation marks, all the separating punctuation marks are placed *inside* them. In this respect, they contrast directly with the linking punctuation marks which are placed *outside*.

The period (.) has the one function of separating declarative subject-predicate sentences (including mild commands) from following sentences. It symbolizes the fall from high to low pitch (h–l) followed by breathing pause. Its grammatical meaning is "end of declarative utterance":

> The mountains enclose a valley.
> Please return the books as soon as possible.

The period can occur after statements not in subject-predicate form if they conclude with the h–l tone-pause pattern.

> The more, the merrier.
> To resume.

It is always inserted *before* end quotation marks:

> He said to me, "Mother is coming."

The question mark (?) separates questions and quoted questions from a following context. It symbolizes two quite distinct final tone-pause patterns of actual speech:

a. A fall from high to low tone (h–l) used when a question contains an interrogative word or word order:

> h———l
> Why did you go to the theater?

b. A rising high tone, usual when a question does not contain an interrogative word or word order:

> l———h
> You went to the theater?

The grammatical meaning of the question mark is "answer needed":

> Are you leaving tonight?
> Is John coming?
> You are in Professor Brown's class?
> "Where is the salt?" he demanded.

It is always inserted *before* end quotation marks:

> He said, "Is this what's wrong?"

The *exclamation point* (!) separates exclamatory sentences or exclamatory words from a following context. It symbolizes various final tone-pause patterns based upon sharply rising or falling tone or a combination of these, or unexpectedly level tone, used in speech when an utterance is surcharged with emotion:

> What a marvelous morning!
> Listen! I hear John coming.

It is always inserted *before* end quotation marks that occur *within* a sentence, but it is placed outside quotation marks at the end of a sentence when the whole sentence is exclamatory:

> "I am finished!" he yelled.
> How horrible was their shout, "We're coming to kill you"!

The *separating comma* (,) originally indicated that a part of a sentence preceding or following it was in some way separated from the remainder. Where it corresponds to anything in speech at all, it generally symbolizes internal grammatical juncture followed by pause in slow-tempo speech. Its use, however, is now highly conventionalized: the comma is often used where speech shows internal juncture unaccompanied by pause but where its omission might lead to misunderstanding. The comma never appears between the main structural elements, the *must* parts, of sentences; i.e., it is never used between the subject and verb, between the verb and a complement, or between two complements, and it is never used before movable modifiers of a sentence if these appear *after* the verb; in short, it is never used to indicate optional internal grammatical junctures. The grammatical meaning of the comma is "dissociation." It is inserted:

a. After each word or word-group in a series terminated by *and, or;* here it may symbolize the high rising tone pattern (h):

> I took bread, butter, tea, and salt with me.
> His cunning, his devious treachery, or his ruthlessness will be enough to make him fight successfully.

b. Between subject-predicate word-groups linked by the coupling conjunctions *and, but, or, not, yet:*

> The book is quite good, and it is relatively inexpensive.
> The food and service were good, yet I was hard to please.

c. After any movable modifier thought of as displaced from a normal end-of-sentence position:

> Instead of the expected twenty, only ten came to the party.
> But: Only ten came to the party instead of the expected twenty.

d. Before any other modifier or modifying word-group thought of as out of its normal sentence position:

> We thought of Goldsmith, poor but genial.
> Talent, Mr. Micawber has; money, Mr. Micawber has not.

e. After an introductory word, word-group, transitional adverb, or vocative expression:

> *This done,* we left the place immediately.
> She didn't like the idea; *nevertheless,* she said she would visit us.
> *Mother,* I have brought my friend to be our guest.

f. After a subject-predicate word-group introducing a direct quotation:

> He exclaimed, "I had no idea that you were in the room."

g. Between elements in sentences and word-groups which might cause confusion if thought of as combined:

> My words are my own; my actions, my ministers'.
> a *bright, blue hat* contrasted with a *bright blue hat*

h. Between items in dates, addresses, books and author references, etc.:

> April 1, 1950
> Mary Johnson, Cleveland, Ohio
> *Oliver Twist,* by Charles Dickens

The comma is always inserted *before* end quotation marks:

> "I am tired of your incompetence," he roared.

Enclosing Punctuation

Paired commas, paired dashes, and parentheses are used to enclose elements outside the main structure of a sentence. They represent a triple scale of enclosure, in which paired commas enclose elements most closely related to the main thought of the sentence and parentheses those elements least closely related. Brackets are merely a specialized type of parentheses. Quotation marks are used principally to enclose the report of words actually spoken.

Paired commas (, . . . ,) have the following uses:

a. To enclose modifying word-groups of the subject-predicate type which are not regarded as essential to the identification of the word which they modify. Such groups are usually called *non-restrictive*.

> NON-RESTRICTIVE: This invention, *which our army rejected,* became Germany's surprise weapon.
>
> RESTRICTIVE: The invention *which our army rejected* became Germany's surprise weapon.

In the first example, the identification is supplied by *this;* the modifying group *which our army rejected* is thus properly enclosed in paired commas. In the second example, the modifying group is needed to identify *invention*.

b. To enclose interpolated words and word-groups, especially when those are transitional adverbs or groups with the function of transitional adverbs:

> Your ideas, *however,* are scarcely valid.
> Your ideas, *as a matter of fact,* are scarcely valid.
> Your ideas, *I conclude,* are scarcely valid.

Paired dashes (— . . . —) enclose elements less closely related to the main thought of a sentence than those enclosed by paired commas but more closely related than those enclosed by parentheses:

> My friends—at that time mostly workers—took me to task for my social attitudes.

They replace paired commas when the enclosed word-group has heavy comma punctuation of its own:

> The artillery—devastating in its sound, fury, and effect—suddenly opened up on us.

Parentheses enclose material which is obviously outside the main scope of the sentence:

> These words (*we might call them determiners*) are important in English but of little importance in many other languages.

Parentheses are used conventionally to enclose the figures numbering parts of a series, and, in legal contexts, to enclose figures expressing monetary value:

> The aims of this course are: (1) to analyze the structure of American English; (2) to examine the resources of its vocabulary; (3) to sketch the history of American English.
> The signer agrees to pay the sum of one hundred dollars ($100.00).

Brackets ([. . .]) are a special kind of parentheses with the following uses:

a. To insert interpolations in quotations:

> As Jarrold said, "It [poetry] is an attempt to express the inexpressible."

b. To insert pronunciations written in the symbols of the International Phonetic Association (IPA):

> The usual pronunciation of *bait* is [bet].

They also enclose parenthetical matter already in parentheses.

Quotation marks (". . .") enclose direct quotations from speech:

> "You may say that," said my father, "but you don't believe it."

They may be used with caution to enclose references to specific words, slang expressions, hackneyed expressions, familiar and well-worn phrases, and terms you do not like:

> My life is one "if" after another.
> His car had the "teardrop" shape of that period.
> While "on campus," Jones was something of a "rod."
> The "liberal arts" curriculum becomes increasingly illiberal.

They are also used to enclose the titles of poems, plays, essays, paintings, etc. (but not the titles of complete volumes or of major works, which are indicated by italics):

> I read Shelley's "Alastor" with distinct pleasure.
> I particularly admired El Greco's "Toledo."
> He was much impressed by the story "Clay" in Joyce's *Dubliners*.

Omission Punctuation

Originally, the *apostrophe* (') indicated the omission of a letter no longer pronounced or deliberately suppressed in pronunciation. This is what it still indicates when used with the possessive singular forms of nouns, contracted forms of verb helpers (auxiliaries), and words with an omitted initial letter:

> the Lord's Prayer (earlier, the Lordes Prayer)
> He's not coming, and he won't come.
> a blot on the 'scutcheon

Its conventional uses are as follows:

a. It precedes *s* in the plurals of figures, signs, symbols, and letters:

> My 8's are difficult to decipher.
> There were three x's in this quotation.
> I have difficulty in writing r's.

b. It precedes *s* in plurals of words which have no normal plural form:

> There were too many if's and but's about the matter.

c. In a purely symbolic function corresponding to nothing actual in speech, it indicates possessive plurals of nouns:

> The generals' orders had to be obeyed.
> the college girls' escorts

d. It indicates the possessive singular forms of nouns already ending in *s:*

> Dr. Caius' (or Caius's) words
> Moses' pronouncements

e. It indicates the possessive singular forms of group names:

> Thomas, Manchester, and Scott's *Rhetoric*
> Chase and Sanborn's coffee

f. It indicates the omission of initial centuries in dates:
> the class of '38

The *omission period* or *dot* (.) indicates the omission of several letters, particularly when words are abbreviated:

> Mr. V. S. Johnson
> Ph.D.
> I enjoy the plays of G.B.S.

It is not used after contractions indicated by the apostrophe, after Roman numerals, after numbered ordinals, after nicknames, or after per cent (for *per centum*); it is now often omitted after the abbreviated names of government agencies, labor organizations, and the like:

> He'll go.   a five per cent bonus
> XXIV   CIC
> 5th, 6th, 7th   FTC
> Dick, Mick, and Ned

When a sentence ends with an abbreviated word, one period punctuates both the abbreviation and the sentence:

> I was talking to Richard Hudson, Ph.D.

Triple periods or *dots* (. . .) indicate a more or less extensive omission of material at the beginning of, or within, a quoted passage; followed by a period (. . . .) they indicate omission at its end:

> . . . language is . . . the thought itself, its confused cross currents as well as its clear-cut issues. . . .

Triple periods are often used to indicate omissions deliberately left to the reader's imagination:

> He took her slowly in his arms . . . from that moment she was his.

In recent advertising practice, this use is greatly extended in order to create appropriate atmosphere:

> Fly to Britain . . . Europe . . . and beyond.
> Industries are discovering . . . with a rush . . . that the Genie of "Opportunity" is at their beck and call.

The *dash* (−) as used in omission punctuation indicates the deliberate suppression of letters in a person's name in order to avoid positive statement of identification:

> My informant, a certain professor *M*−, vouches for the truth of this report.

In earlier writing it was often used to indicate omissions in oaths, etc.:

> "D−n," he said. "I'll see you hanged yet."

No attempt has been made here to deal with all the minute points of punctuation. Such matters as the use of capitals and italics are treated under the appropriate headings in a dictionary: they are matters of format rather than punctuation although they serve a very real purpose in the transference of spoken to written distinctions. What has been attempted here is to present punctuation proper as a system of symbols each one of which contrasts with all others in function. Ideally, the writer should be able to ignore the grammar book or the dictionary when he is faced with a punctuation problem; what he needs most of all is an understanding of the entire system as it determines the individual application.

OTTO JESPERSEN

Spelling

The traditional way of writing English is far from being so
consistent that it is possible, if we know the sounds of a word,
to know how it is to be spelled, or inversely, from the spelling
to draw any conclusions as to its pronunciation. The following
words in their traditional garb and in phonetic transcription may
serve as illustration:

> *though* [ðou]—rhyming with *low*
> *through* [þru]   ”   *true*
> *plough* [plau]   ”   *now*
> *cough* [kɔf]   ”   *off*
> *enough* [i'nʌf]   ”   *cuff*

However chaotic this may seem, it is possible to a great extent
to explain the rise of all these discrepancies between sound and
spelling, and thus to give, if not rational, at any rate historical
reasons for them. A full account of all these anomalies would,
however, require a whole volume; here we must, therefore, content ourselves with a succinct exposition of the chief facts that
have determined the present English spelling.

The alphabet used in England as well as in most European
countries is the Roman alphabet. Though this is better than many
Oriental alphabets, it is far from being perfect as a means of
rendering sounds, as it is deficient in signs for many simple
sounds (*e.g.* the initial consonants of *this* and *thick*, the final one
of *sing*); nor does it possess more than five vowel-letters, where
many languages distinguish a far greater number of vowels.

. . . .

From *Essentials of English Grammar*, 1933, by permission of George Allen
& Unwin Ltd.

At first people could follow no other guide in their spelling than their own ears: writing thus began as purely phonetical. But soon they began to imitate the spellings of others, whose manuscripts they copied, their teachers and their elders generally. As the spoken forms of words tend continually to change, this would mean that older, extinct forms of speech would continue to be written long after they had ceased to be heard. Such traditional spelling, which is found in all languages with a literary history, has become particularly powerful since the invention of the art of printing; in many respects, therefore, modern English orthography represents the pronunciation prevalent about that time or even earlier.

An equally important factor was the influence of French—later also of Latin—spelling. Norman scribes introduced several peculiarities of French spelling, not only when writing words taken over from that language, but also when writing native English words. Our present-day spelling cannot, therefore, be fully understood without some knowledge of the history of French.

The letters *ch* were used in Old French to denote the sound-combination [tʃ] as in *chaste, chief, merchant;* in English this spelling was used not only in originally French words, but also in native words like *child, much*. In French the stop [t] was later dropped, the sound [ʃ] only remaining; hence *ch* in some late loan-words comes to stand for [ʃ]: *machine, chaise* (which is the Modern French form of the same word that in the old form was taken over as *chair*), *chauffeur*.

In words from the classical languages *ch* denotes the sound [k]: *echo, chaos, scheme*. Schedule is pronounced with [sk] in America, with [ʃ] in England.

The sound-history of French also serves to explain some striking peculiarities concerning the use of the letter *g* in English spelling. Written French *gu* originally served to denote the combination of [g] with a following [u] or [w]; but this combination was later simplified in various ways. In the northernmost French dialects [g] was dropped, and English from those dialects adopted such words as *ward, reward, warden* and *war*. But in other parts of French it was inversely the [u]-sound that disappeared, and a great many words were adopted into English with this simple sound of [g], such as *gallop, garrison;* in some cases English kept the spelling *gu* though French now writes without the *u: guard, guarantee.* In both languages the spelling *gu* came to be extensively used as an orthographic device to denote the sound [g] before *e* and *i*, because in that position g was pronounced [dʒ], thus in *guide, guise;* and in English this spelling was even transferred to a certain number of native words like *guess, guest, guild* (sb.), *guilt, tongue,* though it never obtained in some frequently used words like *get, give, begin, gild* (vb.).

In Old French the letter g stood for the sound-combination [dʒ], as Latin g [g] had devoloped in that way before [e] and [i]; hence spellings like *gentle, giant, age, manage,* etc. Sometimes after a short vowel *dg* was written: *judge, lodge;* thus also in native words like *edge, bridge.*

As with the corresponding voiceless combination [tʃ], the stop in [dʒ] was later dropped in French; hence g is in later loan-words pronounced [ʒ]: *rouge, mirage, prestige.*

Another Old French way of writing [dʒ] was *i*, later *j;* hence we have English spellings like *joy, join, journey.* In *bijou j* has the later French value [ʒ].

In OE. the letter *c* was exclusively used for the sound [k], even before *e, i* and *y*, exactly as in Latin. But in French this Latin sound had become first [ts] and later [s] before *e* and *i;* and this value of the letter *c* is consequently found in English, not only in French and Latin words, like *cease, centre, city, peace, pace* —even sometimes where French has *s: ace,* Fr. *as; juice,* Fr. *jus*— but also in some native English words, e.g. *since, hence.* Sc is pronounced in the same way, e.g. *scene, science;* it is writen without any etymological reason in *scent* (from French *sentir*).

C is used for the sound [k] in *can, corn, cup, clean, creep* and many similar words, while *k* is written in *kiss, keep, think,* etc., and *q* before *u: queen,* etc. Instead of *ks, x* is written: *six,* etc., even in *coxcomb* and *coxswain* from *cock*.

French influence is responsible for the use of the digraph *ou* form ME. long [u:] as in *couch, spouse* (later Fr. *épouse*); sometimes also for short [u]: *couple, touch.* This was transferred to native words like *house, loud, out, our,* etc. When the long sound was later diphthongized, the spelling *ou* came to be very appropriate. As this diphthongizing did not take place in Scotch, *ou* is there still found for the sound [u:], as in *Dougall, dour, souter,* "shoemaker."

The simple vowel *u* was used for the short vowel as in *up, us, nut, full,* etc., and for the diphthong [iu] or [ju:], frequent in French words like *duke, use, due, virtue,* but also found in native words, e.g. *Tuesday, hue, Stuart* (the same word as *steward*).

But at a time when angular writing was fashionable, it became usual to avoid the letter *u* in close proximity with the letters *n, m,* and another *u* (*v, w*), where it was liable to cause ambiguity (five strokes might be interpreted *imi, inu, mu, um, uni, uui,* especially at a time when no dot was written over *i*); hence the use of *o* which has been retained in a great many words: *monk, money, honey, come, won, wonder, cover* (written *couer* before *v, o* and *u* were distinguished), *love,* etc.

A merely orthographic distinction is made between *son* and *sun, some* and *sum.*

In ME. vowels were frequently doubled to show length, and many of these spellings have been preserved, e.g. *see, deer, too, brood,* though the sounds have been changed so that they no more correspond to the short vowels of *set, hot.*

But neither *a* nor *u* were doubled in that way; and instead of writing *ii* it became usual to write *y.* This letter, which in Old English served to denote the rounded vowel corresponding to [i] (= Fr. *u* in *bu,* German *ü* in *über*), has become a mere variant of *i* used preferably at the end of words, while *i* is used in the beginning and interior of words; hence such alternations as *cry, cries, cried; happy, happier, happiest, happiness; body, bodiless, bodily,* etc. But *y* is kept before such endings as are felt more or less as independent elements, e.g. *citywards, lady-*

ship, twentyfold, juryman. After another vowel *y* is generally kept, e.g. *plays, played, boys;* cf., however, *laid, paid, said* (but *lays, pays, says:* too much consistency must not be expected). In some cases homophones are kept apart in the spelling: *die* (with *dies,* but *dying,* because *ii* is avoided)—*dye, flys,* 'light carriages,' but otherwise *flies* (sb. and vb.).

Further, *y* is written in many originally Greek words: *system, nymph,* etc.

Before a vowel, *y* is used as non-syllabic [i], i.e. [j], e.g. *yard, yellow, yield, yole, yule, beyond.*

Doubling of consonants has come to be extensively used to denote shortness of the preceding vowel, especially before a weak syllable, e.g. in *hotter, hottest* from *hot, sobbing* from *sob.* Instead of doubling *k, ch* and *g* [= dʒ] the combinations *ck, tch* and *dg* (*e*) are written, e.g. *trafficking* from *traffic, etch, edge.*

On account of the phonetic development, however, a double consonant is now written after some long vowels, e.g. in *roll, all, staff, glass,* which had formerly short vowels.

Though since the introduction of printing a great many minor changes have taken place without any great consistency, such as the leaving out of numerous mute *e's,* only one important orthographic change must be recorded, namely, the regulating of *i* and *j, u* and *v,* so that now *i* and *u* are used for the vowels, *j* and *v* for the consonant sounds, while, for instance, the old editions of Shakespeare print *ioy, vs, vpon, fiue, fauour = joy, us, upon, five, favour.* The old use of *u* for the consonant explains the name of *w: double u.*

Scholars have introduced learned spellings in many words, e.g. *debt, doubt,* on account of Latin *debita, dubito,* formerly written as in French *dette, doute; victuals,* formerly *vittles.* In some cases the pronunciation has been modified according to the spelling; thus [p] has been introduced in *bankrupt,* earlier *bankeroute,* and [k] in *perfect,* earlier *perfit, parfit.* In recent years, with the enormous spread of popular education, combined with ignorance of the history of the language, such spelling-pronunciations have become increasingly numerous.

ROBERT A. HALL, JR.

Our English Spelling System

The real nature of writing in its relation to language is so obvious on a moment's reflection, that it might seem strange that so much misunderstanding could arise about it. Probably the confusion is due to two things: the nature of our English spelling system, and the age at which we start to learn it. People whose languages have a simple, relatively accurate conventional spelling, like Italian, Hungarian, or Finnish, are not confused as to the relation of writing and speech, and are often surprised at the misunderstanding that spellers of English show. But our traditional orthography for English is quite far removed from the reality of speech, and our letters certainly do not stand in a wholly one-to-one relationship with the phonemes of our speech. It takes considerable effort and many years (as we all well know!) to completely master our English conventional spelling; and once we have learned it, it represents a considerable investment. Nobody likes to give up the fruits of any investment, and the more costly it is, the less we want to discard it; and so it is with the spelling of English. Once we have learned it, we have a strong emotional attachment to it, just because we have had considerable difficulty with it and have been forced to put in so much time and effort on learning it.

Furthermore, we learn to speak long before we are able to do any kind of reflective or analytical intellectual work; we learn to speak when we are small children, by a purely unreflecting

. . . .

process of repeated trial and error. But when we go to school and learn to write, we do so consciously and reflectingly. If, in our first school contacts with writing, we were taught a scientifically accurate phonemic spelling, which reflected all the facts of our speech itself, we would have very little trouble and would learn to use such a spelling in a year or two, as do Italian or Hungarian children. But we do not learn an accurate phonemic spelling; we learn our inaccurate, confused traditional English orthography, and we talk about it as we do so. When we were little children learning how to speak, we learned only to speak, not how to analyze our speech. When we are older and learn to spell, we also learn how to talk about spelling and how to analyze it: we are taught to name the letters, to tell how we replace letters by apostrophes or how we drop letters, and so forth. But we still learn nothing whatsoever about how to discuss speech and analyze it in its own terms; the only approach, the only vocabulary we end up with for discussing language is the approach and the vocabulary of spelling. Edith Wharton, in *The Custom of the Country*, says of one of her characters:

> Mrs. Spragg, when she found herself embarked on a wrong sentence, always ballasted it by italicizing the last word.

What Mrs. Wharton meant, of course, was "emphasizing" or "stressing" the last word; but the only term at her disposal was the word *italicizing*, the term that referred to spelling rather than to speech.

This entire situation has given results that are little short of disastrous for the understanding of the true nature of language, throughout the English-speaking world. Very few people have any clear idea of what they actually do when they speak—what organs of their body they use and in what way they use them. Many people find it difficult or downright impossible to conceive of sounds as such, or to hear differences in sound that are not directly related to differences in English spelling. Some even develop emotional blockings on the subject of phonetic analysis, because the strange appearance and use of special symbols in a transcription makes them "feel all funny inside," as one such person put it to me. When it comes to discussing sounds, the only way to identify many sounds in writing for the general reader who knows no phonetics, is to avoid all letters entirely, and to give cumbersome definitions like "the vowel sound of *bit*" or "the initial sound of *thing*"; for, if we were to speak of the *i* of *hit* or the *th* of *thing*, almost everyone would immediately read off those definitions as "the 'eye' (*i*) of *hit*" or "the 'tee aitch' (*th*) of *thing*." Likewise for a discussion of grammar or of syntax, we can recognize grammatical facts which we see reflected in the conventional spelling, like the vowel change in *sing sang sung;* but we find it hard to recognize or discuss those grammatical facts which are not indicated in writing, like the difference between the final consonant sounds of *house* (noun, as in *he has a big house*) and *house* (verb, as in *where can we house them?*), or the change in vowel sound between *you* (stressed, as in *is that you?*) and *you* (unstressed, as in *how do you do?*).

All kinds of misunderstandings and misrepresentations arise as a result of this spelling-induced confusion and ignorance. People often think that spelling a word out is the best way to tell someone how to pronounce it, and think that the names of the letters alone will give a key to the sounds that are involved. I once witnessed a prize example of this confusion when a high-school girl named Carlys (normally pronounced as if spelled *Carleece,* stress on last syllable) was trying to tell my four-year-old boy Philip how to pronounce her name, which he had some difficulty with:

> Philip: Hey, Craleeth!
> Carlys: No, no. Not Craleeth; Carlys. Say that.
> Philip: Craleeth.
> Carlys: No, no, no. Carlys. CAR-LYS.
> Philip: Craleeth.
> Carlys: No! Look; shall I spell it out for you?
> Philip (not knowing what "spelling it out" meant): Yes.
> Carlys: See, ay, ahr, ell, wye, ess. Now say it.
> Philip: Craleeth.
> Carlys: ! ! !

Many times we think that, because a word is spelled with a certain letter, we ought to pronounce some sound to correspond to that letter: we pronounce a *t*-sound in *fasten,* we pronounce three syllables in *Wednesday,* we sometimes even try to pronounce the initial *p* in words like *psychology* or *ptarmigan.* This kind of behavior is known as *spelling-pronunciation;* it almost never occurs where a language has a reasonably accurate system of spelling, but always crops up whenever the spelling ceases to represent the language adequately. Our pronunciation of *author* is a case in point. Older English had a word *autor,* meaning "creator, author," which had been borrowed from the French word *autor* of the same meaning, ultimately taken from Latin *auctor.* In the sixteenth century, people came to realize that many words previously spelled with *t* came from Latin or Greek sources in which they were spelled with *th,* such as *theater, thesis.* It came to be a mark of elegance and learning to write *th* instead of *t;* but some people carried their learning too far and wrote *th* even where it didn't belong, as in *author* for *autor.* Then more and more people, seeing the letters *th* in the elegant spelling of *author,* pronounced the *th* with the sound those letters stand for in *thing;* by now, that spelling-pronunciation has become general and we all pronounce *author* with that sound, not with the *t*-sound it originally had. Needless to say, spelling-pronunciation serves no good purpose, and only introduces confusion and misunderstanding into otherwise clear situations, like those of *autor* or *fasten.* That is, once upon a time *autor* was pronounced with a *t*-sound, and everybody was quite happy about it; now, everybody says it with a *th*-sound and is equally happy about it; but nothing has been gained by the change, and there was no need of the uncertainty that prevailed during the period of transition.

"Correct" spelling, that is, obedience to the rules of English spelling as grammarians and dictionary-makers set them up, has come to be a major shibboleth in our society. If I write *seet* instead of *seat, roat* instead of *wrote,* or *hite* instead of *height,* it makes no difference whatsoever in the English language, i.e. in my speech and that of others around me; yet we are all trained to give highly unfavorable reactions to such spellings, and to be either amused or displeased with people who know no better than to "misspell" in such a way. This shibboleth serves, as does that of "correct" speech, as a means of social discrimination: we can class people among the sheep or the goats according as they measure up to the standards we set in spelling. Spelling which is more nearly in accord with speech, and which we might logically expect to be considered better than the conventional spelling, thus comes to be, not praised, but blamed. Spelling "phonetically" becomes equivalent to spelling incorrectly. I once came across a reference to "phonetic" pronunciation, which at first puzzled me, since pronunciation can by definition never be anything but phonetic; it later turned out that the writer was referring to inaccurate pronunciation of a foreign language, such as French *est-ce que vous avez* "have you?" pronounced in a way which he transcribed *ess-ker-vous-avay*. He had come to use the term "phonetic" as equivalent to "incorrect," through the folk use of the term *phonetic spelling* in the meaning of "incorrect spelling."

When we write down the exact words of people whose speech we consider "incorrect," we often purposely misspell their words to indicate their pronunciation and give the reader an idea of what social level they belong to; the realistic novels of Erskine Caldwell, John Steinbeck and others are full of these spelling devices: for instance, *Elviry done tole me she ain' a-gwineta do no sich thing fer nobuddy*. This shocks purists who are attached to "correct" spelling at all costs; but it is spreading more and more as an element of realism, which of course derives its force from the contrast between normal "correct" spelling and pronunciation, and the "incorrect" speech implied by the "incorrect" spelling. A further development of this device is so-called *eye-dialect*, in which misspellings are used to represent normal pronunciations, merely to burlesque words or their speaker. We all pronounce *women* in the same way; but if we spell it *wimmin*, we imply "The person quoted is one who would use a vulgar pronunciation if there were one." Likewise the spellings *licker* instead of *liquor*, *vittles* instead of *victuals*, *sez* instead of *says*, and the host of reduced forms such as *I wanna* for *I want to*, *ya oughta* for *you ought to, watcher gonna do* for *what are you going to do,* or *I hafta* for *I have to.*

This last group of examples may not, at first, seem accurate, because we are often not aware how much we reduce and telescope such combinations in normal speech; but just try observing yourself and see how many times a day you actually use the full, separate forms of the words in such an expression as *what are you going to do,* or *I have to do it.* In fact, *I have to* with a *v*-sound in *have* would be not only unusual, it would be abnormal. But, because of our conventions of spelling, the more realistic and accurate spellings like *I wanna* or *I hafta* are relegated to the comic strips and are made the objects of prejudice, which can be appealed to in whipping up opposition to phonetic transcription or to the writing of, say, the Italian word for "when" as KWAN-*do* instead of the conventional *quando.*

The situation with respect to spelling is much the same as it is with regard to "correct" speech in our society. In each case, an irrational, meaningless standard is set up as a shibboleth for people to conform to, which in many instances puts a premium on lack of realism and on unnaturalness in speech or its representation. In particular, our society's emphasis on the irregularities of English spelling has brought many of us to a point where we cannot distinguish between speech and writing, and where we cannot even conceive of sounds as existing distinct from and prior to letters. Consequently, anyone who goes through our schooling system has to waste years of his life in acquiring a wasteful and, in the long run, damaging set of spelling habits, thus ultimately unfitting himself to understand the nature of language and its function unless he puts in extra effort to rid himself of all the misconceptions and prejudices that our system has foisted on him.

HAROLD WHITEHALL

Writing and Speech

All of us have a grammar. The fact that we use and understand English in daily affairs means that we use and understand, for the most part unconsciously, the major grammatical patterns of our language. Yet because of the effects of education, many of us have come to think of a relatively formal written English and its reflection among those who "speak by the book" as the only genuine English, and to consider its grammar as the only acceptable English grammar. That is by no means true. The basic form of present-day American English is the patterned, rhythmed, and segmented code of voice signals called *speech*—speech is used in everyday conversation by highly educated people (*cultivated speech*), by the general run of our population (*common speech*), or by some rural persons in such geographically isolated areas as the Ozark Plateau, the Appalachian Mountains, or the woodland areas of northern New England (*folk speech*). From the code of speech, the language of formal writing is something of an abstraction, differing in details of grammar and vocabulary and lacking clear indication of the bodily gestures and meaningful qualities of the voice which accompany ordinary conversation. Thus, serious written English may be regarded as a rather artificial dialect of our language. To acquire that dialect, the would-be writer needs to know a good deal about its structural details, and particularly about those in which it differs from the less formal varieties of speech.

. . . .

Even a moment's reflection will show that the spoken American language is backed by expressive features lacking in the written language: the rise or fall of the voice at the ends of phrases and sentences; the application of vocal loudness to this or that word or part of a word; the use of gesture; the meaningful rasp or liquidity, shouting or muting, drawling or clipping, whining or breaking, melody or whispering imparted to the quality of the voice. Written English, lacking clear indication of such features, must be so managed that it compensates for what it lacks. It must be more carefully organized than speech in order to overcome its communicative deficiencies as compared with speech. In speech, we safeguard meaning by the use of intonation, stress, gesture, and voice qualities. In writing, we must deal with our medium in such a way that the meaning cannot possibly be misunderstood. In the absence of an actual hearer capable of interrupting and demanding further explanation, a clear writer is always conscious of "a reader over his shoulder." All this despite the fact that writing, being permanent, as compared with speech, which is evanescent, allows not only reading but also rereading.

Nor is this all. If written English is somewhat abstract, somewhat artificial, it is also generalized—national, not geographically or socially limited in scope. We must realize that comparatively few of us make use in our day-to-day affairs of a generalized spoken American English that is at all comparable with it. Such a language—a Received Standard Spoken English—exists, but not for the most part in this country where the practical need for it is slight. It exists in England, where the practical need for it is great. In England, many people still start their linguistic careers speaking one or another of the regional dialects, dialects so different from each other in vocabulary and grammar, so quilt-crazy in their distribution, that they form real barriers to generalized, national communication. Yet, in a modern, democratic country, general communication is a necessity. For that reason, Englishmen are willing to accept the notion both of a generalized spoken and a generalized written form of expression on a level above the dialects, and are willing to make the effort of learning them in school and elsewhere. We would be equally willing if our everyday speech happened to resemble this specimen from the English county of Lancaster:

> Nay! my heart misgi'es me! There's summat abeawt this neet's wark as is noan jannock. Look thee here! Yon chap's noan t' first sheep theaw's lifted tax-free fro't' mooar, an' aw've niver been one to worrit abeawt it, that aw hav'nt. But toneet, someheaw, it's noan t'same. There's summat beawn't 'appen— aw con feel it i' my booans. This een, an unconny wind wor burrin' i't'ling, an' not a cleawd i't' sky; an' whin aw went deawn to' t'well for watter, t'bats wor flyin' reawn it in a wid- dershins ring. Mark my words, there's mooar to coom.

In the United States, our language situation is quite different. Ours is probably the only country on earth in which three thousand miles of travel will bring no difficulty of spoken communication. We do have, of course, regional and social differences of language. The speech of Maine does not coincide in all points with that of Texas, nor the speech of Georgia with that of Minnesota. The speech of cultivated people in urban centers is not precisely that of the general mass of our citizens, nor that of rural residents of limited education in geographically secluded areas. Yet, unless we deliberately choose to emphasize disparities for social or other reasons, our regional and social speech differences create no great barriers to the free exchange of opinions and ideas. They consist of flavoring rather than substance.

Precisely for that reason, pressures for the adoption of a generalized national spoken American English comparable in acceptance and prestige with Received Standard Spoken British have proved largely unavailing. In American life, one may use cultivated or common speech Southern, cultivated or common speech Northeastern, or cultivated or common speech North Middle Western without encountering any great practical disadvantage. Our standards of speech are mainly regional standards, and most of us, in actual fact, speak some kind of a patois in which one or another of the cultivated or common speech regional varieties of American English blends quite happily with elements absorbed from reading and the educational process. We are very fortunate in this—fortunate that American historical and sociological conditions have removed difficulties of spoken communication found in most other parts of the world.

In a lesser sense, however, our good fortune is something of a misfortune. Because an American can understand other Americans no matter what regional or social class they come from, he is apt to underestimate the necessity for a generalized and abstract written American English. Because he finds no pressing reason for standardizing his speech, he is likely to misunderstand the necessity for standardizing his writing. He would like to write as he speaks. Moreover, the differences between the various regional and social varieties of American speech, being slight, are often of so subtle a nature that he tends to find difficulty in discriminating them. Slight as they are, when transferred to writing they are sufficient to make a reader pause, to induce a momentary feeling of unfamiliarity, to interrupt his consideration of the *matter* of expression by unwittingly calling attention to the *manner* of expression. Outside frankly literary writing (particularly the writing of poetry), such pauses, such unfamiliarities, such interruptions will hinder rather than help the writer's communicative purpose. If writing must be generalized, it must be generalized with a good reason: to speak with a local accent is not disadvantageous; to write serious prose with a local accent definitely is.

The moral of all this is clear. To gain command of serious written English is to acquire, quite deliberately, an abstract and generalized variety of the language differing by nature and purpose from any social or regional variety whatsoever. It is to sacrifice the local for the general, the spontaneous for the permanent. It is to bring to the study of written American English something of the perspective we normally reserve for the study of foreign languages. It is to master a set of grammatical and vocabulary patterns not because they are "correct" but because experience has proved them efficient in the communicative activity of writing.

The word "correct" is deliberately introduced here. The clear distinctions between spoken and written language mentioned in the paragraphs above have been all too often masked by the pernicious doctrine of "correctness." Perhaps that is to be expected. Without the flexible medium of language, a human society in human terms would be impossible. Without language, there could be no continuous record of experience, no diversification of labor, no great social institutions—the humanity of man could never have been achieved. But social activities breed social rituals and social judgments. Because language is *the* basic social instrument, it has inevitably acquired social attitudes so complex and variegated that they have often been allowed to obscure its primary communicative function. For far too many of us, knowledge of language is confused with knowledge of judgments on language that are socially acceptable. Education in the English language has become, for the most part, education in linguistic niceties—a poor substitute for that real linguistic education which ought to show us the major and minor patterns of our language, the way in which they interlock in function, the ways in which they can be manipulated for effective expression. As a result, the instrument of communication which should be every man's servant has become most men's master. This need not be so. Our self-confidence is immediately bolstered, our attitudes towards the study of writing techniques tremendously improved, once we realize that the difficulties of writing English do not spring from faulty nurture, restricted intelligence, or beyond-the-tracks environment but from the necessary change-over from one kind of English to another—that they are neither unpardonable nor irremediable.

No matter what irrationalities surround the details and the perspectives by which English is normally viewed, the fact that it has so admirably served and is still serving the needs of many fine writers guarantees that it is neither an impossible nor an unworthy instrument of human expression. Let us admit that all languages, spoken or written, are man-made things, that their weaknesses as well as their strengths are implicit in their human origin. Let us admit that the world has never known either a faultless language nor one constructed on what to us seems a strictly logical system. The proper approach to written English is first to understand what the medium is; then to concede its limitations and to use its strengths to the best possible effect. Every communicative medium has a set of resistances that the communicator must overcome. Marble is hard; paint relatively unmanageable; music barely descriptive. No small part of any kind of composition is contributed directly by tensions set up between the craftsman's demands on his medium on the one hand and its inherent resistances on the other. To this, the science, craft, and art of expression in written American English is no exception.

SIMEON POTTER

The Sentence

We do not learn to frame sentences instinctively, as we learn
to breathe or to walk. We repeat sentences from memory and
we vary them by analogy. Imagine for a moment that all the
sentences you have uttered during the course of the last two
weeks are somewhere accurately recorded and that you can now
scrutinize them at leisure. You will probably find them to be
surprisingly varied: long and short; simple, double, multiple,
and complex; statements, commands, wishes, questions, and exclamations; balanced, periodic, and loose. The words have been
largely of your own choosing, but the sentences have seldom
been of your own making. You have inherited them from the
immediate, the distant, and the long-distant past. You have
carried with you in your mind a certain number of sentence-
patterns, few or many according to your individual linguistic
capacity, and into these patterns you have fitted and varied
the words expressing your thoughts and desires.

A child may echo the sounds it hears without being conscious
of the meanings of separate words. Because English is, in the
main, an analytic language (in spite of reviving synthetic tendencies which we were considering in the last chapter), the
sentence is the most important unit of English speech. The
sentence is more important even than the word. Revelling in the
exercise of its imitative faculty, a child will attempt, however
imperfectly, to babble whole sentences. A schoolboy may be
. . . .

word-perfect in his recitation of a long and difficult poem while remaining blissfully ignorant of the poet's intention and meaning. "If hopes were dupes, fears may be liars," I say to console a friend. He may like the words and repeat them, and yet neither of us may pause to reflect upon the astounding personifications implied by Clough in this oft-repeated line. "Genuine poetry," Mr. T. S. Eliot has reminded us, "can communicate before it is understood." A lovely sentence may haunt my memory—

> And I shall have some peace there, for peace comes dropping
> slow,
> Dropping from the veils of the morning to where the cricket
> sings

—and I may often murmur it to myself without being at all conscious of linguistic form, or function, or even of meaning. Nevertheless, the effective speaker and writer of prose is he who does not merely *catch* his sentence-patterns but who *grips* them and wields them with well-controlled purpose. In addition to possessing a ready command of vocabulary, the good speaker must be endowed with an unerring sense of rhythm. Even the most gifted orator, however, cannot depart too far from the speech patterns accepted by the community in which he lives without running the grave risk of being misapprehended or of being only partially understood. In ordinary affirmations the subject is followed by the predicate, consisting of verb and object or complement. In all the Indo-European languages the sentence is normally bipartite. Basically it is a two-in-one. It is a binary unit. The subject is that to which the speaker wishes to draw the hearer's attention and the predicate is that which the speaker has to say about that subject. If I utter a defective sentence it is probably because, for some reason or other, I have failed to keep these two things clear in my mind. In order to put it right, I have only to ask myself the simple questions: What am I talking about? What have I to say about it? Or, in other words: What is my subject? What do I predicate of that subject? As Edward Sapir has so well said (*Language*, p. 36), "The major functional unit of speech, the sentence . . . is the linguistic expression of a proposition. It combines a subject of discourse with a statement in regard to this subject. Subject and predicate may be combined in a single word, as in Latin *dico;* each may be expressed independently, as in the English equivalent, *I say;* each or either may be so qualified as to lead to complex propositions of many sorts. No matter how many of these qualifying elements (words or functional parts of words) are introduced, the sentence does not lose its feeling of unity so long as each and every one of them falls in place as contributory to the definition of either the subject of discourse or the core of the predicate."

The predicate may indeed have preceded the subject in Proto-Indo-European, as in Modern Welsh, as in parenthetical "said he," or as in H. G. Wells's stylistic mannerism "Came a pause." The sentence-type *Down came the rain,* which is as old as Chaucer, finds its normal place in Modern German. Emphatic *down* comes first, the verb retains second place, and so the subject falls into the final position. It has been computed that the subject precedes the predicate in less than half of King Alfred's sentences, and if we study the shapes assumed by certain concrete locutions during the last thousand years or so, we detect a gradual shifting towards the modern order: subject, verb and object. Old English *mē gelīciaþ bēc* "To me are pleasing books" becomes modern English *I like books.* The vocables are identical, but the case of the pronoun has been altered from dative to nominative and the grammatical subject has been shifted from the things to the person. Since loving and liking are primarily active feelings, Modern English, it might be claimed, is here more rational than Old English. The modern grammatical subject becomes identical with the logical and the psychological one. Similarly, both *If you like* and *If you please* have derived historically from *If to you it may be pleasing* (*you* being dative of the pronoun and *like* and *please* third person singular of the present subjunctive) very much as in French *s'il vous plaît,* or Dutch *als 't u blieft* or old-fashioned German *wenn es Ihenen gefällt,* where, however, in all three languages, the verb is in the indicative. A still more striking example of the shifting of the grammatical subject to the first place in the sentence, without any resulting change in the position of the pronoun, is seen in *He was given the book* in which *the book* is "retained object." In the corresponding sentence in Old English, however, *the book* is the grammatical subject, *Him wæs gegiefen sēo bōc,* "(To) him was given the book." Similarly Chaucer's *It am I,* in which the grammatical subject is *I* (Old English *Hit eom ic,* Latin *Ego sum*), becomes Modern English *It is I.* In Chaucer's day the subjective character of *I* was still so strong that, in spite of word order, *It am I* sounded just as natural as Old French *Ce suis je.* French has certainly gone further than English in normalizing *C'est moi.* "L'état, c'est moi," said Louis XIV as long ago as in the seventeenth century, not "L'état, c'est je." *It is me* is regarded by many to be too colloquial for literary use. At the same time, the feeling predominates that, apart from grammatical structure, a verb should be followed by the accusative. No one, as Otto Jespersen pointed out, would venture to suggest changing Shelley's emphatic *me* in *Ode to the West Wind*—

> Be thou, Spirit fierce,
> My spirit! Be thou *me,* impetuous one!

No one is shocked by the ungrammatical *Fare thee well* instead of *Fare (go) thou well.*

In the sentence *It's me* the neuter pronoun *it* has no separate meaning. It is a meaningless substitute which brings this simple statement into the usual pattern of subject, and complement. In the casual observations *It is blowing hard, It is cold,* and *It is raining,* you might too readily assume that the neuter pronoun stands for *the wind, the weather,* and *the rain* respectively. "For the rain it raineth every day" sang the clown at the end of *Twelfth Night,* and Robert Louis Stevenson wrote playfully in his verses for children—

> The rain is raining all around
> It falls on field and tree.

After a little reflection you will probably conclude that *it* in *It is raining* is merely a substitute for the subject of the impersonal verb and that it expresses an action or a condition of things without reference to any agent.

Swift defined a good style as the use of proper words in proper places. The proper places will vary considerably according to degrees of emphasis. Usage has left many parts of the sentence relatively free and these we can vary to suit our purpose. Coleridge laid much stress on the importance of word order. He defined poetry, you may remember, as "the best words in the best order." In the words of the greatest poets "there is," Coleridge asserted, "a reason assignable not only for every word, but for the position of every word." In the well-ordered sentence the hearer or the reader will receive no jolt or check. As Herbert Spencer observed, "things which are to be thought of together must be mentioned as closely as possible together." Naturally we place together such words as are more closely associated in meaning. We say "a big brown dog" rather than "a brown big dog," "a handsome young man" and not "a young handsome man," and "a kind old gardener" and not "an old kind gardener." So, too, we place together those phrases which are most closely associated in our minds. "Delighted to make your acquaintance" we say upon being introduced and not, as in German, "Delighted your acquaintance to make."

The classification of sentences is not a difficult matter. Sentences are of three kinds according to *form:* simple ("I know it"), compound ("I know it and I am proud of it"), and complex ("I know that he will come"). They are of four kinds according to *function:* statement ("I know it"), command-wish ("Long live the King!"), question ("Are you coming?"), and exclamation ("How good you are!"). The verb generally comes before the subject in wishes and questions. As we pass from a simple to a complex sentence we do not, as in some other languages, change the order of the words: "I hope (that) he will come. He will, I hope, come. Presumably he will come." But in German we are bound to say: "Ich hoffe, er wird kommen. Ich hoffe, dass er kommen wird. Hoffentlich (vermutlich) wird er kommen."

Sentences may be further categorized according to *style* as loose, balanced, and periodic, although this division is of its very nature somewhat vague and ill defined. All three types of sentence are good and a master of English will weave them skilfully into the varied fabric of style. In the so-called *loose* sentence the writer or speaker states fact after fact just as these occur to him, freely and artlessly. Daniel Defoe opens *The Life and Adventures of Robinson Crusoe* with a long, loose, rambling sentence which nevertheless grips our attention at once: "I was born in the year 1632, in the city of York, of a good family, though not of that country, my father being a foreigner of Bremen, who settled first at Hull: he got a good estate by merchandise, and leaving off his trade, lived afterward at York, from whence he had married my mother, whose relations were named Robinson, a very good family in that country, and from whom I was called Robinson Kreutznoer; but, by the usual corruption of words in England, we are now called, nay, we call ourselves, and write our name Crusoe, and so my companions always called me." The style is conversational. We seem to hear the author talking quietly to us in the first person and telling us the story of his life. This imaginary autobiography seems at once factual and real. As the writer tells us about the time and the place of his birth, about his parentage and his name, he adds clause to clause pleasantly. The sentence might well have ended after the first clause, "I was born in the year 1632"; or it might have ended in at least thirteen other places after that. On the other hand, it might have gone on and on for many pages. There is no ambiguity, no obscurity, and no tautology. The reader receives no mental check. All is easy and natural. But behind this apparent artlessness there is art concealed, and behind this easy and natural prose—Defoe was writing in the year 1719—lay more than ten centuries of linguistic change and development. There is probably no surer way of appreciating the maturity and concreteness of Defoe's prose than by translating it into some foreign tongue.

In the *periodic* sentence the climax comes at the close. The reader is held in suspense until at last he hears what he has long been waiting for, and only then is he able to comprehend the meaning of the sentence as a whole. It is a style cultivated to good effect by the orators of classical antiquity, Demosthenes and Cicero, as well as those of modern times, Burke and Gladstone. When, in *The Laws of Ecclesiasticall Politie*, Richard Hooker reflected upon what might be the subsequent fate of man if the ordinances of nature should fail, he expressed himself in a stately and sonorous prose far different from Defoe's: "Now if nature should intermit her course, and leave altogether though it were but for a while the observation of her own laws; if those principal and mother elements of the world, whereof all things in this lower world are made, should lose the qualities which now they have; if the frame of that heavenly arch erected over our heads should loosen and dissolve itself; if celestial spheres should forget their wonted motions, and by irregular volubility turn themselves any way as it might happen; if the prince of the lights of heaven, which now as a giant doth run his unwearied course, should as it were through a languishing faintness begin to stand and to rest himself; if the moon should wander from her beaten way, the times and seasons of the year blend themselves by disordered and confused mixture, the winds breathe out their last gasp, the clouds yield no rain, the earth be defeated of heavenly influence, the fruits of the earth pine away as children at the withered breasts of their mother no longer able to yield them relief: what would become of man himself, whom these things now do all serve?" The language is highly rhythmical and the imagery is Biblical, reminiscent of Isaiah, the Psalms, and the Book of Job. The word-picture is painted with consummate art. After a long and steady climb upward over successive terraces of conditional clauses, the reader descends swiftly with the final rhetorical question.

As an example of a shorter but no less effective period we might consider the sentence in his *Autobiography* in which Edward Gibbon describes the birth of the idea of his great *History:* "It was at Rome, on the 15th of October 1764, as I sat musing amidst the ruins of the Capitol, while the barefooted friars were singing vespers in the temple of Jupiter, that the idea of writing the decline and fall of the city first started to my mind." In Rome, ruinous and Christian, late in the afternoon in the fall of the year, the inspiration came to the historian. The word-picture is brief, but it is artistically perfect. The rhythm

is stately and entirely satisfying. The reader is held in suspense
to the end.

Had he wished, and had he been less of an artist, Gibbon
might have said exactly the same things in a different way,
arranging them in their logical and grammatical order: "The
idea of writing the decline and fall of the city first started to
my mind as I sat musing amidst the ruins of the Capitol at
Rome on the 15th of October 1764, while the barefooted friars
were singing vespers in the temple of Jupiter." What has happened? It is not merely that a periodic sentence has been re-
expressed as a loose one. The emphasis is now all wrong and
the magnificent cadence of the original is quite marred. All is
still grammatically correct, but "proper words" are no longer
in "proper places." The passage has quite lost its harmonious
rhythm.

The *balanced* sentence satisfies a profound human desire for
equipoise and symmetry and it has long been at home in English
as in Hebrew, Greek, and Latin, and many other languages both
ancient and modern. It may express two similar thoughts in
parallelism or two opposing ones in *antithesis*. Such proverbial
sayings as *Like master like man, More haste less speed, First
come first served,* and *Least said soonest mended* probably represent a primitive Indo-European sentence-type which survives in
many lands.

"Children sweeten labours," wrote Francis Bacon, "but they
make misfortunes more bitter: they increase the cares of life,
but they mitigate the remembrance of death." Speaking at the
Guildhall, London, on October 9, 1805, just one fortnight after
the Battle of Trafalgar, William Pitt declared: "England has
saved herself by her exertions and will, I trust, save Europe by
her example." No less memorable was the balanced sentence
uttered in the House of Lords by Edward Viscount Grey of
Fallodon on August 3, 1914, on the eve of Britain's entry into
the First World War: "The lamps are going out all over Europe:
we shall not see them lit again in our lifetime."

English sentence-patterns show infinite variety and *loose, periodic,* and *balanced* are only relative terms. The best writers

shape their sentences in such a way as to give just the right degree of emphasis, and this they must achieve, in written language, by word order alone. Now it is certainly not surprising that in a language like ours, with such a long history behind it, some patterns have become blended, mixed, or, to use the technical term, "contaminated," and that some of these "contaminations" have been sanctioned by usage. "I am friendly with him" and "We are friends" ("He and I are friends") have become contaminated and so have produced "I am friends with him." It is an idiom or manner of expression peculiar to English. "I am friends with him" cannot be translated literally into French, German, or Italian, though it is as old as Shakespeare. "I am good friends with my father," says Prince Hal (I *Henry the Fourth,* III. iii. 202), "and may do any thing." "But whom say ye that I am?" (*St. Matthew,* xvi, 15) is frequently quoted from the King James Bible as an example of an ungrammatical accusative *whom* used as the complement of the verb *to be.* Is it, then, an error? Perhaps no direct yes or no can be given in answer to this question. The sentence is a good example of a blending of "Who say ye that I am?" and "Whom say ye me to be?" That is all. The English poets, even the very greatest of them, have occasionally indulged in such contaminations of sentence-structures, refusing to be bound by strict rules. "I should have liked to have been there," someone will say. Clearly this is a blending of "I should like (I wish now as I look back) to have been there" and "I should have liked (but unfortunately I was unable) to be there." "They each did their best" is likewise a mixture of "They all (all of them) did their best" and "Each of them did his best."

If it is true that we repeat sentences from memory and vary them by analogy, and that we do not really frame sentences in any other way, then we should perhaps look upon all analogous creations with a kind and indulgent eye. "Do like I do" is no worse than Elizabethan "Do like as I do." "Do like me" and "Do as I do" mark a desirable distinction, but it would be well to recognize that the distinction is more stylistic than grammatical. "What are you doing of?" is the Cockney's analogous creation, based upon "What are you doing?" and "What are you thinking of?" "I would say" and "I should like to say" are blended and so we hear "I would like to say," an undesirable form which is helped on its way to acceptance by the general tendency, especially in North America and in Ireland, to ignore the (relatively recent) traditional distinctions between *shall* (*should*) in the first person and *will* (*would*) in the second and third. "It looks as though" is now on everyone's lips—"It looks as though there will be a general election (or anything else for that matter) soon." "It looks to me," said Burke in 1790 (*Reflections on the Revolution in France*) "as if I were in a great crisis." The verb to-day would be in the past subjunctive (or subjunctive equivalent) if people were conscious of the precise implication: "It appears as would or might be the case if." But "It looks as though" has come to be a mere substitute for "apparently, probably, by all appearances," and it is now invariably followed by the future tense. "You and I will decide between us" has influenced "Let you and me decide" which becomes "Let you and I decide" on the lips of the heedless, who no longer think of "Let us decide" as "Allow us to decide" supplanting "Decide we," the old jussive. Whatever the grammarians may say, there is abundant evidence in many languages for the use of the superlative degree in a comparison of only two persons or things. Nevertheless, "Which (selective) is the stronger of the two?" is more satisfactory than "Who is the strongest of the two?" If we say "He was one of the kindest men that has ever lived" we break that favourite rule of the prescriptive grammarians which states that the verb in a relative clause should agree with its nearer antecedent. Doubtless we are thereby confusing "He was the kindest man that ever lived" and "He was one of the kindest men that have ever lived." We may confuse "The reason why printing is slow is that paper is scarce" and "Printing is slow because paper is scarce" and, as a result, we say "The reason why printing is slow is because paper is scarce." If we are observant and alert, we shall probably hear many interesting "contaminations," such as these, both tolerable and intolerable, every day of our lives.

Another interesting thing we shall observe is the way in which natural emphasis overrides strict logic in word order. "He only died last week" may be denounced by modern precisians on the ground that it flouts one of those rules of proximity whereby the modifying adverb should be placed as near as possible to the word, phrase or clause it modifies. "He died only last week" or "It was only last week that he died" should stand. Stress, intonation, and pause, however, make everything clear, or even clearer, when *only* is detached. "He only died last week" implies no ambiguity and no misplaced emphasis. Shakespeare himself wrote in Sonnet xciv—

> The summer's flower is to the summer sweet
> Though to itself it only live and die

—and not "Though only to itself" or "Though to itself alone," the latter cadence seeming certainly preferable to my modern ear. Mr. Vernon Bartlett once opened a wireless talk on world affairs with the words: "I am not an expert on China. I have only been there twice in my life." Natural emphasis and intonation were just right: the hearer's attention was arrested at once. "I have been there only twice in my life" would have sounded unnatural and pedantic in comparison. Language, after all, is more psychological than logical. So, too, in regard to the placing of the preposition, we should do well to divest ourselves of the notion that it is "an inelegant word to end a sentence with" and that, just because it is called a *pre-position*, it must therefore "be placed before." In Old English (*ūs betwēonan* "between us") as in Latin (*pāx vōbiscum* "peace be with you"), there were *postpositions* and the tradition has been kept alive through centuries of English poetry: "the table round" (Shakespeare); "stoutly struts his dames before" (Milton); "my heart within" (Scott); "the willowy hills and fields among" (Tennyson); "I will go to France again, and tramp the valley through" (Flecker). The final preposition became a butt for the nineteenth-century grammarians, who averred that the most careful writers avoided it and that the Authorized Version of the Bible contained not one instance of it. As a matter of fact, the curious reader will not go far in the Book of Genesis before encountering an example in Chapter xxviii: "I will not leave thee, until I have done that which I have spoken to thee of." It is a remarkable fact that even Dryden, that acknowledged master of English prose, criticized Ben Jonson's conversational style adversely on the ground that it showed the "common fault" of putting the preposition at the end, a fault which, Dryden added, "I have but lately observed in my own writings." Indeed, when revising his *Essay of Dramatic Poesy*, Dryden went so far as to rewrite the sentences in which an end preposition occurred and his illustrious example was followed by others. To-day we accept the final preposition as permissible and desirable in such natural and spontaneous expressions as "What are you thinking of?" and "I sometimes wonder what the world is coming to." Phrasal verbs, consisting of verbs joined with adverbs and prepositions, are now in such frequent use that, in order to avoid the prepositional ending entirely, a speaker would sometimes be driven to perpetrate an intolerably artificial sentence. Against such a clumsy sentence, according to Sir Ernest Gowers (*Plain Words*, p. 74), Mr Winston Churchill is said to have added the marginal comment: "This is the sort of English up with which I will not put." Sir Ernest goes on to tell the story of a nurse who contrived to get no fewer than four prepositions together at the end of a sentence when she asked a child: "What did you choose that book to be read to out of for?" And did the child understand? If stress, rhythm, intonation, and pause were right, yes. The nurse "said what she wanted to say perfectly clearly, in words of one syllable, and what more can one ask?" You may have observed, by the way, that *out* in "read to out of for" is really an adverb or, if you will, that *out-of* is a prepositional compound consisting of adverb and preposition. At any rate, the dividing line between prepositions and adverbs is often shadowy and vague.

The English sentence, then, is something of a paradox. Word order has become more significant than hitherto, far more important than in Old, Middle, or Tudor English, and yet it has retained enough of its elasticity to give to the skilful speaker all the scope and power he needs. We English have inherited our sentence-patterns, but we have abundant freedom to vary words, phrases, and clauses within those inherited patterns. We shall be effective as speakers and as writers if we can say clearly, simply, and attractively just what we want to say and nothing more. If we really have something worth saying, then we are bound by the nature and necessities of our language to say it as simply as ever we can. If we have something very abstruse and complex to say, then, of course, we cannot say it simply, but we shall endeavour to say it as clearly as the theme permits. We shall vary our style, our vocabulary and our speech-level to suit the occasion and, at the same time, we shall never lose sight of the needs and capacities of our hearers. If, following the wise counsel of Aristotle, we keep these three things constantly in mind—our subject-matter, our purpose, and our audience—all will be well.

IV.

USAGE

A reader new to the subject may feel that modern essays on usage are like an adult western. In place of the old reliable melodrama of hero and villain, correct and incorrect, we are offered a confusing, adult reasonableness. In the first essay, Professor Robert Pooley of the University of Wisconsin shows that the family background of the formerly admired rules of grammar and usage is linguistically disreputable. Puzzled whether to use *slow* or *slowly,* we are no longer referred to a rule but to the history of the word and to our own sense of euphony and appropriateness. One source of puzzlement is the changing status of words and expressions. "Hisn" formed by the analogy with "mine" is not now "correct," but as Robert A. Hall, Jr., observes in the second essay, "today's analogical 'mistakes' are often tomorrow's competing forms, and day-after-tomorrow's 'correct' forms."

Even a dictionary editor cannot reasonably pose as an umpire of usage. His proper job, as Charles Fries argues in the third essay, is to describe rather than to arbitrate. To aid us, the editor classifies his descriptive findings under various labels: *colloquial, British,* and so on. By attending to his labels we may select a language that will make us sound like an illiterate Yankee, a Southern gentleman, or any one of a dozen other characters. But the choice is ours. That is the point of the fourth essay, the account of multiple negation by Professor Allan Hubbell of New York University. If we choose or are brought up to multiply negatives we will sound like an educated Elizabethan or a modern illiterate but not like an educated American.

That class distinctions in usage exist in a democratic society is disturbing. Anger at such inequality colors the famous economist Thorstein Veblen's argument that the use of "correct" language is merely a way of showing off one's social and economic superiority. Professor Donald Lloyd of Wayne University contends further that fear of being "incorrect" muddies our writing. He urges us to have the courage to write as well as we talk. The same fear is the object of humorous satire by the British essayist, Max Beerbohm, who implies that in an effort to be "correct" we lose ourselves in an abject and hypocritical sameness of expression. Mark Twain's entertaining account of Buck Fanshaw's funeral is a reminder of the colorful geographical and class differences in usage which the spread of "correctness" tends to eliminate. In the last essay, the Canadian essayist, Stephen Leacock, discusses slang and swearing, and shows with wise humor that they should not be flatly condemned or approved, but judged on the basis of their vitality and usefulness.

ROBERT C. POOLEY

Historical Backgrounds of English Usage

The English language in the Elizabethan period underwent an enormous expansion in its vocabulary. From travelers on the Continent and in the New World, from the scholars of the classical languages in the universities, and from experiments among English writers there poured in a flood of words, most of which became assimilated into the language. Part of the effervescence of the Elizabethan era found its vent in the game of words—not before or since has English witnessed such absorbing interest in words and their meanings, nor such an enormous increase in the number of words. Grammar, on the other hand, attracted little attention and was taken for granted. While the major outlines of English grammar had become fairly fixed by the time of Shakespeare and were essentially the grammar we know today, it was a popular or traditional, rather than a formal, grammar. A study of the usage of Elizabethan dramatists, for example, reveals far greater freedom in number agreement, in double comparatives, and in double negatives than is tolerated in current writing. Elizabethan dramatic literature, in short, is a faithful reproduction of the normal speech of Elizabethan gentlemen, who wrote as they spoke, unhampered by considerations of formal correctness.

The verbal enthusiasm of the Elizabethan era was followed by a natural reaction toward restraint. From the beginning of the seventeenth century there appeared a critical attitude toward

. . . .

From *Teaching English Usage*. Copyright, 1946, The National Council of Teachers of English. Reprinted by permission of Appleton-Century-Crofts, Inc.

English, voiced at first by a few scattered writers who felt that English was an uncouth and disorderly language, lacking the beauty and regularity of Latin and Greek. Gradually the idea of the impurity and irregularity of English came to be commonly accepted, so that by the end of the seventeenth century the interest in language had shifted almost entirely from vocabulary to grammar and syntax. This change of interest was accompanied by a zeal for reform and by a great increase in the numbers of books on the English language. Prior to 1700 there were few books devoted to language criticism; in the first half of the eighteenth century approximately fifty such books appeared, and in the succeeding half century over two hundred were published. These figures reveal the tremendous interest in language which characterized the latter part of the eighteenth century.

The same spirit which brought about the Augustan Age of English literature, the "improving" of Shakespeare and the editing of Milton, accelerated the purifying and correcting of English. That a large part of the critical work in English was beneficial to the language cannot be denied, but unfortunately there was much bad mixed with the good. Many of the writers on language were retired clergymen and country philosophers, who, though possessing some skill in the classics, had no conception at all of the history of English or the methods of linguistic research. Too frequently their statements on English usage were the product of false philology or of personal prejudice. Moreover, the philosophy of the age was inimical to scientific research in language; the prevailing conceptions of language were (1) that language is a divine institution, originally perfect, but debased by man; (2) that English is a corrupt and degenerate off-spring of Latin and Greek. The first theory gave rise to the application of reason and the analogy of the language in an effort to restore English to its pristine glory; the second resulted in corrections of English idioms to make them conform to classical models. The actual usage of English was ignored or despised by all but one or two of the writers of this age.

Thus we find the laudable effort to improve and correct the grammar and syntax of English sadly handicapped by ignorance of linguistic principles on the one hand and misleading philosophies on the other. Yet the prescriptions of the reformers, whether good or bad, were received, approved, and formulated into rules; the rules were gathered into textbooks and were copied from book to book throughout the nineteenth century and may still be found in the books we are now using. In the meantime the English language has continued its organic growth, only slightly influenced by the rules prescribed for it, until today many of the rules bear no more than a faint resemblance to the language customs they are supposed to describe. It is small wonder that English teachers are perplexed in trying to reconcile dead rules with a living language!

The links between the reformers of the eighteenth century and the textbooks of today may be easily traced. One of the most influential of the eighteenth-century writers on language was Bishop Lowth, whose *Short Introduction to English Grammar* appeared in 1762. In 1795 an American named Lindley Murray wrote a grammar, nearly all of which he copied from Lowth. Murray's book enjoyed an enormous popularity; it is estimated that over a million copies were sold in America before 1850. Murray's successors copied freely from his book, so that the direct influence of Lowth persisted well into the latter part of the nineteenth century. The vast expansion of the United States since the Civil War, the accompanying increase in the numbers of textbooks, and the greatly improved theories and methods of education have resulted in textbooks very different in character from those of Lowth and Murray; but whereas in organization and technique the books have made great forward strides, in actual content they still retain much of the theory and practice of the eighteenth and nineteenth centuries.

The teaching of English usage is still further confused by the conflict between the traditional rules, whose origins we have just traced, and the modern science of linguistics, which is giving us entirely new concepts of language and its functions. Linguistics teaches us to look at language from the viewpoints of history, psychology, and sociology, and to understand and interpret modern usage in the light of these factors rather than upon a set of traditional authorities. Some examples of the application of these principles may be interesting to include here.

History. Many textbooks contain warnings against the use of the word *slow* as an adverb, pointing out that *slow* is an adjective with a corresponding adverb *slowly*. But when we look back into the history of English, we discover that adverbs were formed in two ways in early English; sometimes by adding *-lic* (the ancestor of *-ly*) and sometimes by just adding *-e*. Thus the descendant of *slow-lic* is *slowly*, a regular adverb, and the descendant of *slow-e* is *slow*, an irregular or "flat" adverb. Both are correct, native English; both have been used in English literature; and both may be used today. The decision as to when to use one or the other is a matter of euphony and appropriateness in the sentence; one need never hesitate to say, "Drive slow!"

Psychology. Textbooks warn us about placing *only* in the sentence so that it is next to the word it modifies; for example, a sentence like this would be called incorrect by many textbooks: "I *only* had five dollars." Logically it is incorrect, because *only* appears to modify the pronoun *I*, but psychologically it is correct, because custom has established the pattern of the sentence beyond possibility of misunderstanding. If you wanted to say that you were the only one to have five dollars, you would have to say, "I *alone* had five dollars," or "*Only* I had five dollars." The regular pattern, "I *only* had five dollars," has but one meaning, namely, that you possessed no more than five dollars. In this manner the psychology of sentence patterns supersedes logic.

Sociology. The only valid basis for the creation, preservation, or extinction of a word is its usefulness to society. If the people need a word it will live; if it is no longer needed it will die. For this reason the Old English word *a*, which meant *law*, was completely eradicated by the Scandinavian word *law* because the latter was less open to confusion, and therefore more useful to society. In similar fashion a modern need is establishing the foreign word *data* as a singular noun meaning *information* or *collection of facts,* despite the fact that it is a Latin plural. There is little doubt that a few more years will establish "The *data is* complete," not because of logical correctness, but because society finds the word *data* useful as a singular noun. These are but a few of the hundreds of examples which might be cited.

The Determination of "Correct" English

In the year 1712 Dean Swift wrote a letter to the Earl of Oxford outlining a plan for the foundation of an English academy similar to the French Academy for the purpose of regularizing and establishing correct English. Although his plan was received with interest, it was never acted upon, and many later attempts to found an academy have failed. The purists of the later eighteenth century did much of what Swift desired, but fortunately for the life and vigor of our tongue it has never been submitted to the restraint of a board of authorities. Several theories of "correctness" in English have therefore been formulated and have influenced writers and teachers of the past and present. One of the most important of these theories was that enunciated by George Campbell in 1776, that "correctness" rests in good custom, defined as "national," "reputable" and "present." This definition was accepted by practically all the nineteenth-century grammarians (although they frequently did it violence in specific instances), and may be found in a number of the high-school composition books of the present day. Another theory, really a modification of Campbell's, proposed by Fitzedward Hall and other nineteenth-century students of language, is that "good usage is the usage of the best writers and speakers." This definition is also very widely used in the textbooks of today, and is probably the expressed or implied standard of good English in almost every American schoolroom. Both of these definitions, useful as they have been and are, present many difficulties in application to the teaching of current usage.

The chief difficulty lies in the interpretation of the terms "reputable" and "the best writers and speakers." For example, nearly all grammar books list as undesirable English the use of the split infinitive, the dangling participle or gerund, the possessive case of the noun with inanimate objects, the objective case of the noun with the gerund, the use of *whose* as a neuter relative pronoun, and many others; yet all of these uses may be found in the authors who form the very backbone of English literature and who are "reputable" and the "best writers" in every sense of the words. If the standard-makers defy the standards, to whom shall we turn for authority? Moreover, the use of literary models tends to ignore the canon of *present* usage, for by the time an author has come to be generally recognized as *standard* his usage is no longer *present*. And among present speakers, who are best? The writer has heard a large number of the most prominent platform speakers of the day, yet he has still to hear one who did not in some manner violate the rules of the books. Are all great writers and speakers at fault, or is it possible that the rules are inaccurate?

The way out of this perplexity is to shift the search for standards away from "authorities" and traditional rules to the language itself as it is spoken and written today. Just as the chemist draws his deductions from the results of laboratory experiments, the biologist from his observation of forms of life, and the astronomer from his telescope, so must students of language draw their deductions from an observation of the facts of language. In establishing the laws of language, our personal desires, preferences, and prejudices must give way to the scientific determination and interpretation of the facts of language. What language we use ourselves may take any form we desire, but the making of rules and the teaching of rules must rest upon objective facts. We must take the attitude of a distinguished scholar who said recently of *due to*, "I don't like it, but there is no doubt about its establishment in English."

If we discard the authority of rules and of "reputable" writers, to what can we turn for a definition of "correct" English? At the outset it must be acknowledged that there can be no absolute, positive definition. "Correct English" is an approximate term used to describe a series of evaluations of usage dependent upon appropriateness, locality, social level, purpose, and other variables. It is a relative term, in decided contrast with the positive nature of (1) *reputability*, the determination of good usage by reference to standard authors; (2) *preservation*, the obligation to defend and maintain language uses because they are traditional, or are felt to be more elegant; (3) *literary*, the identification of good usage with formal literary usage. By discarding these traditional conceptions, and turning to the language itself as its own standard of good usage, we may find the following definition adequate for our present needs. <u>Good English is that form of speech which is appropriate to the purpose of the speaker, true to the language as it is, and comfortable to speaker and listener. It is the product of custom, neither cramped by rule nor freed from all restraint; it is never fixed, but changes with the organic life of the language.</u>

Such a definition is linguistically sound because it recognizes the living, organic nature of language; it is historically sound, for the language of the present is seen to be the product of established custom; it is socially sound in recognizing the purpose of language and its social acceptability in *comfort* to speaker and writer.

Teachers of English will recognize that the acceptance of this or a similar definition of good English necessitates great changes in the presentation of usage in textbooks and in the classroom. Those who are accustomed to rule and authority, to an absolute right and wrong in language, will find great difficulty in making the mental readjustment imperative for a relative rather than an absolute standard of usage. Much of the conventional teaching of grammar and correctness will have to be vastly modified or discarded. There will be much confusion and some distress. But eventually there will grow up in the schools a new theory of good English so closely knit with the language itself that the perplexity now arising from the discrepancies between rule and usage will no longer have cause for existence. But in discarding an absolute right and wrong for a relative standard of appropriateness and social acceptability, we shall have to determine the areas or levels of language usage, to define and illustrate them, and to apply them as standards for the written and spoken English in the schools.

ROBERT A. HALL, JR.

Analogy

Internal borrowing, or *analogy*, is the kind of change that takes place when a child says *foots* instead of *feet, oxes* instead of *oxen, sticked* instead of *stuck*, or *breaked* instead of *broke*. We usually call such forms as *foots, oxes, sticked, breaked* "mistakes" and all of us—even the most illiterate users of sub-standard English—train our children to say *feet*, not *foots*, and so on. Yet what lies at the root of these "mistakes" is an extremely widespread process, which we call *analogical replacement*. What has happened when the child has said *foots* or *sticked?* Simply this: he has heard and learned a whole host of "regular" forma-tions—plural formations such as *root—roots, hat—hats, book—books, map—maps, box—boxes*, and past formations like *kick —kicked, lick—licked, trick—tricked, rake—raked*, in the hundreds and thousands. He has simply made his new formation of a plural for *foot* or *ox* by abstracting (unconsciously, for the most part) the "regular" ending *-s, -es* and adding it to *foot* or *ox*. Likewise, he has taken the "regular" past ending *-ed* or *breaked* "on the analogy" of other pasts like *kicked, raked*, and so on. He is making what we often call an *analogical new-formation*, by borrowing an element of linguistic form or construction (here the noun-plural suffix *-s -es* or the verb past suffix *-ed*) from one part of our linguistic structure (here the "regular" forma-tions) and adding it to another (here the "irregular" forms). This is a kind of borrowing, just like external borrowing; but the
. . . .

From *Leave Your Language Alone!* Copyright 1950 by Robert A. Hall, Jr. Reprinted by permission of the author.

source of borrowing is not somewhere outside but within the language itself, and so we call it internal borrowing.

Analogical changes of this kind are often presented in the shape of proportional formulas, with x standing for the new-formation, thus

> *hat: hats = foot:* (*"hat* is to *hats* as *foot* is to x")
> *box: boxes = ox: x*
> *kick: kicked = stick: x*
> *rake: raked = break: x*

Sometimes, objections are made to our statement of analogical replacements in a proportional formula, such as those we have just given; critics say that naive speakers would not be capable of exact enough reasoning to make up a formula of this sort and carry it out. There are two answers to this objection: 1) that what we are giving here is a description of what takes place, not a statement of reasoning that we might necessarily expect from a naive speaker, who speaks normally without abstract analysis and who habitually does perfectly many things he could not possibly describe; and 2) that even naive speakers from time to time are perfectly conscious of the basis for their analogical formations. The great Danish linguistician Otto Jespersen tells the story of a Danish child who should, according to normal Danish usage, have said *nikkede* "nodded" as the past of *nikker* "nod," but said *nak* instead on the analogy of *stak* "stuck," whose present is *stikker*. When the child was corrected, he immediately retorted "*Stikker—stak, nikker—nak,*" showing that he knew perfectly well on what analogy he had made the new past tense form, and stating it in the form of a proportion.

From the point of view of the present language, analogical new-formations like *oxes* or *taked* are "mistakes," forms that would be uttered only by children or others learning the language, or by adults when tired or flustered (that is, as "slips of the tongue"), and that would not be accepted by any native speaker at present. But there are always some forms with regard to which our usage is not fully settled, even that of normal adult native speakers of the language, and for which we may use first one and then another alternative. We have, for instance, the "irregular" plural formation *hoof—hooves,* and the "strong" past tenses *wake—woke, dive—dove;* yet we often hear and make regularized forms for these words: *hoofs, waked, dived.* That is to say, in some respects our usage is *fluctuating;* and in the course of time, we will gradually come to favor one competing form over the other (say, *dived* over *dove*), until at last one is triumphant and drives out the other completely in normal everyday usage.

What we often fail to realize, however, is that some forms which seem fully fixed in our present language were, in earlier times, analogical new-formations, and went through a period of newness, and then of fluctuation, before displacing older forms entirely. Our plurals *days* and *cows* are both analogical replacements of earlier forms which would have sounded quite different if they had developed normally into Modern English. Old English had the singular *dag* "day," plural *dagas,* and *cū* "cow," plural *cȳ* (in which the letter *y* stands for a vowel like that spelled *u* in French or *ü* in German); the Old English plurals, had they developed normally, would have given *dawes* and *kye* (rhyming with *high*) in present-day English. But we do not say *day—dawes* or *cow—kye;* we use the regularized plurals *days* and *cows* instead. This is because around the year 1200, our linguistic ancestors made an analogical new-formation, borrowing the stem *day* from the singular to replace the stem *dawe-* in the plural before the ending *-s.* In the plural of *cow,* there were two successive analogical formations. Around the year 1300, people started to use the plural *kyn,* with the analogical plural ending *-n* (which was then very frequent, but survives now only in *oxen, children, brethren*). The form *kyn* survives at present as an archaism, *kine;* in its turn, it was replaced around 1600 by the plural *cows,* in which the plural ending *-s* was borrowed from the majority of nouns and added to the singular *cow.* There must have been a time when *days* seemed as much of a "mistake" as *foots* does now, and—slightly later—a period when *days* and *dawes* were in competition just as *hoofs* and *hooves* are now. If we extend our time-perspective far enough back, we can see that we use relatively few plural formations which are direct continuations of those in use four or five thousand years ago.

These considerations are of importance when it comes to judging forms like *hisn, hern,* and so forth, or *he done.* When an "ignorant" person borrows the ending *-n* from the possessive pronoun *mine* and adds it to the adjectives *his, her, our, your* and *their,* to make the distinctive possessive pronouns *hisn, hern, ourn, yourn, theirn,* this procedure on his part is not due to ignorance or stupidity. It is due to exactly the same process of analogizing, of regularizing the forms of the language, that we saw in the instances of *cows* or *days,* and that has gone on in producing a great many other forms we now use. The analogy in this instance is, of course:

$$my : mine = his : x$$

and so forth. Likewise, such a past tense as *he done* is traceable to some such analogy as this:

$$he \ has \ kicked : he \ kicked = he \ has \ done : x$$

That such forms as *hisn* or *he done* are not accepted as part of the standard language is not due to any defect in the forms themselves—they are perfectly respectable analogical forms, with as much right to existence as *cows* and *days;* the thing that makes them unacceptable is simply the connotation of social disfavor which has been attached to them.

Very often, internal borrowing (analogy) comes into play when linguistic forms become irregular and grammatical relationships are obscured as a result of changes in phonemes. This is what happened in the case of English *day—dawes;* it has happened in recent centuries in such instances as those of the old plurals *eye—eyen, shoe—shoon, brother—brethren,* which have now been replaced by the more transparent and easily understandable formations *eyes, shoes, brothers* respectively; or in such past tenses of verbs as *help—holp, work—wrought,* now regularized by analogy in the new-formations *helped, worked.*

In English noun plurals and verb pasts and past participles, the trend of development is slowly but surely towards analogical leveling of irregularities; even though forms like *gooses, mouses* or *drinked, writed* are simply "errors" or "blunders" now, they may perhaps be perfectly normal by two or three hundred years from now. Today's analogical "mistakes" are often tomorrow's competing forms, and day-after-tomorrow's "correct" forms.

CHARLES C. FRIES

Usage Levels and Dialect Distribution

Even a very superficial examination of the language practices of
native speakers of English will reveal many differences in those
practices from person to person. A hasty glance at the materials
gathered for the *Linguistic Atlas of New England* not only will
confirm the impression one receives from casually listening to the
speech of those who talk English but will furnish convincing evidence that the differences of usage among native speakers of English are much greater and much more intricate than is usually believed. These differences of English usage occur not only in
matters of vocabulary but also in matters of grammar and
especially in matters of pronunciation. It is these differences in
the practice of those who speak English that give rise to the
many discussions concerning our language and often send students and others to our dictionaries for the information necessary
to understand these differences. Ever since the publication of
Samuel Johnson's *English Dictionary* in 1755 the "dictionary"
has been looked to and consulted as the "authority" concerning
the acceptability of words and the proper use of word meanings.
"What does *the* dictionary say?" occurs as the common question
in all our disputes concerning our language—as if there were
but one dictionary with ultimate authority and as if the statements recorded in any dictionary were valid for all time. Those
who ask "What does the dictionary say?" practically never inquire
concerning the publication date of the particular dictionary con-

. . . .

From *American College Dictionary*. Copyright Random House, Inc., 1947,
1948. Reprinted by permission of the publisher.

sulted or the qualifications of those who have produced it. The desire for an easily accessible "authority" on the part of the general public has created an enormous market for many cheap dictionaries, often produced by unscrupulous publishers who have achieved cheapness by reprinting old dictionary materials upon which the copyright has expired—adding, of course, a few of the well-known new words in order to give the appearance of being up-to-date.

Attitudes toward Usage Differences

Part of the difficulty lies in the common and traditional view of the differences of English usage. Often it is assumed that there exist in any language only two kinds of words, word meanings, and pronunciations: those that are correct and proper and those that are incorrect or mistakes. The "mistakes" are thought to be derived by ignorance and carelessness from the correct or proper uses. It is assumed also that the separation and labeling of the mistakes is a simple process and that grammarians and lexicographers have long ago made the proper decisions and the results of their work need only be preserved and made known to succeeding generations. It is assumed that all dictionaries will incorporate these "accepted" decisions and therefore there is no reason to inquire concerning the qualifications of the editors of a new dictionary or even the means employed to make the assignment of usage labels valid.

Necessity of Recording Usage

From the point of view of modern linguistic science these common naïve assumptions concerning the differences of usage in English must be discarded. They belong to a prescientific period in the study of language—to an age that still believes the earth to be flat and denies the circulation of the blood. The modern dictionary editor who is aware of the principles and methods of the modern scientific study of language and of the accumulations of knowledge concerning our language built up by the patient study of many scholars cannot in honesty follow the easy path of copying the usage labels as they are attached to words and word meanings in former dictionaries. He cannot, as Samuel Johnson often did, condemn words and word meanings in accord with his special prejudices. Johnson, in spite of the fact that his quotations show that the word *excepting* is used by Dryden and Collier, condemns it with the label "an improper word." In similar fashion he attaches the label "low words" to *budge, fun,* and *clever,* although his own quotations give examples of these words from Shakespeare and from Moore, from Addison, Pope, and Arbuthnot.

Constant change—in pronunciation, in grammatical structure, in word meanings, and in the words themselves—is, as far as we know, the normal condition of every language spoken by a living people. The careful study of these changes by the rigorous techniques developed by linguistic science has given us linguistic history. A hundred years of scholarly work has gone into establishing the details of the history of the English language and has forced us to turn away from the methods of "authority" as they are represented in Samuel Johnson's *Dictionary* and its successors. It has demanded the patient recording of the facts of usage as the language is and has been employed by the hosts of speakers of English in this country and in the other countries where English is the language in which the major affairs of the people are conducted. The editor of a modern dictionary is thus confronted with a wide range of constantly changing differences in English usage that cannot be easily separated into correct and proper forms on the one hand and mistakes on the other. These changes in usage render the older dictionaries inaccurate and make necessary continually new examinations of the status of the words and word meanings in English. A dictionary can be an "authority" only in the sense in which a book of chemistry or of physics or of botany can be an "authority"—by the accuracy and the completeness of its record of the observed facts of the field examined, in accord with the latest principles and techniques of the particular science. Older "authorities" in the uses of words are thus superseded by those which incorporate the latest results of the more scientific investigations in the English language.

Regional Differences

In the matter of English usage it is not always possible to define precisely the boundaries within which a word or a word meaning is used or recognized. The facilities of travel have so developed in modern times that many speakers of English hear constantly the language of those from other geographical areas. And the radio has brought into even the most secluded communities the speech of all sections of the country. This mixing of speech forms from various geographical areas is not by any means limited to the upper classes.

> "I knowed you wasn't Oklahomy folks. You talk queer kinda—That ain't no blame, you understan'."
> "Ever'body says words different," said Ivy. "Arkansas folks says 'em different, and Oklahomy folks says 'em different. And we seen a lady from Massachusetts, an' she said 'em differentest of all. Couldn' hardly make out what she was sayin'."
> (J. Steinbeck, *The Grapes of Wrath*, p. 168.)

In the great mass of differences of usage that appear in the practice of English speakers, however, some words and word meanings and some pronunciations are in common use in special parts of the English-speaking world and appear much less frequently or never in other areas. For these this dictionary marks the geographical areas of special use. Some of the areas thus indicated within this country are New England, the old South, and the Southwest for such words as the following: *selectman, sharpie, levee* [1] (def. 1), *granny* (def. 4), *corn pone, alamo, chaps, chuck wagon* (see the definitions of these words).

British usage differs from the usage of the United States in such words as *lift* (def. 21), *navvy, lorry* (def. 1), *petrol* (def. 1), *gorse* (see the definitions of these words, and the preface by A. W. Read on "British and American Usage," page xxviii).

And Australia has its particular words and word meanings, as *paddock* (def. 3), *swag* [2] (def. 2), *billabong, billy* (def. 3) (see the definitions of these words).

Many words and word meanings are characteristic of certain fields of human activity. Each trade and occupation and sport has its technical vocabulary. Some of this technical vocabulary consists of special words used only in science, art, trade, or sport, such as *Binet test, electrode, binnacle, chiaroscuro, silo, forward pass* (see the definitions of these words).

Much of these technical vocabularies, however, consists of special meanings and uses of words that are employed generally in the language. The *field* in baseball has a special sense, as does *sacrifice, run, hit, out, plate, pitcher.* In the preparation and marketing of alcoholic beverages, the words *proof, dry, mash,* and *smooth* are used with special meanings.

"Levels" of Usage

Most frequently, however, discussions of language center upon what are often called the "levels" of usage. Some words and word meanings are frequently called "slang." The term "slang" has suffered such a wide extension of its signification and has been applied to so many varieties of words that it is extremely difficult to draw the line between what is slang and what is not. The difference between slang and not-slang does not rest in the meanings of the words themselves. To say that a man is "recalcitrant" is using an acceptable and somewhat learned word; to call him "a kicker" in the same situation is using slang, although the meanings are similar. Some clipped words, as *gent*, are often regarded as slang; others, such as *piano, phone,* and *cello*, are not slang. Slang cannot be defined in terms of either the forms or the strict meanings of the words themselves; it can, however, be characterized in terms of the suggested feelings accompanying certain words—their connotations rather than their denotations. Flippant humor marks the expressions we call slang. Some examples are *Java* (def. 3), *ice* (def. 8), *croak* (def. 4), *hangout, corking* (see the definitions of these words).

Some expressions appear only in poetry. They suggest then those circumstances in which they usually occur. Others are now found only in the written material of books. To mark them *"Poetic"* and *"Literary"* serves to record the special areas in

which they are commonly used. Some examples are *gloaming,
e'er, lidless* (def. 3), *naught* (def. 2), *scarce* (def. 4) (see the
definitions of these words).

Many expressions occur primarily in conversation rather than
in formal writing. The occasions for their use are chiefly conversational situations. These are marked "*Colloq.*" Even teachers of
English frequently misunderstand the application of the label
Colloquial in our best dictionaries. Some confuse it with *localism*
and think of the words and constructions marked "colloquial"
as peculiarities of speaking which are characteristic of a particular locality. Others feel that some stigma attaches to the
label "*Colloquial*" and would strive to avoid as incorrect (or as
of a low level) all words so marked. The word *colloquial,* however, as used to label words and phrases in a modern scientifically edited dictionary has no such meaning. It is used to
mark those words and constructions whose range of use is primarily that of the polite conversation of cultivated people, of
their familiar letters and informal speeches, as distinct from
those words and constructions which are common also in formal
writing. The usage of our better magazines and of public addresses generally has, during the past generation, moved away
from the formal and literary toward the colloquial.

Some words and expressions occur primarily in the language
of those without much conventional education. These expressions are often called "illiterate" or "vulgar English," and are
considered "incorrect." As a matter of fact, many of these expressions are survivals from an older period of the language and
are "incorrect" only in the sense that they do not occur in the
usage of standard English—the practice of the socially accepted,
those who are carrying on the important affairs of English-speaking people. Much of the language spoken by the uneducated
is the same as that of the polite conversation of cultivated people
and also duplicates the expressions of formal literary discourse.
The usage labels in a dictionary attempt to mark only those expressions that are peculiar to a particular type or dialect of
English. If one ignores the differences that characterize the
various geographical areas and the differences of the separate

fields of human activity, of trades and vocations and sports, the situation may be roughly represented by the following diagram:

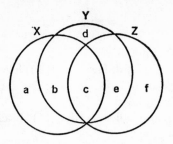

The three circles X, Y, Z represent the three sets of language habits indicated above.

X—formal literary English, the words, the expressions, and the structures one finds in serious books.

Y—colloquial English, the words, expressions, and the structures of the informal but polite conversation of cultivated people.

Z—illiterate English, the words, the expressions, and the structures of the language of the uneducated.

b, c, and e represent the overlappings of the three types of English.

c—that which is common to all three: formal literary English, colloquial English, and illiterate English.

b—that which is common to both formal literary English and colloquial English.

e—that which is common to both colloquial English and illiterate English.

a, d, and f represent those portions of each type of English that are peculiar to that particular set of language habits.

The following is a list of some of the other usage labels used in this dictionary with typical examples under each of the particular words and expressions to which each label is assigned.

Archaic: impose (def. 8), hugger-mugger (def. 2), glister (def. 1), lief (def. 2), angle² (def. 3).

Colloq.: angel (def. 6), brass tacks, fizzle (def. 2), flimflam, goner.

Humorous: celestial (def. 5), human (def. 4).

Obs.: loblolly boy, lust (def. 5), flittermouse, murther, drugget (def. 2).

Obsolesc.: saloon (def. 6), regimen (def. 5).

Rare: image (def. 17), impassionate, faulty (def. 2), instancy (def. 2), genial [1] (def. 3).

Scot.: chap [1] (def. 5), laird, hag [2] (def. 1), icker.

Scot. and N. Eng.: unco, kirk (def. 1), ilk (def. 2), braw, bairn.

South African: laager, kraal (def. 3).

U.S.: chain lightning, challenge (def. 14), biscuit (def. 1), boss (def. 2), quilting bee.

ALLAN F. HUBBELL

Multiple Negation

"I couldn't find nobody there." This sentence, as anyone who will read this probably knows, contains a double negative, a construction with a fascinating history. Today in all parts of the English-speaking world, its use or avoidance is one of the clearest marks of differentiation between different social groups. Among those who have had comparatively little formal schooling and whose social and occupational status is relatively low, the construction is extremely common. Among the well-educated and more "privileged," it is rare almost to the point of non-existence. In many circles, in fact, a double negative uttered by a presumably educated person would cause the same embarrassed silence as a loud belch in church.

The avoidance of this usage by the more cultivated members of the English speech-community is roughly about three hundred years old. In earlier English, the doubling, tripling, or even quadrupling of negatives was frequent even in the most formal literary styles. King Alfred, for example, in a translation made late in the ninth century, writes a sentence which in modern form would read: "No man had never yet heard of no ship-army." A little later, in the oldest English version of the Gospels, we read: "The five foolish maidens took lamps, but didn't take no oil with them." In the fourteenth century, Chaucer writes of his "gentle knight" that "in all his life he hasn't never yet said nothing discourteous to no sort of person" (four negatives!). As late as Shakespeare's time, the construction was still possible

. . . .

From *Inside the ACD*, October 1957 issue. © 1957 by Random House, Inc.

in Standard English, particularly in speech. Thus, in *Romeo and Juliet*, when Mercutio is confronted by Tybalt, he cries out, "I will not budge for no man's pleasure."

In the course of the seventeenth century, however, the multiple negative began to go out of educated use. Undoubtedly the chief cause of its gradual disappearance was the influence of classical literary Latin, then considered the most nearly perfect language. The fact that Cicero and Caesar did not multiply negatives even in the most emphatic statements of negation weighed heavily with those who aspired to write well. In the latter half of the century, furthermore, there developed a growing distaste for the extravagance and exuberance of Elizabethan English. The piling up of negatives was presumably felt to be one of the extravagances to be shunned.

After 1700 it is rather difficult to find examples of the multiple negative in educated written English. We of course know less about the spoken usage of the eighteenth century and it may be that for a time many avoided doubling negatives in writing but not in speech. But speech too in time conformed and since then Standard English has been quite uniform in this avoidance.

Our school grammars commonly tell us that the double negative is improper because "two negatives make an affirmative," that is, because "I couldn't find nobody there" really means "I could find somebody there." This curious notion appears to have been first set afloat by an eighteenth-century grammarian, Lowth, and it quickly came to be repeated on every side. It rests primarily on an analogy with algebra, where two negative signs cancel one another in certain operations. But ordinary language is not the language of algebra and utterances containing a double negative are regularly interpreted in the sense intended by the speaker and never in an opposite sense. Furthermore, if the reasoning were sound, a triple negative like King Alfred's or like "I won't give you no bubble gum for nothing" would be quite acceptable in modern Standard English. Of course it is not.

Nonstandard English, in this respect as in some others, is intensely conservative and tenacious of past practice. For two hundred years now, school children have had it dinned (and sometimes beaten) into them that they must not double or triple their negatives. For some of them the instruction is quite superfluous, for they have already learned Standard English at their mothers' knees. The usage of some others comes to be altered. There are those who determine quite early in life that they are going to move up the social ladder and who sense that their inherited speechways will be a bar to advancement. But the usage of a very considerable number is almost unaffected by the school instruction they receive. They leave high school continuing to use a nonstandard variety of the language and, among other things, still multiplying negatives in a fourteenth-century profusion.

Observing this "perverse" adherence to inherited patterns, teachers sometimes think despairingly that there must be some really fundamental fault in their methods. There must be, they feel, some pedagogical device not yet hit upon which could produce much greater results. But to think in this fashion is to misconceive the situation. An individual's linguistic usage is among other things the outward sign of his most deepseated group loyalties. If the usage of the group or groups with which he identifies himself is not that of Standard English, the schools are not likely to have much effect on his practice. For the blunt fact is that only if his loyalties shift will his grammar change. In a democratic society, the schools have an obligation to make a knowledge of the standard language available to everyone. And teachers have an obligation to make this instruction as interesting and meaningful as possible. They should not be surprised, however, if the nonstandard forms of English continue to flourish. They are hardy growths and will be with us for a long time to come.

THORSTEIN VEBLEN

The Higher Learning

. . . lately, since college athletics have won their way into a recognized standing as an accredited field of scholarly accomplishment, this latter branch of learning—if athletics may be freely classed as learning—has become a rival of the classics for the primacy in leisure-class education in American and English schools. Athletics have an obvious advantage over the classics for the purpose of leisure-class learning, since success as an athlete presumes, not only a waste of time, but also a waste of money, as well as the possession of certain highly un-industrial archaic traits of character and temperament. In the German universities the place of athletics and Greek-letter fraternities, as a leisure-class scholarly occupation, has in some measure been supplied by a skilled and graded inebriety and a perfunctory duelling.

The leisure class and its standards of virtue—archaism and waste—can scarcely have been concerned in the introduction of the classics into the scheme of the higher learning; but the tenacious retention of the classics by the higher schools, and the high degree of reputability which still attaches to them, are no doubt due to their conforming so closely to the requirements of archaism and waste.

"Classic" always carries this connotation of wasteful and archaic, whether it is used to denote the dead languages or the obsolete or obsolescent forms of thought and diction in the

· · · · · · · · ·

From *The Theory of the Leisure Class*. Reprinted by permission of The Viking Press, Inc., N.Y.

living language, or to denote other items of scholarly activity or apparatus to which it is applied with less aptness. So the archaic idiom of the English language is spoken of as "classic" English. Its use is imperative in all speaking and writing upon serious topics, and a facile use of it lends dignity to even the most commonplace and trivial string of talk. The newest form of English diction is of course never written; the sense of that leisure-class propriety which requires archaism in speech is present even in the most illiterate or sensational writers in sufficient force to prevent such a lapse. On the other hand, the highest and most conventionalised style of archaic diction is—quite characteristically—properly employed only in communications between an anthropomorphic divinity and his subjects. Midway between these extremes lies the everyday speech of leisure-class conversation and literature.

Elegant diction, whether in writing or speaking, is an effective means of reputability. It is of moment to know with some precision what is the degree of archaism conventionally required in speaking on any given topic. Usage differs appreciably from the pulpit to the market-place; the latter, as might be expected, admits the use of relatively new and effective words and turns of expression, even by fastidious persons. A discriminate avoidance of neologisms is honorific, not only because it argues that time has been wasted in acquiring the obsolescent habit of speech, but also as showing that the speaker has from infancy habitually associated with persons who have been familiar with the obsolescent idiom. It thereby goes to show his leisure-class antecedents. Great purity of speech is presumptive evidence of several successive lives spent in other than vulgarly useful occupations; although its evidence is by no means entirely conclusive to this point.

As felicitous an instance of futile classicism as can well be found, outside of the Far East, is the conventional spelling of the English language. A breach of the proprieties in spelling is extremely annoying and will discredit any writer in the eyes of all persons who are possessed of a developed sense of the true and beautiful. English orthography satisfies all the requirements of the canons of reputability under the law of conspicuous waste. It is archaic, cumbrous, and ineffective; its acquisition consumes much time and effort; failure to acquire it is easy of detection. Therefore it is the first and readiest test of reputability in learning, and conformity to its ritual is indispensable to a blameless scholastic life.

On this head of purity of speech, as at other points where a conventional usage rests on the canons of archaism and waste, the spokesmen for the usage instinctively take an apologetic attitude. It is contended, in substance, that a punctilious use of ancient and accredited locutions will serve to convey thought more adequately and more precisely than would the straightforward use of the latest form of spoken English; whereas it is notorious that the ideas of today are effectively expressed in the slang of today. Classic speech has the honorific virtue of dignity; it commands attention and respect as being the accredited method of communication under the leisure-class scheme of life, because it carries a pointed suggestion of the industrial exemption of the speaker. The advantage of the accredited locutions lies in their reputability; they are reputable because they are cumbrous and out of date, and therefore argue waste of time and exemption from the use and the need of direct and forcible speech.

DONALD J. LLOYD

Our National Mania for Correctness

Every now and then the editors of the university presses let
out a disgruntled bleat about the miserable writing done by
scholars, even those who are expert in literary fields; and from
time to time there are letters and editorials in our national
reviews bewailing some current academic malpractice with the
English language. At present, even *PMLA* (the Publications of
the Modern Language Association), traditionally the repository
of some of the worst writing done by researchers, is trying to
herd its authors toward more lucid exposition. And at two recent
meetings of the august Mediaeval Academy, one at Boston and
one at Dumbarton Oaks, bitter remarks were passed about the
failure of specialists in the Middle Ages to present their findings
in some form palatable to the general reader, so that he can
at least understand what they are writing about.

Even admitting that a really compelling style is the result of
years of cultivation, much scholarly writing is certainly worse
than it needs to be. But it is not alone in this. Generally speaking,
the writing of literate Americans whose primary business is
not writing but something else is pretty bad. It is muddy, backward, convoluted and self-strangled; it is only too obviously
the product of a task approached unwillingly and accomplished
without satisfaction or zeal. Except for the professionals among
us, we Americans are hell on the English language. I am not
in touch with the general run of British writing by non-profes-
. . . .

From *The American Scholar*, Summer 1952. Reprinted by permission of the
publisher.

sionals, but I suspect that it is nothing to make those islanders smug, either.

Furthermore, almost any college professor, turning the spotlight with some relief from himself and his colleagues to his students, will agree that their writing stinks to high heaven, too. It is a rare student who can write what he has to write with simplicity, lucidity and euphony, those qualities singled out by Somerset Maugham; far more graduating seniors are candidates for a remedial clinic than can pass a writing test with honors. And freshman writing is forever the nightmare of the teachers of composition, as it would be of their colleagues if the latter could not escape to the simple inanities of their objective tests.

Yet it was not always so. I have on my desk a little manuscript from the fourteenth century written by an unknown author, which I am in the process of editing. When I read it to one of my classes, as I occasionally do, with no more modernization than my own Great Lakes pronunciation and the substitution of a word for one which has become obsolete, it is a simple, clear and engaging document. "Where is any man nowadays that asketh how I shall love God and my fellow-Christians?" it begins. "How I shall flee sin and serve God truly as a true Christian man should? What man is there that will learn the true law of God, which he biddeth every Christian man to keep upon pain of damnation in hell without end? . . . Unnethe [scarcely] is there any lewd man or lewd woman that can rightly well say his Pater Noster, his Ave Maria, and his Creed, and sound the words out readily as they should. But when they play Christmas games about the fire, therein will they not fail. Those must be said out without stumbling for dread of smiting. But if a lewd man should be smited now for each failing that he maketh in saying of his Pater Noster, his Ave Maria, and his Creed, I trowe he should be smited at the full." And so on, to the beautiful poetic line, "Then think it not heavy to dwell with thy mother in her wide house, thou that laist in the strait chamber of her womb." The spelling in the original is hectic, and the capitalization and punctuation sporadic, to say the least.

Yet there was a man who knew what he had to say and set out about saying it, with no nonsense and no fumbling. He aimed for his audience and, judging by the dog-ears and sweat-marks on the book, which is about the size of one of our pocket books, he hit it. Why cannot we do as well in our time? Indeed, the eighteenth century was about the last age in which almost any man, if he was literate at all, could set down his thoughts —such as they were—so that they did not have to be excavated by the reader. We have an abundance of letters, diaries, pamphlets, and other papers from that period, and they are well written. It was the age, we may recall, not only of Boswell and Johnson, but of Pepys and Franklin as well, and of a host of other men whose main legacy to us was a simple, direct, workmanlike style, sufficient to the man and to the occasion, which said what it had to say and said it well. With the end of that century we go into the foggy, foggy darkness, and God knows whether we shall ever find our way out of it—as a people, that is, as a nation of thinking men and women with something to say.

Nevertheless, there is no question what makes our writing bad, or what we shall have to do to better it. We shall simply have to isolate and root out a monomania which now possesses us, which impedes all language study and inhibits all mastery of our native tongue—all mastery, that is, on paper; for as speakers of English, we Americans are loving and effective cultivators of our expression. I recall the gas station attendant who was filling my car. The gasoline foamed to the top of the tank, and he shut off the pump. "Whew!" I said, "that nearly went over." "When you see whitecaps," he replied, "you better stop." "You better had," I said, lost in admiration. But if you had given him a pencil, he would have chewed the end off before he got one word on paper.

The demon which possesses us is our mania for correctness. It dominates our minds from the first grade to the graduate school; it is the first and often the only thing we think of when we think of our language. Our spelling must be "correct"—even if the words are ill-chosen; our "usage" must be "correct"—even though any possible substitute expression, however crude, would be perfectly clear; our punctuation must be "correct"—even though practices surge and change with the passing of years, and differ from book to book, periodical to periodical. Correct! That's what we've got to be, and the idea that we've got to be correct rests like a soggy blanket on our brains and our hands whenever we try to write.

This mania for correctness is another legacy from the eighteenth century, but it did not get a real grip on us until well into the nineteenth. Its power over us today is appalling. Among my other tasks, I teach advanced courses in the English language to students preparing to teach. Most of these are seniors and graduate students, and in the summer especially, there is a sprinkling of older men and women, experienced teachers, who are sweating out a master's degree. They have had courses in "English" throughout their schooling. But of the nature and structure of the English language, the nature of language habits, the relation of speech to writing, and the differences in usage which arise from dialect and from differing occupational and educational demands—of all these, they know nothing at all. Nor do they come to me expecting to learn about these. They want to know two things: what correct usage is and how you beat it into the kids' heads. That there are other considerations important to an English teacher is news to many of them. What they get from me is a good long look at their language.

To trace this monolithic concentration on usage is to pursue a vicious circle, with the linguists on the outside. The literate public seems to get it from the English teachers, and the teachers get it from the public. The attitudes and pronouncements on language of a Jacques Barzun, a Wilson Follett, a Bernard De Voto, or a Norman Lewis ("How Correct Must Correct English Be?") mean more to English teachers than anything said by the most distinguished professional students of language—such as Leonard Bloomfield, Robert Hall or Charles Carpenter Fries. Correct usage is pursued and discussed, furthermore, without much reference to the actual writing of literary men. Now and again I amuse myself by blue-penciling a current magazine such as the *Saturday Review* or *Collier's* against the rules. I have to report that error is rampant, if variation is to be considered error. The boys just don't seem to pay attention to the rules. Moreover, having seen some of their first drafts, I am pretty sure that what conformity they do display is the work of their wives, secretaries, editors, proofreaders and typesetters, rather than their own. It takes a determined effort to beat the old Adam out of a readable manuscript.

Thus it is only the determined, consciously creative professional who can build his work on the actual language of men. In a recent issue of the *Saturday Review,* I stumbled on a quotation from Wolfgang Langewiesche. "Well, it isn't crowned by no castle, that's for sure," he wrote, "and by no cathedral either." My eyes popped, and I read it again. I liked it. It looked right; it sounded right; it had a fine Chaucerian swing to it. But I bet it cost him some blood and a fifth of Scotch to get it into print. In my own limited publication, I find "a historical" changed to "an historical," all my "further's" changed to "farther" and all my "farther's" to "further," "than us" watered down to "than we," and many, many more. How E. M. Forster got by with "the author he thinks," and got it reprinted in a freshman handbook a few pages along from the prohibition of such locutions baffles me. A phony standardization of usage appears in print, the work of editors unconscious of the ultimate meaning of what they do.

The result of all this is that a wet hand of fear rests on the heart of every nonprofessional writer who merely has a lot of important knowledge to communicate. He writes every sentence with a self-conscious horror of doing something wrong. It is always a comfort to him if he can fit himself into some system, such as that of a business or governmental office which provides him with a model. It is thus that gobbledegook comes into being. I once braced a distinguished sociologist, a student of occupational myths and attitudes, about the convoluted, mainly nominal turgidity of his writing. He apparently admitted verbs into his sentences the way we admit DP's into the United States, reluctantly and with pain. In speech he was racy, confident and compelling, a brilliant lecturer. "It's the only way I can get my work into the periodicals," he told me blandly. "If it's clear and simple, they don't think it's scholarly." With what relief the pedagogues subside into pedagese!

If we really want to get good writing from people who know things, so that we can come to learn what they know as easily as we learn from their talk, we can do it in a generation or so. In school and out, in print and out, we can leave usage to its natural nurse, the unforced imitation of the practices which are actually current among educated people. We can use our English courses in school and college, not to give drill on questionable choices among common alternatives, demanding that one be taken as right and the others as wrong, but to give practice in reading and writing. We can learn to read and write for the idea, and go for the idea without regard for anything else. Then our young people will come to maturity confidently using their pencils to find out what they think and get it down on paper; then our scholars will come to write simply, clearly and brilliantly what they brilliantly know.

In our speech we have arrived, I think, at a decency of discourse which is conducive to effective expression. We listen, with a grave courteous attention, to massive patterns of speaking different from our own because they come from differences in dialect and social status; we listen without carping and without a mean contempt. Furthermore, we participate; we go with a speaker through halts and starts, over abysses of construction, filling in the lacunae without hesitation; we discount inadvertencies and disregard wrong words and we arrive in genial good will with the speaker at his meaning. In this atmosphere, our speech has thrived, and the ordinary American is in conversation a confident, competent expressive being. In writing he is something else again.

No one flourishes in an atmosphere of repression. It is possible, of course, for a person with special aptitudes and a special drive to bull his way past the prohibitions and achieve an individual style. But with the negative attitude that attends all our writing, those whose main interest lies elsewhere are inhibited by fear of "error" and the nagging it stirs up from setting pen to paper, until the sight of a blank white page gives them the shakes. It is no wonder that their expression is halting and ineffective. They cannot fulfill the demands of a prissy propriety and trace the form of an idea at the same time. They thus arrive at adulthood victims of the steely eye of Mr. Sherwin Cody, whose bearded face stares at them from the countless ads for his correspondence school, demanding, "Do YOU make these mistakes in English?" The locutions he lists are not mistakes, and Mr. Cody knows they are not; but his readers do not know it, and they do not know that they don't matter anyway.

For usage doesn't matter. What matters is that we get done what we have to do, and get said what we have to say. Sufficient conformity is imposed upon us by the patterns of our language and by the general practices of its users so that we do do not have to run the idea of conformity into the ground by carping about trivial erratics in expression. Why in this matter of language alone complete conformity should be considered a virtue—except to typists, printers and typesetters—it is difficult to see (unless, perhaps, we are using it as a covert and pusillanimous means of establishing our own superiority). In our other concerns in life, we prize individuality; why in this one matter we should depart from a principle that otherwise serves us well is a puzzle for fools and wise men to ponder, especially since there is no general agreement on what to conform to, and one man's correctness is another's error. Not until we come to our senses—teachers, editors, writers and readers together—and stop riding each other's backs, will the casual, brisk, colorful, amused, ironic and entertaining talk of Americans find its way into print. We should all be happy to see it there.

MAX BEERBOHM

How Shall I Word It?

It would seem that I am one of those travellers for whom the railway bookstall does not cater. Whenever I start on a journey, I find that my choice lies between well-printed books which I have no wish to read, and well-written books which I could not read without permanent injury to my eyesight. The keeper of the bookstall, seeing me gaze vaguely along his shelves, suggests that I should take "Fen Country Fanny" or else "The Track of Blood" and have done with it. Not wishing to hurt his feelings, I refuse these works on the plea that I have read them. Whereon he, divining despite me that I am a superior person, says "Here is a nice little handy edition of More's 'Utopia'" or "Carlyle's 'French Revolution'" and again I make some excuse. What pleasure could I get from trying to cope with a masterpiece printed in diminutive grey-ish type on a semi-transparent little grey-ish page? I relieve the bookstall of nothing but a newspaper or two.

The other day, however, my eye and fancy were caught by a book entitled "How Shall I Word It?" and sub-entitled "A Complete Letter Writer for Men and Women." I had never read one of these manuals, but had often heard that there was a great and constant "demand" for them. So I demanded this one. It is no great fun in itself. The writer is no fool. He has evidently a natural talent for writing letters. His style is, for the most part, discreet and easy. If you were a young man writing "to Father

. . . .

of Girl he wishes to Marry" or "thanking Fiancée for Present"
or "reproaching Fiancée for being a Flirt," or if you were a
mother "asking Governess her Qualifications" or "replying to
Undesirable Invitation for her Child," or indeed if you were in
any other one of the crises which this book is designed to allevi-
ate, you might copy out and post the specially-provided letter
without making yourself ridiculous in the eyes of its receiver—
unless, of course, he or she also possessed a copy of the book.
But—well, can you conceive any one copying out and posting
one of these letters, or even taking it as the basis for composition?
You cannot. That shows how little you know of your fellow-
creatures. Not you nor I can plumb the abyss at the bottom
of which such humility is possible. Nevertheless, as we know
by that great and constant "demand," there the abyss is, and
there multitudes are at the bottom of it. Let's peer down
. . . No, all is darkness. But faintly, if we listen hard, is borne
up to us a sound of the scratching of innumerable pens—pens
whose wielders are all trying, as the author of this handbook
urges them, to "be original, fresh, and interesting" by dint of
more or less strict adherence to sample.

Giddily you draw back from the edge of the abyss. Come!—
here is a thought to steady you. The mysterious great masses
of helpless folk for whom "How Shall I Word It?" is written are
sound at heart, delicate in feeling, anxious to please, most loth
to wound. For it must be presumed that the author's style of
letter-writing is informed as much by a desire to give his public
what it needs, and will pay for, as by his own beautiful nature;
and in the course of all the letters that he dictates you will
find not one harsh word, not one ignoble thought or unkind
insinuation. In all of them, though so many are for the use of
persons placed in the most trying circumstances, and some of
them are for persons writhing under a sense of intolerable injury,
sweetness and light do ever reign. Even "yours truly, Jacob
Langton," in his "letter to his Daughter's Mercenary Fiancé,"
mitigates the sternness of his tone by the remark that his "task
is inexpressibly painful." And he, Mr. Langton, is the one writer
who lets the post go out on his wrath. When Horace Masterton,

of Thorpe Road, Putney, receives from Miss Jessica Weir, of Fir Villa, Blackheath, a letter "declaring her Change of Feelings," does he upbraid her? No; "it was honest and brave of you to write to me so straight-forwardly and at the back of my mind I know you have done what is best. . . . I give you back your freedom only at your desire. God bless you, dear." Not less admirable is the behaviour, in similar case, of Cecil Grant (14, Glover Street, Streatham). Suddenly, as a bolt from the blue, comes a letter from Miss Louie Hawke (Elm View, Deerhurst), breaking off her betrothal to him. Haggard, he sits down to his desk; his pen traverses the note-paper—calling down curses on Louie and on all her sex? No; "one cannot say good-bye for ever without deep regret to days that have been so full of happiness. I must thank you sincerely for all your great kindness to me. . . . With every sincere wish for your future happiness," he bestows complete freedom on Miss Hawke. And do not imagine that in the matter of self-control and sympathy, of power to understand all and pardon all, the men are lagged behind by the women. Miss Leila Johnson (The Manse, Carlyle) has observed in Leonard Wace (Dover Street, Saltburn) a certain coldness of demeanour; yet "I do not blame you; it is probably your nature"; and Leila in her sweet forbearance is typical of all the other pained women in these pages: she is but one of a crowd of heroines.

Face to face with all this perfection, the not perfect reader begins to crave some little outburst of wrath, of hatred or malice, from one of these imaginary ladies and gentlemen. He longs for—how shall he word it?—a glimpse of some bad motive, of some little lapse from dignity. Often, passing by a pillar-box, I have wished I could unlock it and carry away its contents, to be studied at my leisure. I have always thought such a haul would abound in things fascinating to a student of human nature. One night, not long ago, I took a waxen impression of the lock of the pillar-box nearest to my house, and had a key made. This implement I have as yet lacked either the courage or the opportunity to use. And now I think I shall throw it away . . . No, I shan't. I refuse, after all, to draw my inference that the bulk of the British public writes always in the manner of this handbook. Even if they all have beautiful natures they must sometimes be sent slightly astray by inferior impulses, just as are you and I.

And, if err they must, surely it were well they should know how to do it correctly and forcibly. I suggest to our author that he should sprinkle his next edition with a few less righteous examples, thereby both purging his book of its monotony and somewhat justifying its sub-title. Like most people who are in the habit of writing things to be printed, I have not the knack of writing really good letters. But let me crudely indicate the sort of thing that our manual needs. . . .

Letter from Poor Man to Obtain Money from Rich One

(The English law is particularly hard on what is called blackmail. It is therefore essential that the applicant should write nothing that might afterwards be twisted to incriminate him.—Ed.)

Dear Sir,

Today, as I was turning out a drawer in my attic, I came across a letter which by a curious chance fell into my hands some years ago, and which, in the stress of grave pecuniary embarrassment, had escaped my memory. It is a letter written by yourself to a lady, and the date shows it to have been written shortly after your marriage. It is of a confidential nature, and might, I fear, if it fell into the wrong hands, be cruelly misconstrued. I would wish you to have the satisfaction of destroying it in person. At first I thought of sending it on to you by post. But I know how happy you are in your domestic life; and probably your wife and you, in your perfect mutual trust, are in the habit of opening each other's letters. Therefore, to avoid risk, I would prefer to hand the document to you personally. I will not ask you to come to my attic, where I could not offer you such hospitality as is due to a man of your wealth and position. You will be so good as to meet me at 3.0 A.M. (sharp) tomorrow (Thursday) beside the tenth lamp-post to the left on the Surrey side of Waterloo Bridge; at which hour and place we shall not be disturbed.

I am, dear Sir,
Yours respectfully
James Gridge.

Letter from Young Man Refusing to Pay His Tailor's Bill

Mr. Eustace Davenant has received the half-servile, half-insolent screed which Mr. Yardley has addressed to him. Let Mr. Yardley cease from crawling on his knees and shaking his fist. Neither this posture nor this gesture can wring one bent farthing from the pockets of Mr. Davenant, who was a minor at the time when that series of ill-made suits was supplied to him and will hereafter, as in the past, shout (without prejudice) from the housetops that of all the tailors in London Mr. Yardley is at once the most grasping and the least competent.

Letter to Thank Author for Inscribed Copy of Book

Dear Mr. Emanuel Flower,

It was kind of you to think of sending me a copy of your new book. It would have been kinder still to think again and abandon that project. I am a man of gentle instincts, and do not like to tell you that "A Flight into Arcady" (of which I have skimmed a few pages, thus wasting two or three minutes of my not altogether worthless time) is trash. On the other hand, I am determined that you shall not be able to go around boasting to your friends, if you have any, that this work was not condemned, derided, and dismissed by your sincere well-wisher, *Wrexford Cripps.*

Letter to Member of Parliament Unseated at General Election

Dear Mr. Pobsby-Burford,

Though I am myself an ardent Tory, I cannot but rejoice in the crushing defeat you have just suffered in West Odgetown. There are moments when political conviction is overborne by personal sentiment; and this is one of them. Your loss of the seat that you held is the more striking by reason of the splendid manner in which the northern and eastern divisions of Odgetown have been wrested from the Liberal Party. The great bulk of the newspaper-reading public will be puzzled by your extinction in the midst of our party's triumph. But then, the great mass of the newspaper-reading public has not met you. I have. You will probably not remember me. You are the sort of man who would not remember anybody who might not be of some definite use to him. Such, at least, was one of the impressions you made on me when I met you last summer at a dinner given by our friends the Pelhams. Among the other things in you that struck me were the blatant pomposity of your manner, your appalling flow of cheap platitudes, and your hoggish lack of ideas. It is such men as you that lower the tone of public life. And I am sure that in writing to you thus I am but expressing what is felt, without distinction of party, by all who sat with you in the late Parliament.

The one person in whose behalf I regret your withdrawal into private life is your wife, whom I had the pleasure of taking in to the aforesaid dinner. It was evident to me that she was a woman whose spirit was well-nigh broken by her conjunction with you. Such remnants of cheerfulness as were in her I attributed to the Parliamentary duties which kept you out of her sight for so very many hours daily. I do not like to think of the fate to which the free and independent electors of West Odgetown have just condemned her. Only, remember this: chattel of yours though she is, and timid and humble, she despises you in her heart.

I am, dear Mr. Pobsby-Burford,
Yours very truly,
Harold Thistlake.

Letter from Young Lady in Answer to Invitation from old Schoolmistress

My dear Miss Price,

How awfully sweet of you to ask me to stay with you for a few days but how *can* you think I may have forgotten you for

of course I think of you so very often and of the three years I
spent at your school because it is such a joy not to be there
any longer and if one is at all down it bucks one up directly
to remember that *thats* all over atanyrate and that one has
enough food to nurrish one and not that awful monottany of
life and not the petty fogging daily tirrany you went in for and
I can imagin no greater thrill and luxury in a way than to come
and see the whole dismal grind still going on but without me
being in it but this would be rather beastly of me wouldn't it
so please dear Miss Price dont expect me and do excuse mistakes
of English Composition and Spelling and etcetra in your affectionate old pupil,

Emily Therese Lynn-Royston.

ps, I often rite to people telling them where I was edducated and
highly reckomending you.

Letter in Acknowledgment of Wedding Present

Dear Lady Amblesham,

Who gives quickly, says the old proverb, gives twice. For this
reason I have purposely delayed writing to you, lest I should
appear to thank you more than once for the small, cheap,
hideous present you sent me on the occasion of my recent
wedding. Were you a poor woman, that little bowl of ill-imitated
Dresden china would convict you of tastelessness merely; were
you a blind woman, of nothing but an odious parsimony. As
you have normal eyesight and more than normal wealth, your
gift to me proclaims you at once a Philistine and a miser (or
rather did so proclaim you until, less than ten seconds after I
had unpacked it from its wrappings of tissue paper, I took it to
the open window and had the satisfaction of seeing it shattered
to atoms on the pavement). But stay! I perceive a possible flaw
in my argument. Perhaps you were guided in your choice by
a definite wish to insult me. I am sure, on reflection, that this
was so. I *shall not forget.*

Yours, etc.,
Cynthia Beaumarsh.

P.S. My husband asked me to tell you to warn Lord Amblesham to keep out of his way or to assume some disguise so complete that he will not be recognized by him and horsewhipped.

PPS. I am sending copies of this letter to the principal London and provincial newspapers.

Letter from . . .

But enough! I never thought I should be so strong in this line. I had not forseen such copiousness and fatal fluency. Never again will I tap these deep dark reservoirs in a character that had always seemed to me, on the whole, so amiable.

MARK TWAIN

Buck Fanshaw's Funeral

Somebody has said that in order to know a community, one must observe the style of its funerals and know what manner of men they bury with most ceremony. I cannot say which class we buried with most eclat in our "flush times," the distinguished public benefactor or the distinguished rough—possibly the two chief grades or grand divisions of society honored their illustrious dead about equally; and hence, no doubt the philosopher I have quoted from would have needed to see two representative funerals in Virginia before forming his estimate of the people.

There was a grand time over Buck Fanshaw when he died. He was a representative citizen. He had "killed his man"—not in his own quarrel, it is true, but in defence of a stranger unfairly beset by numbers. He had kept a sumptuous saloon. He had been the proprietor of a dashing helpmeet whom he could have discarded without the formality of a divorce. He had held a high position in the fire department and been a very Warwick in politics. When he died there was great lamentation throughout the town, but especially in the vast bottom-stratum of society.

On the inquest it was shown that Buck Fanshaw, in the delirium of a wasting typhoid fever, had taken arsenic, shot himself through the body, cut his throat, and jumped out of a four-story window and broken his neck—and after due deliberation, the jury, sad and tearful, but with intelligence unblinded by its sorrow, brought in a verdict of death "by the visitation of God." What could the world do without juries?

Prodigious preparations were made for the funeral. All the

vehicles in town were hired, all the saloons put in mourning, all the municipal and fire-company flags hung at half-mast, and all the firemen ordered to muster in uniform and bring their machines duly draped in black. Now—let us remark in parenthesis—as all the peoples of the earth had representative adventurers in the Silverland, and as each adventurer had brought the slang of his nation or his locality with him, the combination made the slang of Nevada the richest and the most infinitely varied and copious that had ever existed anywhere in the world, perhaps, except in the mines of California in the "early days." Slang was the language of Nevada. It was hard to preach a sermon without it, and be understood. Such phrases as "You bet!" "Oh, no, I reckon not!" "No Irish need apply," and a hundred others, became so common as to fall from the lips of a speaker unconsciously—and very often when they did not touch the subject under discussion and consequently failed to mean anything.

After Buck Fanshaw's inquest, a meeting of the short-haired brotherhood was held, for nothing can be done on the Pacific coast without a public meeting and an expression of sentiment. Regretful resolutions were passed and various committees appointed; among others, a committee of one was deputed to call on the minister, a fragile, gentle, spiritual new fledgling from an Eastern theological seminary, and as yet unacquainted with the ways of the mines. The committeeman, "Scotty" Briggs, made his visit; and in after days it was worth something to hear the minister tell about it. Scotty was a stalwart rough, whose customary suit, when on weighty official business, like committee work, was a fire helmet, flaming red flannel shirt, patent leather belt with spanner and revolver attached, coat hung over arm, and pants stuffed into boot tops. He formed something of a contrast to the pale theological student. It is fair to say of Scotty, however, in passing, that he had a warm heart, and a strong love for his friends, and never entered into a quarrel when he could reasonably keep out of it. Indeed, it was commonly said that whenever one of Scotty's fights was investigated, it always turned out that it had originally been no affair of his, but that

out of native goodheartedness he had dropped in of his own accord to help the man who was getting the worst of it. He and
Buck Fanshaw were bosom friends, for years, and had often
taken adventurous "pot-luck" together. On one occasion, they
had thrown off their coats and taken the weaker side in a fight
among strangers, and after gaining a hard-earned victory, turned
and found that the men they were helping had deserted early,
and not only that, but had stolen their coats and made off with
them! But to return to Scotty's visit to the minister. He was
on a sorrowful mission, now, and his face was the picture of
woe. Being admitted to the presence he sat down before the
clergyman, placed his fire-hat on an unfinished manuscript
sermon under the minister's nose, took from it a red silk hand-
kerchief, wiped his brow and heaved a sigh of dismal impres-
siveness, explanatory of his business. He choked, and even shed
tears; but with an effort he mastered his voice and said in lugu-
brious tones:

"Are you the duck that runs the gospel-mill next door?"

"Am I the—pardon me, I believe I do not understand?"

With another sigh and a half-sob, Scotty rejoined:

"Why you see we are in a bit of trouble, and the boys thought
maybe you would give us a lift, if we'd tackle you—that is, if
I've got the rights of it and you are the head clerk of the dox-
ology-works next door."

"I am the shepherd in charge of the flock whose fold is next
door."

"The which?"

"The spiritual adviser of the little company of believers whose
sanctuary adjoins these premises."

Scotty scratched his head, reflected a moment, and then said:

"You ruther hold over me, pard. I reckon I can't call that hand.
Ante and pass the buck."

"How? I beg pardon. What did I understand you to say?"

"Well, you've ruther got the bulge on me. Or maybe we've
both got the bulge, somehow. You don't smoke me and I don't
smoke you. You see, one of the boys has passed in his checks

and we want to give him a good send-off, and so the thing I'm on now is to roust out somebody to jerk a little chin-music for us and waltz him through handsome."

"My friend, I seem to grow more and more bewildered. Your observations are wholly incomprehensible to me. Cannot you simplify them in some way? At first I thought perhaps I understood you, but I grope now. Would it not expedite matters if you restricted yourself to categorical statements of fact unencumbered with obstructing accumulations of metaphor and allegory?"

Another pause, and more reflection. Then, said Scotty:

"I'll have to pass, I judge."

"How?"

"You've raised me out, pard."

"I still fail to catch your meaning."

"Why, that last lead of yourn is too many for me—that's the idea. I can't neither trump nor follow suit."

The clergyman sank back in his chair perplexed. Scotty leaned his head on his hand and gave himself up to thought. Presently his face came up, sorrowful but confident.

"I've got it now, so's you can savvy," he said. "What we want is a gospel-sharp. See?"

"A what?"

"Gospel-sharp. Parson."

"Oh! Why did you not say so before? I am a clergyman—a parson."

"Now you talk! You see my blind and straddle it like a man. Put it there!"—extending a brawny paw, which closed over the minister's small hand gave it a shake indicative of fraternal sympathy and fervent gratification.

"Now we're all right, pard. Let's start fresh. Don't you mind my snuffling a little—becuz we're in a power of trouble. You see, one of the boys has gone up the flume—"

"Gone where?"

"Up the flume—throwed up the sponge, you understand."

"Thrown up the sponge?"

"Yes—kicked the bucket—"

"Ah—has departed to that mysterious country from whose bourne no traveler returns."

"Return! I reckon not. Why pard, he's *dead!*"

"Yes, I understand."

"Oh, you do? Well I thought maybe you might be getting tangled some more. Yes, you see he's dead again—"

"*Again?* Why, has he ever been dead before?"

"Dead before? No! Do you reckon a man has got as many lives as a cat? But you bet you he's awful dead now, poor old boy, and I wish I'd never seen this day. I don't want no better friend than Buck Fanshaw. I knowed him by the back; and when I know a man and like him, I freeze to him—you hear *me*. Take him all round, pard, there never was a bullier man in the mines. No man ever knowed Buck Fanshaw to go back on a friend. But it's all up, you know, it's all up. It ain't no use. They've scooped him."

"Scooped him?"

"Yes—death has. Well, well, well, we've got to give him up. Yes indeed. It's a kind of a hard world, after all, *ain't* it? But pard, he was a rustler! You ought to seen him get started once. He was a bully boy with a glass eye! Just spit in his face and give him room according to his strength, and it was just beautiful to see him peel and go in. He was the worst son of a thief that ever drawed breath. Pard, he was *on* it! He was on it bigger than an Injun!"

"On it? On what?"

"On the shoot. On the shoulder. On the fight, you understand. *He* didn't give a continental for *any*body. *Beg* your pardon, friend, for coming so near saying a cuss-word—but you see I'm on an awful strain, in this palaver, on account of having to cramp down and draw everything so mild. But we've got to give him up. There ain't any getting around that, I don't reckon. Now if we can get you to help plant him—"

"Preach the funeral discourse? Assist at the obsequies?"

"Obs'quies is good. Yes. That's it—that's our little game. We are going to get the thing up regardless, you know. He was always nifty himself, and so you bet you his funeral ain't going to be no slouch—solid silver door-plate on his coffin, six plumes on the hearse, and a nigger on the box in a biled shirt and a plug hat—how's that for high? And we'll take care of *you*, pard. We'll fix you all right. There'll be a kerridge for you; and whatever you want, you just 'scape out and we'll 'tend to it. We've got a shebang fixed up for you to stand behind, in No. 1's house, and don't you be afraid. Just go in and toot your horn, if you don't sell a clam. Put Buck through as bully as you can, pard, for anybody that knowed him will tell you that he was one of the whitest men that was ever in the mines. You can't draw it too strong. He never could stand it to see things going wrong. He's done more to make this town quiet and peaceable than any man in it. I've seen him lick four Greasers in eleven minutes, myself. If a thing wanted regulating, *he* warn't a man to go browsing around after somebody to do it, but he would prance in and regulate it himself. He warn't a Catholic. Scasely. He was down on 'em. His word was, 'No Irish need apply!' but it didn't make no difference about that when it came down to what a man's rights was—and so, when some roughs jumped the Catholic bone-yard and started in to stake out town-lots in it he *went* for 'em! And he *cleaned* 'em, too! I was there, pard, and I seen it myself."

"That was very well indeed—at least the impulse was—whether the act was strictly defensible or not. Had deceased any religious convictions? That is to say, did he feel a dependence upon, or acknowledge allegiance to a higher power?"

More reflection.

"I reckon you've stumped me again, pard. Could you say it over once more, and say it slow?"

"Well, to simplify it somewhat, was he, or rather had he ever been connected with any organization sequested from secular concerns and devoted to self-sacrifice in the interests of morality?"

"All down but nine—set 'em up on the other alley, pard."

"What did I understand you to say?"

"Why, you're most too many for me, you know. When you get in with your left I hunt grass every time. Every time you draw, you fill; but I don't seem to have any luck. Let's have a new deal."

"How? Begin again?"

"That's it."

"Very well. Was he a good man, and—"

"There—I see that; don't put up another chip till I look at my hand. A good man, says you? Pard, it ain't no name for it. He was the best man that ever—pard, you would have doted on that man. He could lam any galoot of his inches in America. It was him that put down the riot last election before it got a start; and everybody said he was the only man that could have done it. He waltzed in with a spanner in one hand and a trumpet in the other, and sent fourteen men home on a shutter in less than three minutes. He had that riot all broke up and prevented nice before anybody ever got a chance to strike a blow. He was always for peace, and he would *have* peace—he could not stand disturbances. Pard, he was a great loss to this town. It would please the boys if you could chip in something like that and do him justice. Here once when the Micks got to throwing stones through the Methodis' Sunday school windows, Buck Fanshaw, all of his own notion, shut up his saloon and took a couple of six-shooters and mounted guard over the Sunday school. Says he, 'No Irish need apply!' And they didn't. He was the bulliest man in the mountains, pard! He could run faster, jump higher, hit harder, and hold more tangle-foot whisky without spilling it than any man in seventeen counties. Put that in, pard—it'll please the boys more than anything you could say. And you can say, pard, that he never shook his mother."

"Never shook his mother?"

"That's it—any of the boys will tell you so."

"Well, but why *should* he shake her?"

"That's what I say—but some people does."

"Not people of any repute?"

"Well, some that averages pretty so-so."

"In my opinion the man that would offer personal violence to his own mother, ought to—"

"Cheese it, pard; you've banked your ball clean outside the

string. What I was a drivin' at, was, that he never *throwed off*
on his mother—don't you see? No indeedy. He give her a house
to live in, and town lots, and plenty of money; and he looked
after her and took care of her all the time; and when she was
down with the small-pox I'm d—d if he didn't set up nights
and nuss her himself! *Beg* your pardon for saying it, but it
hopped out too quick for yours truly. You've treated me like a
gentleman, pard, and I ain't the man to hurt your feelings inten-
tional. I think you're white. I think you're a square man, pard.
I like you, and I'll lick any man that don't. I'll lick him till he
can't tell himself from a last year's corpse! Put it *there!*" [An-
other fraternal handshake—and exit.]

The obsequies were all that "the boys" could desire. Such a
marvel of funeral pomp had never been seen in Virginia. The
plumed hearse, the dirge-breathing brass bands, the closed marts
of business, the flags drooping at half mast, the long, plodding
procession of uniformed secret societies, military battalions and
fire companies, draped engines, carriages of officials, and citizens
in vehicles and on foot, attracted multitudes of spectators to the
sidewalks, roofs and windows; and for years afterward, the
degree of grandeur attained by any civic display in Virginia
was determined by comparison with Buck Fanshaw's funeral.

Scotty Briggs, as a pall-bearer and a mourner, occupied a
prominent place at the funeral, and when the sermon was finished
and the last sentence of the prayer for the dead man's soul
ascended, he responded, in a low voice, but with feeling:

"Amen. No Irish need apply."

As the bulk of the response was without apparent relevancy,
it was probably nothing more than a humble tribute to the memory of the friend that was gone; for, as Scotty had once said, it
was "his word."

Scotty Briggs, in after days, achieved the distinction of becoming the only convert to religion that was ever gathered from the
Virginia roughs; and it transpired that the man who had it in
him to espouse the quarrel of the weak out of inborn nobility of
spirit was no mean timber whereof to construct a Christian. The
making him one did not warp his generosity or diminish his

courage; on the contrary it gave intelligent direction to the one and a broader field to the other. If his Sunday-school class progressed faster than the other classes, was it matter for wonder? I think not. He talked to his pioneer small-fry in a language they understood! It was my large privilege, a month before he died, to hear him tell the beautiful story of Joseph and his brethren to his class "without looking at the book." I leave it to the reader to fancy what it was like, as it fell, riddled with slang, from the lips of that grave, earnest teacher, and was listened to by his little learners with a consuming interest that showed that they were as unconscious as he was that any violence was being done to the sacred proprieties!

STEPHEN LEACOCK

Good and Bad Language

English superiority and American slang—The English steal the lan-
guage, the Americans the continent—Canadians and Eskimos out
of it—Luxuriance of American slang—Seventeen kinds of guys in
one Wisconsin high school—American sky-pilots and British incum-
bents—The New Realism—A hero with guts—How to swear in print
—Foul oaths, then fouler and foulest—The panorama man and the
peasant in the Swiss More-Ass

Quite apart from the technical aspect of the art of narration,
there is the broader general question of good and bad language,
of where speech ends and slang begins. To what extent must
the language of literature and cultivated discourse accept and
assimilate the innovations, the irregularities and the corruptions
that perpetually appear in all languages as spoken by the mass
of the people? To what extent are we to think of our language
as a moving current, never the same except in its identity, and
to what extent should we wish to check the flow of the current,
so that stiller waters may run deeper! Obviously there is a limit
in each direction. A current totally arrested means stagnation.
Waters that run too fast end in the sand. Somewhere there may
be a happy mean between the two.

Now this question arises for all languages. But it has a very
peculiar importance for the English language since here the
current flows in two parts, the American and the British; and
many people are inclined to think that one tends to run too fast

. . . .

From *How To Write* by permission of Dodd, Mead & Company, Inc. Copyright 1943 by Dodd, Mead & Company, Inc.

and the other tends to slacken. In other words we have here the problem of the American language and American slang. Every now and then controversy breaks out in regard to British English and American English—or it used to before the war stilled all babble—and it sometimes had a rather nasty edge to it. It carried in it one of the last faint survivals of the Stamp Act and the Boston Tea Party. Great quarrels die away to leave only generous memories; little quarrels live on. Hence the question of "slang" as between England and America (England, not Scotland; the Scots are not worrying) keeps its edge; all the more so, in that a lot of Americans think in their hearts, that the reason why the English don't use much slang is that they can't make it up, and a lot of English people think that the Americans use slang because they weren't brought up properly—or, no, they don't think it, they know it. That's the provoking thing about the English (say the Americans); they don't think things, they know them. They did all their thinking years and years ago.

I can write on this controversy with the friendly neutrality of a Canadian. In Canada we have enough to do keeping up with two spoken languages without trying to invent slang, so we just go right ahead and use English for literature, Scotch for sermons and American for conversation.

Perhaps the highest point of controversy is reached in the discussion whether there is, whether there ought to be, whether it is a shame that there isn't, an "American" language. Some people feel very strongly on this point. They think that having your own language is a mark of independence like owning your own house, driving your own car and having your own shaving mug in the barber shop. Gangs of boys make themselves up a "language" and revel in its obscurity. The leading boys in the respect are the Irish, so anxious to have their own language that they are trying to learn Gaelic. If they are not careful, first thing they know they'll get to talk it and then they'll be sorry.

On the other hand, some people feel just the other way about it. A most interesting article appeared a little while ago in one of the leading British Quarterlies, written by an American, and deprecating all idea of the creation of an American language as dangerous to our mutual dependence and kinship.

My own feeling about this, if I may put it in slang, is "I should worry." Or, in other words, there is not the faintest chance of there ever being an American language as apart from English. The daily intercommunication of telegraph, telephone, literature and the press, fuses all forms of "English" toward one and the broadcast and the talking pictures even fuse the toned voice. In the world of today languages cannot separate. That process belonged to epochs of distance and silence unknown now. Even then it was long. It took Latin a thousand years to turn into French.

The situation in the world today is this: There is a language called "English." It is too bad, if you like, that one country should seem to have stolen or to monopolize the claim to the name. But if the English stole the name of a language, the "Americans" stole the whole of two continents. Humble people, like the Canadians, and the Eskimos, have to live in "America" and speak "English," without fretting about it.

English is spoken by the people in England; is also spoken by the Scots, by the unredeemed Irish, the Australians—a lot of other people than Americans. Who speaks it best, no one knows; it's a matter of taste. Personally I think I like best the speech of a cultivated Scot, and perhaps least a certain high-grade English which calls a railroad a "wailwoad." I myself talk Ontario English; I don't admire it, but it's all I can do; anything is better than affectation.

Now by slang is meant the unceasing introduction into language of new phrases, and especially new nouns as names for things. There is no doubt that this peculiar fermentation of language has reached in America higher proportions than ever known anywhere else. For example—and my authority here is Mr. Eric Partridge, who cannot be wrong—a test was taken not long ago in a Wisconsin high school to see how many different words the boys and girls employed to express a low opinion of a person. Their list reads, *mutt, bonehead, guy, carp, highbrow, tightwad, grafter, hayseed, hot-air artist, rube, tough-nut, chump* and *peanut.* Perhaps they thought of more after they got home; these no doubt were only some of the things they called their teachers.

Many people, without being students of language, have observed the extraordinary number of ways in which American slang can indicate that a man has had too much drink. The chief authority on the subject (I refer to American slang and don't want to be ambiguous), H. L. Mencken, gives a partial list, brought up to 1923, and including *piffled, fiddled, spiflicated, tanked, snooted, stewed, ossified, slopped, jiggered, edged, loaded, het up, frazzled, jugged, soused, cornered* and *jagged.*

Slang passes as it comes. It lives only when it deserves to live, when the word has something about it that does a real service. In the Wisconsin students' list above I can detect only two words that look permanent, *guy* and *highbrow. Guy* is a word with a history; it comes down to us from poor Guy Fawkes (Guido Faukes), tortured and executed for trying to blow up the English Parliament. His "Fifth of November" crime was kept alive in memory—still is—by toting around a tattered figure on a stick in a procession with the cry, "Oh, please to remember the fifth of November, with gunpowder, treason and plot." So the word came to mean a tattered-looking person and then just a queer-looking person, like a professor. From that it began to mean just a person: *I was out with another guy last night.*

The fact is we are always hard up for neutral words to mean "just a person"; each new one gets spoiled and has to be replaced. Be careful how you call a "woman" a "woman," and a "lady" is apt to be worse; don't call a Frenchman an "individual," or an Englishman a "fellow." Hence the need for "guy," which will gradually rise from ridicule to respectability, as already indicated. At some future British coronation the Archbishop of Canterbury will say to the Queen, "Will you take this guy to be your husband?" And for all we know the queen will answer, "Sez-you."

The other word, *highbrow,* will live for another reason. We need it. It is a little different from *intellectual, learned, cultivated.* It started like most slang as a brilliant image, or metaphor, taken from the sweeping forehead, smooth as an egg, of a Shakespeare or a Hall Caine. But, with perhaps a change of spelling, the thought of *brow* will disappear and we shall use the term naturally and effectively—a *highbrow audience;* the *opinion of highbrows,* etc.

The making of slang is, as I say, a sort of living process of language like the scum on wine. Without it there is no wine, no life, no fermentation. Later on, the scum passes as dust and dregs and leaves behind the rich fluid of the wine. A language that has ceased to throw off slang has ceased to live. Thus came all our language. Every syllable of it since the dawn of speech has been rolled over and over in endless renewal. Our oldest words, our oldest names, were once bright with the colours of the morning, striking some new metaphor that brought into full relief the image of the thing seen. Centuries ago some Roman called his fellow-Roman's head a "pot" and put the word *testa* (tête) into the French language. His genius for seeing resemblances was no greater than that of his American successor who perceived that the human head was a *bean.*

Now, the process of creating slang is not confined to America. But I think the fermenting, slang-making process is livelier far in America than in England. This would seem to be the consequence of setting a language in a new country—with new lives, new scenes to turn it to, and with the débris of other languages jostling beside it. Under the wide canopy of heaven above the prairies a preacher became a *sky-pilot.* In England he remained, among other things, an *incumbent,* still sitting there. A newcomer in the West was a *tenderfoot* or a *greenhorn,* a locomotive an *iron horse,* and so on. Little snips of foreign *idiom* like the *something else again* of German, and *I should worry* of Yiddish, came snuggling into the language. *Yes, we have no bananas* carries with it the whole Mediterranean migration.

This process of change, like invention itself, became much more conscious in America than in England. What the English did for lazy convenience or by accident, the Americans did on purpose. Hence American slang contains a much greater percentage of cleverness than English. A lot of English slang words are just abbreviations. To call a professional at cricket a *pro*, or breakfast *brekker*, or political economy *pol. econ.*, saves time but that is all. To call a pair of trousers *bags*, is a step up; there is a distinct intellectual glow of comparison. But it is only twilight as compared with such American effects as *lounge-lizard, rubber-neck, sugar-daddy, tangle-foot* and *piece of calico*.

It is, moreover, a peculiar merit of American slang that a lot of it has the quality of vitality—vital force of renewed life. Take such words as a *hide-out* and *frame-up*, or a *tie-up* (on a railway). To make these involves the process of *starting over again*, forming language from the beginning. Compare *sob-stuff, fade-out, send-off, side-track* and a host of others.

Everything, as the French say, has the defects of its merits. American slang forces the pace, and hence a lot of it *is* forced, pointless, of no literary or linguistic value. Especially tiresome is the supposed slang of the criminal class, as used in crime novels to heighten the reader's terror. Every one recognizes such language as *See, here, pal, if the narks grab you for doing in that moll, the beak will send you up, see, and you'll burn.* I don't know whether any people really use this stuff. I hope not. If they must be criminals, they might at least talk like gentlemen. But in any case English crime stories often run to the same kind of stuff; indeed I am not sure just where the words above belong.

But no one need be afraid that slang will really hurt our language, here or in England. It cannot. There is no dictatorship behind it. Words and phrases live only on their worth; they survive only on their merits. Nor does slang tend to separate America and England. As a matter of fact, the rising generation in England reach out eagerly for American slang. If that means they're not rising but sinking, it's too bad. But anyway we'll sink together.

. . .

So much for the toleration of slang as bad language turning into good, or dying from its very badness. What are we to say of bad language in the other sense, the kind that really is bad?

Are we to put it in or leave it out? When we write a story our characters, if they are what are called "red-blooded" men and women, are apt to get profane; and even if they are thin-blooded they are apt to get nasty, in fact the thinner the nastier. The problem which all writers of fiction have to try to solve, and none have solved yet, is how to swear in print. Some writers of today think that they can solve the problem by ignoring it —just go ahead and swear. We open the pages of a typical novel and our eyes bounce off with a start at the expression . . . *You miserable bastard!* . . .

This is not said to the reader. It is what the hero says to, or rather *throws at* the villain, who has said something unbecoming in the presence of a girl, something that a girl ought not to hear. The hero is a splendid fellow. He has *guts*. The books says so. In fact that's why the girl likes him. It says, "She threw her arms about his neck and pressed her slim body close to him. 'You have guts,' she murmured." You see, she herself is so aw-fully slim that naturally—well, you get the idea. If not, you can read it all for yourself in any new book, under such a title as *Angel Whispers,* or *Undertones* or something like that, on the outside. On the inside it's full of *guts*. The new books are like that.

But we are not talking about any particular book but about the problem that is suggested—the question of how to deal with profanity in fiction—how can you swear in print?

. . .

We must, I fear, dismiss at once the old-fashioned Victorian expedient of telling the reader that one of the characters in the story said something "with a terrible oath." That won't do now-a-days. We want to hear it. What was it? This formula was the one used in the pirate stories written for boys and girls.

For example:

"Har! har!" shouted the pirate with a foul oath. "They are in our power."

"They certainly are," said the second pirate with an oath fouler than the first.

"I'll say so," said the third pirate with an oath fouler still—a lot fouler.

The fourth pirate remained silent. He couldn't make it.

.   .   .

Now that won't do. We'll judge for ourselves how foul the oath is. If you can't say it, just whisper it. It's got to be pretty foul to get past us.

And I need hardly say, that it won't do to fall back on that old-fashioned trick that is used in novels "laid" in the Middle Ages—I mean the trick of making up a lot of fanciful stuff and calling it swearing.

Here's how it runs:

"Odd's piddlekins," cried Sir Gonderear, "by my halidome, thou art but a foul catiff. Let me not, or I'll have at you."

"Nay, by the Belly of St. Mark," answered the Seneschal, "I fear thee not, false paynim . . . Have one on me!" (Or words to that effect.) That was all right, as we shall see in the discussion of historical romances, from Sir Walter Scott. It won't do now. Such an epithet as *foul catiff* has been replaced by *you big stiff*, and a *paynim* is a *lobster*.

.   .   .

There used to be a special kind of swearing reserved by convention for the use of sailors in sea-stories. "Shiver my timbers!" cried the bosun, "you son of a swob! Lift a finger, you lobscouse, and I'll knock the dead lights out of you." After which he spat a quid—a *quid pro-quo*—into the lee scuppers.

Fenimore Cooper is a case in point. The public of his day was too strict in its ideas to allow a sailor even to shiver his timbers in print. A glance at any of Cooper's famous sea stories will reveal such terrible profanity as d—l, apparently hinting at *devil*, and d—e, which may be interpreted with a thrill as "damme." Oddly enough, in Cooper's day the word "bloody" had not yet taken on in America its later offensive connotation, so that Cooper was at liberty to write, "D—e," said the bosun, "what the d—l does the bloody fellow mean?" But we may leave that to Fenimore Cooper. At present you couldn't navigate even a car ferry with a truck on it on that language.

You see, it was much easier to get away with such things a hundred years ago, at the beginning of modern fiction, than it is now. Take the case of Charles Dickens. He couldn't, of course, put real swearing into his books, and anyway he wouldn't have wanted to. So he set up a sort of jargon that he took straight out of the blood and thunder of the cheap London theater of which, as an impecunious youth, he was inordinately fond.

An example is seen in the language used by Bill Sykes, the murderer, in *Oliver Twist*. There is a scene, in which he is just going to do the murder—no, has just done it and is trying to escape. A child has got in the way and Sykes says to his associates, "Open the door of some place where I can lock this screeching hell babe . . ." Why he didn't "bump the child off," I forget just now. The present point is the language he used. He would have had just as good a phrase for bumping it.

Compare the *hell's accursed,* and the *foul fiend,* and such mild phrases. With objurations of that sort you sometimes couldn't tell whether the characters were cursing or praying; in fact in origin the two are one.

That reminds me of the language I once heard used by a man showing a "picture panorama"—the kind of thing they used to have long ago before the real "pictures" replaced it. In these pictures, when the successive scenes were shown, there was a man who did the talking. "Here you see this," and "now you see that . . ." and so on, as the scene went by. The man I speak of was showing a scene representing a Swiss peasant, getting swallowed up in a morass, or nearly swallowed up, till an angel appeared to save him. I was quite unable, and I still am, to distinguish whether the Swiss peasant and the angel were praying or swearing. In fact I don't think the picture man had thought it out. He took a chance.

His talk ran:

> Here you see the Swiss Alps. In the foreground is one of those dangerous more-asses, where the treacherous surface, with all the aspect of firm ground, offers no real support. Here

*you see a Swiss peasant. Look! He is stepping out on the
more-ass. The ground yields beneath his feet. He moves forward more rapidly to escape. He begins to sink. He tries in
vain to withdraw his feet. He is slowly sinking to his doom.
Look, he lifts his hands and cries aloud: "Oh, Heaven," he
says, "get me out of this more-ass. Oh, God, this is the
damnedest more-ass. Christ! this is awful."*

*His prayer is heard. An angel appears, bending out from
the clouds, her hand outstretched. "You poor soul," she says
in a voice vibrating with pity. "You poor nut, you poor
bastard . . . give me your hand, and come up." She takes
him to her bosom, and he is saved.*

So he would be, of course.

. . .

But to turn back again to advice to writers. Don't think you
can get away with swearing by putting something very close to it,
something nearly as good and much cheaper, by a shift of a
letter or two. Some writers try, for instance, to use "ruddy"
to stand for "bloody." This is used especially in the mouths of
English army sergeants and such. It is supposed to give a bar-
rack-room touch. But it is really just a left-over piece of Victorian
evasion. Rudyard Kipling used this trick, not so stale in his
hey-day as it is now. One recalls his Soudanese negro Fuzzy-
wuzzy, who was described as a "big, black, bounding beggar,
who broke a British Square."

That's all right. Fuzzy-wuzzy was pretty close to that, but not
just exactly that.

And here's another thing:

Don't try to get around the difficulty by turning the profanity
into strokes(————), or making it into asterisks (****). That's
just feeble.

. . .

Asterisks and dots and strokes are hopeless. You can't *swear*
with those things. They won't read right. . . . Read aloud, as
they are, they would turn the pirate story into:

"Three asterisks!" shouted the Pirate.
"Four," shouted the next.
"I'll make it six," yelled a third, adding a stroke and a colon.

. . .

A person still young and inexperienced might think—surely there is no problem here. The true method would be to write down the very words that an actual person would actually use, to put the swearing in the book exactly as people swear it. But that, of course, would never do. Leaving out all question of whether the law allows it, art forbids it. It wouldn't sound right. Try it. Put down a set of foul, profane, obscene words—not samples, but the whole set used in what is called a string of profanity. It would sound awful for one paragraph, flat and stale after two, and beyond that utterly nauseating—in fact just like swearing. And you know how that sounds.

The only advice that can be given to the writer is, don't go further than others do. In fact, keep just a little behind them. If they say "guts," you say "bowels of compassion."

Aids to Study

I. DICTIONARIES, WORDS, AND MEANINGS

WHITEHALL, The Development of the English Dictionary

1. Why were the first glossaries and English-foreign language dictionaries made?
2. What is an *inkhorn* term? Where do you suppose the phrase comes from?
3. Distinguish between the chief contributions to dictionary-making of the eighteenth- and nineteenth-century lexicographers.
4. Examine your own desk dictionary. Does it have all the characteristics described on p. 11 as typical of modern American dictionaries?
5. Locate in your library the *New English Dictionary (Oxford English Dictionary)*, the *Dictionary of American English*, the *Dictionary of Americanisms*, the *Century Dictionary* and the Merriam-Webster *New International Dictionary of the English Language*, 2nd. ed. You will have occasion to refer to them all.

JOHNSON, Preface to the *Dictionary*

1. Examine the one-sentence paragraph beginning "When I took the first survey of my undertaking . . ." and, omitting no idea, reduce Johnson's remarks to a series of simple sentences. What has he gained by the style he has employed? How would you describe his style?
2. What was Johnson's attitude toward the English spelling of his time?
3. Consult the *Oxford English Dictionary (NED or OED)* for the derivations of *enchantment, incantation,* and *entire.* Are Johnson's etymological discussions accurate?
4. Johnson speaks of "the genius of our tongue." (p. 18) What does he mean by *genius*? Will your desk dictionary help you? What does the *OED* record about this use of *genius*?
5. Johnson speaks (p. 20) of words related "by descent or cognation." What does he mean by *cognation*?

6. Make a list of words from Johnson's own prose which are un-familiar to you. Which ones are words apparently no longer in common use? How can you be sure? Which are words whose meanings have changed appreciably from Johnson's day to ours?

7. What are some of the difficulties Johnson had in making his dictionary?

8. Johnson decided to limit his researches into the older English language to the Renaissance and after (pp. 23–4). How accurate do you think his remarks on this matter are, especially those in the famous paragraph beginning "But as every language has a time of rudeness . . ."?

9. One of the best things about Johnson's *Dictionary* is the Preface, perhaps in large part because of the personality which emerges. If this is the first time you've read Johnson, how would you characterize him, judging from the Preface? If you've read him—or read about him, perhaps in Boswell's famous biography—how does the personality here square with the impression you already had?

10. What are Johnson's views on linguistic change?

MATHEWS, Meanings and Etymologies,

AND Dictionaries Contain Surprises

1. Examine your own desk dictionary to learn what principle dictates the order of the listing of meanings.

2. What is *etymology?*

3. If you have a desk dictionary other than *Webster's New World Dictionary*, compare its entry for *anecdote* with the entries from other dictionaries quoted by Professor Mathews. How do they differ?

4. Here are some questions suggested by Professor Mathews; try to answer them by looking up the etymologies of the italicized words:

   (a) Why should an *acrobat* walk on his tiptoes?
   (b) The name of what animal is preserved in *arctic?*
   (c) Should a *diploma* be flat or folded once in the middle?
   (d) Should *athletes* be given prizes?
   (e) Where would you expect a *hippopotamus* to live?
   (f) Why should a *volume* be round?
   (g) Should you give a *parasite* food or a night's lodging?
   (h) Why would it be impossible to collect *poll tax* from the headless horseman who appears in Irving's "Legend of Sleepy Hollow"?
   (i) Which of the following animals would you expect a *polecat* to like best: duck, chicken, pig, turkey?

(j) In what school subject should a *glamour* girl excel?

(k) If a goat could act on the stage would he do better in *tragedy* or in *comedy?*

(l) How tall would you expect a *pygmy* to be?

(m) In ancient times where did people think the voice of a *ventriloquist* came from?

(n) Should a *pugnacious* animal fight with its teeth or its claws?

(o) Would you expect a *planet* to stay in the same spot?

(p) What was the occupation of the first *pedagogues?*

(q) Would you expect an *alligator* and a *lizard* to resemble each other?

(r) How should a *candidate* dress when out electioneering?

(s) In Latin *rostrum* meant the beak of a bird. What does it mean now? Does your dictionary tell how it came to have its present meaning?

(t) Would you feel flattered if someone called you a *dunce?* Look up the etymology of the word in a large dictionary.

(u) From what animals were the first *bugles* made?

(v) What objects were the first to be *considered?*

(w) From what old law-court phrase does *culprit* come?

5. What does Emerson mean by the word *cant* in the epigraph for "Dictionaries Contain Surprises"?

6. Among the several dictionaries discussed in Professor Mathews' essays, where do you suppose you would find (a) the best information about current American pronunciation of a word; (b) the latest information about current U.S. meanings of a word; (c) the fullest historical account of a word?

7. Use an unabridged dictionary, preferably the *OED*, to see if you can answer the following questions posed by Professor Mathews:

(a) How did Arabian girls use *alcohol* 2,000 years ago?

(b) In what way is it said that a certain nobleman's love of gambling led to the presence of *sandwich* in the English language?

(c) The nickname of what Admiral is said to be preserved in the word *grog?*

(d) In Matthew 3:4 it is said that John the Baptist ate locusts and wild honey. Did the *locusts* he ate belong to the animal or the vegetable kingdom?

(e) When you *curry favor* with someone, what part does a chestnut-colored horse play in your activity?

(f) Where would you look to find the *signature* of a plant? How were doctors formerly guided by these signatures?

(g) What habit of the *moose* gave the animal its name?

(h) What does it mean *to tell out of school?*

(i)   In what condition is one who has a *bee in his bonnet?*

(j)   What should one do who is asked to *tell it not in Gath?*

ROBERTSON AND CASSIDY, Changing Meanings and Values of Words

1. What further examples of the "etymological fallacy" can you think of? Check them in an unabridged dictionary to see what happened to their meanings.
2. Consult the *Oxford English Dictionary* for the following words: *affair, awful, minister, gentle, shade, sergeant, shears, scissors, cad, boor, gossip, hussy.* What processes of semantic change does each illustrate?
3. Look up the noun *romance* in the *OED* and in your desk dictionary. Write an essay in which you discuss all its changes of meaning since it entered the language, and try to explain why these changes might have occurred. When did it take on its current meaning, synonymous with *love affair?*
4. What are some of the possible causes of semantic change?

MENCKEN, Euphemisms

1. What new examples of American euphemisms can you think of?
2. What reasons can you find to explain all the various classes of euphemisms Mencken cites?
3. Is a euphemism a bad thing?
4. Mencken himself makes vigorous use of the language: he speaks of "the advance of human taxidermy," and he describes morticians' "expectant hauling of the ill." Reread his discussion of *mortician* and the other euphemisms connected with that trade, and then write an essay in which you show how Mencken manages to make clear his amusement and disgust while appearing merely to present a factual discussion.

SULLIVAN, The Cliché Expert Testifies on the Atom

1. Make a list of "atomic clichés" which have appeared in the decade since Mr. Sullivan wrote his dialogue.
2. Try your hand at writing a cliché-expert dialogue.
3. What is it that makes clichés amusing? Why do English instructors object to them in student writing?
4. Is it possible to talk without using clichés?

SCHLAUCH, Semantic Rejuvenation

1. What do these words and phrases mean as Miss Schlauch uses them: *jejune, context, the original metaphoric synthesis, evinced,* and *rejuvenation?*
2. What does your desk dictionary tell you about the meaning of *ambiguity?* Note how the double force of old and new meanings works in the poetry Miss Schlauch cites.
3. How do Miss Schlauch's remarks about the usefulness of knowing older and etymological meanings square with the conclusions of Professors Robertson and Cassidy?
4. Under what circumstances should you ignore what "the dictionary says"? Use some examples and write an essay on this subject.
5. What is the term used on your campus for a short, unannounced quiz? For a class which didn't meet because the teacher didn't appear? For unexcused absences? For a course said to be ridiculously easy? Write an essay in which you discuss the origins of some of these terms, using dictionaries where they will help you and what you have learned about semantic change where they will not.

II. THE HISTORY OF ENGLISH

SCHLAUCH, Family Relationships among Languages

1. Study the several Germanic versions of "Yes, Mother, I have three." Then write as many statements as you can to describe the similarities among them. Remember that *sounds* are more important than *spellings*.
2. Look up the word for *father* in as many English-foreign language dictionaries as possible. From the list of words can you pick out family relationships among languages?
3. Study the Romance-language versions of "Yes, Mother, I have three." Make a list of descriptive statements about the similarities, being as complete as possible. Now compare and contrast the statements you've made for the Romance languages with those you've made for the Germanic languages.
4. Why is *Indo-European* a better term for the parent language than *Aryan* or *Indo-Germanic?* Consult a map for the locations of all the members of the Indo-European group.

HOOK AND MATHEWS, Changes in the English Language

1. Consult your desk dictionary for the dates usually given to the "Old English" and "Middle English" periods. How do you suppose these dates are arrived at?
2. What are some of the grammatical differences between Chaucer's English and yours?
3. What sort of influence has Latin had on English since the two languages first made contact?
4. What kinds of contribution did the Norsemen make to the English language?
5. What effect did the Norman Conquest have on English?
6. Select at random a page in your desk dictionary and make a list of the languages of origin mentioned in the etymological entries. How many different languages appear? Which ones occur most often?
7. What current words—perhaps from the daily newspaper—has American English borrowed recently from foreign languages? How many of them are in your desk dictionary?

MARCKWARDT, The Language of the Colonists

1. What dates do most historians use to include the American Colonial period?
2. Where, in England, did the main groups of colonists come from? Which group probably spoke the London dialect?
3. How do puns and rimes from Shakespeare's plays help us discover the sounds of his language?
4. Make a list of the vowels in Shakespeare's English which are different from our modern ones.
5. What differences in stress does Professor Marckwardt describe in comparing Elizabethan and modern American English?
6. What was Shakespeare's practice with second person pronouns? How did it differ from ours?
7. Rewrite the passage from William Bradford's *History*, using good modern English. What differences, in addition to those Professor Marckwardt discusses, do you find in your version?

FRIES, What Language Matters To Teach

1. Examine the seven quotations from eighteenth-century authors and make a list of the differences between their use of the language and yours. What words do you find which have changed their meaning today? How does their punctuation differ from yours?

2. What did these eighteenth-century writers want to do with English?
3. What is the difference between "functional" and "formal" grammar as Professor Fries describes them?
4. What are the three kinds of grammar-teaching which Professor Fries says we have tried in this country? Which one—or what combination—of these methods was used in your high school?
5. According to Professor Fries, what kinds of things should we teach you in a course in English composition?

MARCKWARDT, The Future of English

1. What are the two dangers some experts feel will keep English from achieving any further status? How do these views contradict each other?
2. Why does Professor Marckwardt feel that the second danger is greater?
3. How do Professor Marckwardt's views (published in 1958) of what we should be teaching and learning about English compare with those of Professor Fries in the preceding essay (published in 1940)?

III. THE STRUCTURE OF ENGLISH

GLEASON, Language

1. What is the difference between *expression* and *content* in language?
2. From your knowledge of a foreign language, find a good example of difference in content between that language and English.
3. Vocabulary "is the least stable and even the least characteristic of the three components of language." Explain why this should be so, illustrating from the things you have learned about words and their changes in meaning in Sections I and II.
4. In learning a second language, says Professor Gleason, vocabulary is the easiest matter, yet students fear it most. Read (or perhaps your instructor will read to you) Mark Twain's essay, "The Wonderful German Language." Does the American humorist agree with the fearful students or with the linguists about what offers the greatest difficulty in learning a language?
5. What is a phoneme? a morpheme? What is the significant difference between them?
6. Get good definitions (try your desk dictionary) for *phonology, morphology, syntax, grammar,* and *rhetoric*.

THE EDITORS OF THE G. & C. MERRIAM Co., The International Phonetic Alphabet

1. What is the difference between *acoustic* and *articulatory* phonetics? Which sort does this selection represent?
2. Read carefully all three transcriptions in the selection. Which one agrees most closely with *your* speech? Listen closely to your own voice; do you habitually pronounce any of the words differently from the way they are recorded in the dialect you speak?
3. Practice making a few simple phonetic transcriptions, being certain that you record the actual sounds you usually make. Transcribe your full name, the way you would say it in response to a question. Transcribe these words: *clothes, interesting, machinery, roof, psychology, execute, executive, screams.* Transcribe this sentence, exactly as you would normally say it: "How do you get to the bookstore from here?"

ROBERTS, Intonation

1. Define each of the three features of intonation: stress, pitch, and juncture.
2. Using Professor Roberts' symbols for *primary, secondary, tertiary,* and *weak* stress, mark the stresses in these utterances as you would normally say them:
    (a) an ice cream cone; a handsome man; a handyman
    (b) a ball point pen display
    (c) There's the cigarette machine.
    (d) There's nobody in the house.
    (e) Please don't talk to the elevator operator.
3. Using the line symbols employed by Professor Roberts, mark the pitch patterns in the following utterances, and describe the differences in meaning which may be obtained by the use of different patterns for each utterance.
    (a) What time is it
    (b) You're going home now
4. Mark the junctures in the following dialogue, using the symbols Professor Roberts uses, and making certain that the junctures reflect the way you actually speak the words.
    (a) "Why don't you come over to my house?" John asked.
    (b) "Because I've got to go to the store, where Mother said she'd wait for me," I answered.
5. Now, referring to the chart on pages 157–8, transcribe the passage in question 4 into the phonetic alphabet. Then mark stress, pitch, and junctures, using Professor Roberts' symbols.

Whorf, Linguistics as an Exact Science

1. Explain Whorf's "linguistic relativity principle." How does this idea correspond to Professor Gleason's remarks on the differences in *structures of content* among languages?
2. Make up an English nonsense word you've never heard before and test it against the formula for one-syllable words in English.
3. Test these words against the formula: *gout, bill, snarf, duz, glib.*
4. Linguistics is also called a *social science*. What assumptions underlie such a statement? How do these fit with what Professor Whorf says about linguistics as an *exact* science?
5. Why does Professor Whorf think scientific study of language is important? Can you think of other arguments, either for or against his conclusions?

Fries, A Classification of Grammatical Phenomena

1. Look closely at the dialogue in the comic strips in your daily newspaper. What substandard or Vulgar English do you find there? Do Professor Fries' remarks about comic writers' use of such language seem to be borne out?
2. What are the three types of device English uses to express grammatical ideas? Find new examples of each.

Brown, Brown, and Bailey, Grammar in a New Key, and Grammatical Distribution

1. Distinguish between "vocabulary" elements and "grammatical" elements, and give some examples of each.
2. Write out some English sentences which employ the grammatical symbols used in the sentences on page 200. Simply fill in the vocabulary elements.
3. What are the arguments the authors use to urge the study of grammar?
4. What do the authors mean by "grammatical distribution"?
5. Examine the uses of the word *round* on page 210. What *are* the other devices that make clear *round's* part of speech in each sentence?
6. Write a number of short sentences using *like* in as many different parts of speech as possible. How do we know what is meant?

Whitehall, The System of Punctuation

1. Punctuate these utterances, following the suggestions Professor Whitehall makes:

(a) I've ordered books stationery and a new typewriter ribbon
(b) She turned and asked Do you want me to come with you or would you prefer to go alone
(c) Stop I cried and I was never more angry in my life or I'll

2. Punctuate the following passage:
   If I were you I told him I'd have nothing more to do with them Their remarks their appearance their very names the whole business seems if you'll take my advice too silly to fool with

3. Make a phonetic transcription of the passage in question 2 above, and then mark stress, pitch, and junctures. Now, what relationships do you see between intonation and punctuation?

4. What sort of assistance does your desk dictionary afford you in problems of conventional punctuation?

JESPERSEN, Spelling

1. Make a list of one- and two-syllable English words which use the letter *a* as a vowel, and then transcribe the words phonetically. How many different sounds do you find for the English letter *a*?

2. Consult your desk dictionary for the origin of the word *ye* in phrases like *Ye Olde Tea Shoppe*. What other spelling curiosities are traceable to writing and printing?

3. George Bernard Shaw is usually credited with inventing this "logical" English spelling of a common word: *ghoti—gh* as in *rough, o* as in *women,* and *ti* as in *motion; ghoti:* a perfectly reasonable spelling of *fish.* See what similar horrors of English spelling you can invent, the sort that a foreigner trying to spell English phonetically might conceivably propose.

HALL, Our English Spelling System

1. Why is English spelling so complicated to master?

2. Why have Americans put so much social stress on accurate spelling?

3. Find in literature some examples of *eye-dialect.* What, actually, does the writer do: vary the spelling to conform to standard English sounds, vary it to conform to sub-standard or geographical dialect sounds, or both?

4. What does Professor Hall seem to think we ought to do about our spelling system? If you are a poor speller, are you comforted by his remarks?

WHITEHALL, Writing and Speech

1. What seem to be the chief differences between written and spoken English?

2. How does the British linguistic situation differ from the American? Consult your desk dictionary for its remarks on British pronunciation. What *is* Received Standard British English, and who speaks it?

3. What sort of things must one do in a course in English composition, according to Professor Whitehall's last paragraph? How has your own school work in English composition tried to meet these needs?

POTTER, The Sentence

1. What limitations are there to the number and variety of sentence patterns you may be able to employ?

2. What are the three kinds of sentence-*forms?* What are the four kinds of sentences classified as to *function?*

3. Professor Potter quotes a number of remarks about style in writing. He speaks also of classifying *sentences* as to *style:* loose, balanced, and periodic. Try your hand at a definition of style. What sorts of things must you discuss in such a definition?

4. How would you classify the *style* of these sentences from Ernest Hemingway's *A Farewell to Arms:*

> Now in the fall the trees were all bare and the roads were muddy. I rode to Gorizia from Udine on a camion. We passed other camions on the road and I looked at the country. The mulberry trees were bare and the fields were brown. There were wet dead leaves on the road from the rows of bare trees and men were working on the road, tamping stone in the ruts from piles of crushed stone along the side of the road between the trees. We saw the town with a mist over it that cut off the mountains. We crossed the river and I saw that it was running high. It had been raining in the mountains. We came into the town past the factories and then the houses and villas and I saw that many more houses had been hit. On a narrow street we passed a British Red Cross ambulance. The driver wore a cap and his face was thin and very tanned. I did not know him. I got down from the camion in the big square in front of the Town Major's house, the driver handed down my rucksack and I put it on and swung on the two musettes and walked to our villa. It did not feel like a homecoming.

And these, from Joseph Conrad's *The Heart of Darkness:*

> The *Nellie,* a cruising yawl, swung to her anchor without a flutter of the sails, and was at rest. The flood had made, the wind was nearly calm, and being bound down the river,

the only thing for it was to come to and wait for the turn of the tide.

The sea-reach of the Thames stretched before us like the beginning of an interminable waterway. In the offing the sea and the sky were welded together without a joint, and in the luminous space the tanned sails of the barges drifting up with the tide seemed to stand still in red clusters of canvas sharply peaked, with gleams of varnished spirits. A haze rested on the low shores that ran out to sea in vanishing flatness. The air was dark above Gravesend, and farther back still seemed condensed into a mournful gloom, brooding motionless over the biggest, and the greatest, town on earth.

IV. USAGE

POOLEY, Historical Backgrounds of English Usage

1. Read Shakespeare's *Love's Labour's Lost,* IV. ii. What kinds of peculiar usage are being made sport of here?
2. Consult an unabridged dictionary for the meaning of "aureate diction" as the Renaissance employed the term. Find some examples of it.
3. How does variation in pattern of intonation further complicate the sentence "I only had five dollars."
4. Why should anyone object to *due to?*
5. What does Professor Pooley think "correct English" is?

HALL, Analogy

1. Think of some more examples of "mistakes" resulting from *internal borrowing* or *analogy.* For example, what is the past tense of the verb *sneak?*
2. Why are some analogical forms respectable while others are unacceptable?
3. What are the plurals of *mongoose, moose, stadium?* Why should you hesitate over some of these? What about *data* and *agenda?* Write down the singular and plural forms *you* would use, and then see what your desk dictionary records for all these words.
4. Look up *analogy* in your desk dictionary, and compare the meanings marked *Philology* or *Linguistics* with the one labeled *Logic.* How does this distinction bear on the problems of grammar and usage we've been treating thus far in this book?

FRIES, Usage Levels and Dialect Distribution

1. Where do the greatest differences in English usage occur: in grammar, in pronunciation, or in vocabulary?
2. Make a list of the usage labels used in your desk dictionary. Where will you hear or see or use words bearing each of these labels?
3. What are the chief dialects of American English?
4. How accurate a term does the word *levels* appear to be in describing usage?

HUBBELL, Multiple Negation

1. When did the multiple negative cease to be acceptable in good English?
2. What arguments does Professor Hubbell use against the "logical" prohibition of multiple negatives?
3. Why does Professor Hubbell think the double negative continues to be a problem, despite all the teaching aimed against it?
4. How *can* we teach Standard English, according to the author? Does he agree with the views on this subject expressed by Professor Fries?

VEBLEN, The Higher Learning

1. How do "archaism and waste," the leisure class "standards of virtue," reflect themselves in linguistic practice?
2. Consult your desk dictionary for the meanings of *classic*.
3. What is the flavor of "Biblical English"? Is this what Veblen means by "the highest and most conventionalized style of archaic diction"?
4. "A discriminate avoidance of neologisms is honorific . . ." Put this clause into language suitable for an essay *you* might write. Is Veblen seriously choosing such words? How would you decide?
5. How do Veblen's views of English spelling fit with Jespersen's and Hall's?
6. How do Veblen's remarks in his final paragraph bear on the current furor over gobbledegook and jargon in business, the law, education, social science, and the like?

LLOYD, Our National Mania for Correctness

1. ". . . . we Americans are hell on the English language." ". . . their writing stinks to high heaven too." Does Professor Lloyd write Standard English? How will you decide?
2. Our "mania for correctness" is the cause to which the author attrib-

utes our loss of the eighteenth-century facility for writing. What other possible causes can you think of?

3. What does the author mean by the phrase "to beat the old Adam out of . . ." (p. 289)?

4. What is *pedagese*? Is it in your desk dictionary? *Should* it be there? What usage label ought it to have?

5. Professor Lloyd appears to want us to write as we speak. If we did so, do you think it would be literally true that "usage doesn't matter"?

6. How do Professor Lloyd's views square with those of Professor Fries?

Beerbohm, How Shall I Word It?

1. How does the existence of "letter-writers" such as Beerbohm describes support Professor Lloyd's remarks about our desire for linguistic conformity?

2. What is a *pillar-box*? What other peculiarly British words and meanings do you see in Beerbohm's essay?

3. What qualities do Beerbohm's own sample letters have in common? Do these qualities seem desirable? Is this sort of letter a good illustration of the kind of tone Professor Lloyd wants to restore to our writing?

4. In Johnson's Preface to the *Dictionary*, the writer's personality came through quite clearly. Beerbohm's personality—that "character that had always seemed to me, on the whole, so amiable"—comes through clearly here. What do you think he was like? How does his use of the language help you to know his character?

Twain, Buck Fanshaw's Funeral

1. The sketch is really both funny and sad. How is language at the root both of the humor and the pathos?

2. The vivid speech of the man called Scotty is clearly not Standard English. What is peculiar about the clergyman's speech?

3. Twain defends Scotty's colorful language. Why? Would he do the same for the minister? Would Professor Lloyd?

4. Does Twain try to suggest the *sound* of the two dialects here? How?

5. Where does the chief difference between these two dialects lie, in vocabulary, in grammar, or in phonology?

Leacock, Good and Bad Language

1. Leacock says that in Canada "we just go right ahead and use English for literature, Scotch for sermons and American for con-

versation." This is perhaps a subjective description of language, perhaps an impressionistic description of national character. How much linguistic truth is there in it?

2. What does Leacock think of Gaelic and the Irish?

3. Irony is a quality of use of language; how does Leacock manage to achieve it in this sentence: "Humble people, like the Canadians, and the Eskimos, have to live in 'America' and speak 'English,' without fretting about it."

4. Leacock says "anything is better than affectation." Would Messrs. Lloyd, Fries, and Veblen agree?

5. Leacock does not fear slang. He himself is in complete control of it. How does he use it to evoke laughter?

DATE DUE
